Baseball Gods in Scandal

Praise for *Baseball Gods in Scandal*

"The first full-length study of the scandal that led to baseball's stance on betting and judgments on rule-breakers. All the characters, players (on and off the field), dramas, and unsolved mysteries come alive in *Baseball Gods in Scandal*."
—Gerald C. Wood, author of *Smoky Joe Wood: The Biography of a Baseball Legend*, winner of the 2014 SABR Seymour Medal for best book on the history of baseball

"The definitive account of an affair that could have wrecked major league baseball. In 1926, only six years after the infamous Black Sox scandal, superstars Ty Cobb and Tris Speaker were implicated in a game-fixing scheme. Kahanowitz brings this little-known episode to vivid life, reminding us that—then as now—celebrity celebrity, money, and power trump all."
—Jerald Podair, author of *City of Dreams: Dodger Stadium and the Birth of Modern Los Angeles*, winner of the 2018 SABR Seymour Medal for best book on the history of baseball

"An absorbing tale that's part detective story, part baseball yarn, involving two of game's all-time greats. The 'Black Sox' and Pete Rose top the list of gambling scandals in the national pastime, but it's time to make room for the Dutch Leonard Affair."
—Tim Wendel, author of *Summer of '68* and *Castro's Curveball*

Baseball Gods in Scandal

Ty Cobb, Tris Speaker, and the Dutch Leonard Affair

by Ian S. Kahanowitz

SUMMER
GAME
BOOKS

ISBN: 978-1-938545-87-0 (print)
ISBN: 978-1-938545-88-7 (ebook)

For information about permissions, bulk purchases, or additional distribution, write to

Summer Game Books
P. O. Box 818
South Orange, NJ 07079

or contact the publisher at www.summergamebooks.com

Dedication

To my wife, Ann-Marie, and my two sons, Jacob and Ryan, whose love carries me every day through my journey in life.

Philippians 4:13

I can do all things through Christ who strengthens me.

About the Author

Ian S. Kahanowitz was born and raised in Brooklyn, New York. After moving to Massachusetts in 1993 to attend law school, he has practiced law for the last twenty-two years. Ian is also an historian whose major focus is on the events of the 20th Century.

Ian's love for baseball, combined with his love for the law and history, led him to publish his first book: *Baseball Gods in Scandal: Ty Cobb, Tris Speaker, and the Dutch Leonard Affair*.

Ian has published many articles on baseball, and has a sports/entertainment podcast called Genesis. The podcasts can be downloaded at YouTube.

He currently resides in North Attleboro, Massachusetts with his wife and two sons.

Author's Facebook Pages

Home page:
https://www.facebook.com/ian.kahanowitz

Ty Cobb, Tris Speaker, and the Dutch Leonard Affair:
https://www.facebook.com/ikahanowitz/

Ty Cobb and The Deadball Era:
https://www.facebook.com/groups/298293513693402/

The History of Women In Baseball:
https://www.facebook.com/groups/377195966007965/

The Tiger Den:
https://www.facebook.com/groups/THETIGERDEN65/

The Dugout:
https://www.facebook.com/groups/Iansbaseballdugout/

The Historical Negro League Baseball Site:
https://www.facebook.com/groups/1495857187357173/

The History of The New York Yankees:
https://www.facebook.com/groups/869959186361373/

Broadcasting Baseball Back In The Day:
https://www.facebook.com/groups/backinthedaybaseball2015/

The Minnesota Twins:
https://www.facebook.com/groups/587054438067768/

Acknowledgments

Many people helped me on my journey to completing *Baseball Gods in Scandal*. First, I would like to thank my publisher, Walter Friedman, for doing a great job of helping me put all the puzzle pieces together to craft the book; to Gerald C. Wood, whose book on Joe Wood propelled my interest in the Dutch Leonard Affair. I'd also like to thank Eldon Ham, who is a professor of law at IIT/Chicago-Kent College of Law (where he has taught Sports, Law & Society since 1994 and won the Distinguished Service Award in 2010), whose advice was priceless; I would also like to thank Matt Novak for helping with my research at the Chicago History Museum; I would also like to thank the librarians at the Detroit Public Library for all their help in finding material I could not get elsewhere.

A big thank you goes out to George Rugg, Curator of the Hesburgh Libraries - Department of Special Collections, at Notre Dame University for providing me with the unpublished Joe Wood transcripts with Lawrence Ritter, author of the essential *The Glory of Their Times*. Another big assist came from Peter Elwell at the Cleveland Public Library who provided me with the 1975 Eugene Murdock interviews with Joe Wood. A big thank you is also due to Hank Thomas, grandson of the great Walter Johnson, who provided me insight into the Dead Ball Era and who edited the audio tapes for *The Glory of Their Times*.

I'd also like to thank the following, whose love and support truly made this lonely journey more bearable: To my mother and sister in New York City, for listening to me discuss the steps I took to create the book; to my mother-in-law and father-in-law, who are always there for me; to my brothers-in-law and sisters-in-law, who showed me how to be part of a big family; to my podiatrist and surgeon, Dr. Barry Rosenbloom, who has helped me with my health issues and who is a baseball aficionado like myself.

Sincere thanks to Perry Barber, who has shown me baseball through the eyes of an umpire, and who has cultivated women's involvement in baseball for four decades. To Dr. Kat Williams, Donna Eden Cohen, Maybelle Blair, Mary Moore, Shirley Burkovich, and all of the members of the International Baseball Women's Center, who continue to inspire me with their dedication to promoting baseball for women of all ages. To Ralph Tyko, aka The Zig Zag man, for giving me the chance to broadcast my radio show "Genesis" on his "Comfortably Zoned Radio Network." To Vincent Serpico, who was my sounding board, and who encouraged me daily to trudge forward in completing the book.

And great thanks and appreciation to Irene Hodges, daughter of the great Gil Hodges, whose chats about baseball expanded my knowledge about the sport in the 1960s and 1970s; to former major league player, Fritz Peterson, who became my close friend and told me first-hand accounts about the "Horace Clarke Years" for the New York Yankees; to Carol Sheldon, who has helped me understand baseball from the 1800's onward, and how women played a major role in the sport from its earliest inception; to former major leaguer, Brett Boone, who showed me what goes on behind the scenes in the game, and the X's and O's of strategy in baseball; to Mary Ann Derbin, for all of her love and support on a daily basis; and finally, but far from least—to all of the administrators caring for my Facebook baseball pages—thank you so much for sharing this baseball journey with me.

Contents

Introduction

The National League's first major game-fixing scandal took place in 1877, a year after its formation, when four members of the Louisville team—star pitcher Jim Devlin, outfielder George Hall, shortstop Bill Craver and substitute Al Nichols—were accused of throwing three exhibition games and some league games.[1] In a precedent-setting decision, league president William Hulbert permanently banned the four players from organized baseball. The scandal and its consequences scared straight many players for a generation afterward, but gambling and questionable on-the-field play continued, and by the turn of the 20th century, betting on baseball had reached its zenith. Baseball's powers that be did little to discourage this behavior because attendance was soaring and many fans enjoyed wagering, too. Even when faced with evidence of their own players being involved with game-fixing, baseball executives looked the other way.[2]

The Black Sox Scandal of 1919, in which some of the key players on the Chicago White Sox conspired to lose the World Series to the underdog Cincinnati Reds, overshadowed the game of baseball for decades after, and even now, 100 years later, is part of baseball history that even most casual fans have heard of. But while the fixing of the 1919 World Series may have, in the words of F. Scott Fitzgerald, "destroyed the faith of fifty million people," dishonest acts like it certainly were nothing new in baseball.[3]

Because it involved the World Series, the Black Sox Scandal was much bigger than the scandals that came before it. Just the thought of gamblers and ballplayers plotting to fix one of the greatest events in all of sport has the power to enrage and disgust lovers of the game. The principal characters that took part in the scandal were like the fictional underworld characters you see in the movies like "The Godfather," or "Goodfellas." There was a reputed mobster who was involved in organizing the whole scheme; bookies

The 1919 Chicago White Sox.

everywhere were taking bets on the information that the White Sox would throw the series; and the players were supposed to receive a large chunk of that money for throwing the series.

To make matters even more interesting, the written testimonies of the players went missing from the district attorney's office, which prevented the case from being tried. In turn, American League President Ban Johnson conducted his own investigation, even using some of his own money, to gather the evidence needed to bring the case to court. Although the court ruled that the players were not guilty of throwing the 1919 World Series, the new commissioner did not agree. In a stunning act, Commissioner Kenesaw Mountain Landis ignored the not guilty verdict of the court and banished all eight players allegedly in on the fix permanently from baseball. The message he sent was loud and clear to both the players and the public: big league baseball had its own set of rules and its own enforcer—one who would show zero tolerance for gambling or game-fixing.[4] That was the message Landis wished to convey. The reality may have turned out a little differently, as we will see.

Pete Rose's banishment from baseball in 1989 for gambling on baseball continues to be a topic of major interest to fans, as Rose, one of the game's all-time great players, remains ineligible for the Hall of Fame. Rose and the Black Sox, with 70 years between them, are the two most iconic gambling-related scandals in baseball. But they were far from isolated incidents. Despite the best efforts of Kenesaw Landis and Bart Giamatti, and baseball authorities before and after them, gambling has always been a part of the game.

Another gambling scandal that rocked the baseball world is far less well remembered than the Black Sox and Pete Rose, but at the time—between the 1926 and 1927 seasons—caused great upheaval and nearly destroyed the sport itself. The scandal gripped the press and public for months, while the owners and the ruling body of baseball grappled with what to do. The "Dutch Leonard Affair" implicated two of baseball's long-time superstars and greatest heroes of the game at the time, Ty Cobb and Tris Speaker. While largely forgotten today, the story headlined every major newspaper during the winter of 1926 and shook the baseball world to its core.

While judgments were reached in the Black Sox and Rose scandals, and the guilt of the parties is nearly universally agreed upon, there is far less certainty about exactly what happened in the Dutch Leonard Affair and the innocence or guilt of the parties.

The Dutch Leonard Affair revolved around a game played on September 25, 1919 between the Cleveland Indians and Detroit Tigers, whose star players were Tris Speaker and Ty Cobb. The Chicago White Sox had already clinched first place and Cleveland had already wrapped up second. The stakes were high for Detroit, however, as the Tigers were in a battle for third place with the New York Yankees, and in those days the top three finishers got a share of the World Series money. Given the virtual slave wages paid in those days, this extra money was very important to the players, so Detroit wanted very much to win.

In May, 1926, nearly seven years after that game was played, now-former major leaguer Dutch Leonard made a trip from his home in California to Detroit and Chicago to inform Tigers' owner, Frank Navin, and American League President, Ban Johnson, that he had proof in the form of two letters that Ty Cobb and Tris Speaker had fixed and bet on that game back in 1919.

Leonard's accusations, of course, came seven years after the Black Sox Scandal and five years after the expulsion of the Black Sox Eight by Commissioner Kenesaw Mountain Landis, who had a fanatical disdain for anything even remotely resembling gambling. Landis's words and actions had set baseball on a new, clean course, as far as its millions of fans were concerned. So the allegation that a game had been fixed and wagered on—by two true Gods of the game—caused great public turmoil and threatened to sink baseball into another sordid controversy.

The story was kept under wraps until the fall of 1926, when suddenly both Cobb and Speaker quit baseball and resigned their positions as player-managers, shocking the public and leaving the press wondering what was going on. The experience for the two Baseball Gods was gut-wrenching, as it appeared both their careers and reputations might be destroyed.

Equally dramatic, and equally consequential in the annals of baseball history, was the battle between American League President Ban Johnson and Commissioner Kenesaw Mountain Landis over how to resolve the scandal. When the dust had cleared in that battle, the power structure of the lords of baseball had been changed forever.

The other key figure in the Dutch Leonard Affair was one-time Red Sox great Smoky Joe Wood, best known for having one of the most dominating seasons for a pitcher in baseball history, in 1912, when he went 34-5. Wood, a teammate and friend of Speaker's, provided key testimony in the hearings that attempted to exonerate Cobb and Speaker.

Decades later, Wood recounted the events of the scandal and the trial in the seminal oral history *The Glory of Their Times*, by Lawrence Ritter, published in 1966. In Wood's interview, he essentially reiterated his version of the events surrounding that fateful game and the role each of the men played. But there was a lot more to the interview than what came out in the book, and in the unpublished portion of the interview, Joe Wood told a very different version of the Dutch Leonard Affair. In fact, had Wood told this version of the affair during his original testimony before Commissioner Landis, the verdict might have been different, and the careers and destinies of Cobb and Speaker might have been altered significantly. Things might have turned out differently for one-time Czar of baseball Ban Johnson, too.

What might be called Wood's confession was so explosive it was buried in the archives for 50 years—never known to the game's historians and scholars—until a few years ago when author Gerald C. Wood mentioned the interview in his book on Smoky Joe Wood. Thanks to the Hesburgh Libraries — Department of Special Collections Notre Dame University, we have obtained the transcript of the **complete** Joe Wood interview about the Dutch Leonard Affair with Lawrence Ritter, which is presented in this book.

Endnotes

1. Longoria, Rico. *Baseball's Gambling Scandals*. ESPN Classic. Aired July 30, 2001. https://www.espn.com/classic/s/2001/0730/1233060.html. Accessed February 15, 2019.
2. ibid.
3. Nathan, David. *Say It Is So: A Cultural History of the Black Sox Scandal*. University of Illinois Press, Champaign, IL. 2002. Quoting from *The Great Gatsby*, by F. Scott Fitzgerald.
4. Spink, J. G. Taylor. *Judge Landis and 25 Years of Baseball: The Story of America's First Commissioner of Baseball*. NightHawk Books, Taos, NM. Kindle Edition. Locations 1343 to 1364.

CHAPTER 1

Baseball's Dirty, Not-so-Little Secret

By the time the Dutch Leonard Affair was publicized in December of 1926, gambling was presumed to be all but gone from the major leagues, since commissioner Kenesaw Mountain Landis permanently banned the eight Chicago White Sox players five years earlier. But when Dutch Leonard's accusations came to light, baseball's clean image began to be questioned once again.

Despite baseball's improved reputation during the early 1920's, minor incidents had occurred during those years, but they had been dealt with swiftly and unilaterally by Commissioner Landis before much damage could be done. Landis's hatred of gambling and his obsession with keeping gamblers out of the game, and his very public display of that attitude, went a long way in restoring fans' faith in the game.

It wasn't always that way. In the early history of professional ball, gambling and baseball had gone hand in hand with each other. Unlike professional baseball from the last 100+ years, which is played in large metropolitan areas, early on the game was played in small country towns. It was basically a game among farmers and farming towns. Local town rivalries quickly developed between neighboring teams, and games were often played on Sundays, because that was the only day the farmers were free from their chores. What was noticeable in these games was that it featured heavy gambling by both the players and fans alike.

Those who organized baseball games quickly realized that people would be more interested in the game if they could make side bets, and that the endeavor would also be profitable for the gambling halls themselves.

The lawless environment of 19th Century baseball is illustrated to (slightly) exaggerated effect in this *Sporting Life* commentary at left. The turn of the century provided little hope of improvement as a monopolistic and near-corrupt National League blindly trudged on.

The Rucker Archive (inset): Library of Congress

Gambling and game-fixing have been a part of baseball since its earliest days.

Baseball historian John Thorn believes that without any type of gambling, baseball would not have become America's national pastime:

> "I don't think you could have had the rise of baseball without gambling...It was not worthy of press coverage. What made baseball seem important was when gamblers figured out a way to spur interest in it...In the beginning, there were people who turned their noses up at gambling but they recognized the necessity of it. You would not have had a box score. You would not have had an assessment of individual skills. You would not have had one player of skill moving to another club if there were not gambling in it."[1]

David Vaught, head of the history department at Texas A&M and a baseball historian, authored *The Farmer's Game: Baseball In Rural America*, where he describes the nature of gambling during these baseball games by the fans:

> "It was very often a winner-take-all event where players would bet on their team to win, and the fans would bet on just about anything they could...Fans would bet on how many hits or runs a team might score, how many pitches might be thrown, how many innings the game might last, and on and on. Since the players were not really paid a regular salary, the only way they could make any money was by betting, and every game featured plenty of it. There was rarely a game played that did not involve some type of gambling, unlike today when gambling on baseball can get a player or manager barred from the game for life...[gambling] was just as much a part of baseball as pitching, hitting, and running."[2]

During the period from 1870 to 1885, as baseball evolved from an amateur game into a professional one, corruption and gambling continued in the sport and continued to gather strength. Part of the blame could be attributed to the players being susceptible to being bribed to fix games. Most of the blame, however, rested with the owners and organizers of the leagues. Owners, lacking no model to guide players by, made the mistake of establishing early franchises like a successful business venture during the period known as the Gilded Era. By doing this, baseball's early owners mishandled the sport's transition from amateur to professional, causing problems with labor relations, gambling, and financial solvency.[3]

Gambling was most prominent in the National Association, the professional league that pre-dated the National League, with games played from 1871 until 1875. Interestingly, at the start, gamblers feared that the new professional league would pay its players enough that they would not be as easily bought. They soon discovered, however, that the new professionals could be bought just as easily as the amateurs they replaced.

Baseball executive Albert Spalding commented "that no game was played in the National Association without some sort of betting."[4] In addition, Henry Chadwick, editor of the *New York Clipper*, went so far as to say that the National Association, "died of pool-selling."[5] As a result of the constant gambling, the practice of players throwing games (as well as horse races and other sporting affairs), known as "hippodroming," was alarmingly common. The National Association's entire 1874 season was a financial flop due to rampant accusations of gambling. As a result of this season, the National Association strengthened the wording of its anti-gambling rule, but the new rule, like the previous one, was not enforced.[6]

In 1875, the *Brooklyn Eagle* newspaper named an "All Star Team of Rogues," listing the most corrupt players in baseball. These were players whose names appeared multiple times in connection with throwing games, and the surprising thing is that the vast majority of them were established starters and even stars. These players were allowed to continue playing and to continue throwing games because of the very lenient stance taken on gambling by the National Association.[7] In Brooklyn, gambling was so common that one area of the stands was called "The Gold Board," since the exchange of money was comparable to the stock market.[8] As a result of payments from gamblers, players lived like royalty, with jewelry, champagne, and other luxuries. This was the nature of the corrupt play in the National Association.

When the National League was formed, the organizers promised to keep gambling out of the league, but their attempts were largely unsuccessful. An article in the *New York Clipper* noted that "1876 was marked by numerous instances of "crooked work," while the public sought "an honest contest."[9] When the National League was created in 1876, a team from Philadelphia was excluded from the league because of rumors about gambling. The rumors indicated that, "players, whose dishonest acts were the common talk of all lovers of the game throughout the country, have been allowed to sell game after game."[10]

A year after it began league play, the National League experienced its first big gambling scandal with the Louisville scandal of 1877. After a

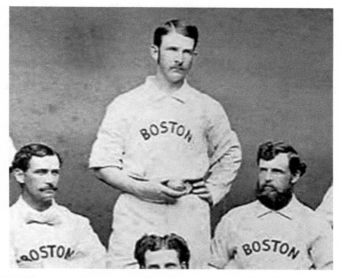

Albert Spalding, star pitcher in the National Association and pioneer in the sporting goods business, fought hard against the rampant gambling in 1870's baseball, but to little avail.

great run early in the season, the first place Louisville Grays mysteriously lost seven games in a row. During this losing streak, several players were observed wearing expensive diamond stickpins, and the *Louisville Courier-Journal* soon became suspicious. An investigation soon followed and Grays' owner, Charles Chase, finally caught four players, George Hall, Bill Craver, Jim Devlin, and Al Nichols for their roles in fixing the games.[11] In return, National League founder, William A. Hulbert, banned all four from baseball. The players claimed they threw the games because their owner had failed to meet payroll obligations and begged for forgiveness, but Hulbert would hear none of it and the players were never reinstated. Nonetheless, in general, the National League failed to remove other "suspected players" and lacked sufficient rules to eliminate gambling and game fixing.[12]

As the 1880's and 1890's passed into the new century, gambling and financial woes continued to plague the sport. Ban Johnson, a Cincinnati newspaper sports editor, bought the financially strapped Western League in 1894. For the next six years, Johnson would put most of his energy building up the league's finances, curtailing rowdyism and drunkenness among the fans, and cracking down on any perceived gambling. Johnson's league was so successful that he changed the name of the league to the "American League" in 1900 and began to cultivate this new league into a "major league." Johnson's goal was to elevate his league to be on the same footing with the already established major league, the National League.

The period of 1900 to 1919 is known as "The Deadball Era" in baseball history. During the Deadball Era, baseball relied much more on stolen bases, hit and run plays and similar strategies than on home runs. These strategies emphasized speed, perhaps by necessity. Teams played in spacious ball parks that limited hitting for power, and, compared to modern baseballs, the ball used then was "dead" from both its composition and its overuse. Balls were not constantly discarded as they are today, and the longer a single ball was used in a game, the more it resembled a head of cabbage with the leaves falling off.

Unfortunately for Major League Baseball, gambling continued to corrupt the sport during the Deadball Era, even with Ban Johnson trying to keep the gamblers out. One problem was that professional athletes liked to hang out in gambling denizens, such as saloons and pool halls, where underworld types ran rampant. Johnson couldn't monitor players' activities 24 hours a day, and many of them cultivated friendships with gamblers who bet heavily on baseball. These friendships were mutually beneficial. For ballplayers, they enjoyed the leisure of being around gamblers with large sums of money to profit off of. For the gamblers, they could gain an inside edge in betting from these ballplayers, such as finding out who was pitching the next day, or when a star player was injured. Chick Gandil, later banished in the Black Sox Scandal, claimed that he had frequently supplied Boston gambler Joseph "Sport" Sullivan with inside information going back to his days with the Washington Senators.[13]

No player had more friends in the gambling world than "Prince" Hal Chase. Some of his peers called him the best defensive first baseman ever. Chase's talents were legendary: He made one-handed catches with astonishing ease, played farther off the bag than anyone had ever seen, and charged sacrifice bunts with speed and agility. He also earned the reputation of being the best hit-and-run batter in the American League and frequently ranked among league leaders in batting average, RBI and stolen bases.[14]

In looking at Chase's 15-year baseball career, his performance was unpredictable from game to game. On some days he looked like a superstar who could do no wrong, both in the field and at bat. On other days he looked like an amateur, as he committed errors on easy plays and fanned against inferior pitchers. Chase's Jekyll and Hyde performances led to accusations of game-fixing. Two of his managers with the New York Highlanders (later the Yankees), George Stallings and Frank Chance, accused him of "laying down" on the team. He missed signs frequently (especially on the hit-and-run, causing base runners to be hung out to dry) and dropped balls from his infielders in such a subtle way that it made their throws look like errors. But whenever fingers were pointed at Chase's play, club owners Frank Farrell and Big Bill Devery sided with their star first baseman, and even made him the manager once, a decision that satisfied no one. Chase lasted just one full season in the role.[15]

Farrell and Devery themselves were involved in the underworld and in gambling. Farrell owned some of the top casinos in New York City, along with saloons and horse racing stables. Devery was an influential New York Tammany Hall figure, a corrupt police official and politician who was "constantly under indictment or administrative charge for extortion, bribery and other misconduct," according to SABR biographer Bill Lamb.[16]

Farrell and Devery were in good company, as other owners and officials in the major league engaged in gambling as well. In 1906, Cincinnati Reds owner Garry Herrmann (who was also the chairman of baseball's ruling body, the National Commission), and who would bring Hal Chase to the Reds later on, admitted to betting thousands of dollars with three New York gamblers, hedging that the Pittsburgh Pirates would not win the pennant. One of the bookies was a Pirates fan who informed the team, and Herrmann was forced to cancel the bet.[17]

Another example of baseball ownership intermingling with the underworld was New York Giants owner Charles Stoneham and Hall of Fame manager John McGraw, who co-owned a race track and casino in Cuba. In addition, McGraw's business interests also included a Manhattan poolroom that he co-owned with Arnold Rothstein, who later was suspected of orchestrating the fixing of the 1919 World Series.[18]

During that tumultuous year of 1919 in baseball, Chicago Cubs secretary John O. Seys testified that he was the stakeholder for bets placed during the 1919 Series by two of the gamblers who helped organize the fix, Abe Attell and Lou Levi. Attell and Levi were well-known by baseball insiders, and Seys apparently thought nothing of holding bets for these gamblers.[19]

There were even attempts to fix Major League Baseball's inaugural World Series, in 1903. Trouble started when a reported bribery attempt was made to Boston's star pitchers, Cy Young and Lou Criger. Criger immediately informed Ban Johnson, who publicly denounced the plot. Criger was rewarded for his honesty as Johnson paid him a pension out of American League funds for many years after his career ended.[20]

Other early World Series were beset by rumors of bribery. In 1905, after the Philadelphia Athletics had clinched the American League pennant, star pitcher and future Hall of Famer, Rube Waddell, suffered a suspicious late-season injury and missed the Series against the New York Giants. The official story was that Waddell injured his valuable left shoulder in a playful wrestling match with a teammate, but rumors have long persisted that he was paid off by gamblers and may have faked the injury.[21]

If Waddell's curious injury wasn't enough to spark concern, Giants' Manager, John McGraw, bet on his team to beat the Philadelphia Athletics in the series. McGraw would win $400 from that bet, as his Giants won the 1905 World Series. Led by Christy Mathewson's three shutouts (thrown in a span of six days), the Giants beat the A's in five games. If that happened in present day baseball, McGraw would be banned from baseball permanently.[22]

Seven years later, during the 1912 World Series, then Red Sox ace Smoky Joe Wood, manager Jake Stahl, and team owner James McAleer were involved in some very questionable activities that made it appear some sort of fix was on in their match with the New York Giants. This episode is covered in depth in chapter 11.

Bribes weren't the only manifestation of the gambling culture in baseball. With money on the line and the pennant race already over, players routinely "eased up" during meaningless late-season contests. This form of game-fixing led to some peculiar events on the field. Hall of Famer Sam Crawford once claimed that his friend Walter Johnson would throw batting practice fastballs to him when he needed a hit to raise his batting average.[23]

The most famous "easing up" incident occurred in 1910, when popular Cleveland Indians star Napoleon Lajoie was credited with an improbable eight hits in eight at-bats during a season-ending doubleheader against the St. Louis Browns. Lajoie and Ty Cobb of the Detroit Tigers were in a down-to-the-wire race to win the coveted batting title and a new car from the Chalmers Automobile Company.

As Ban Johnson later learned, Browns manager Jack O'Connor had ordered rookie third baseman John "Red" Corriden to play well behind third base.[24] O'Connor didn't do it for selfish or financial reasons; he simply hated Cobb and wanted the popular Lajoie to win the title. With Corriden playing so deep, Lajoie laid down six bunt singles and beat them all out. Browns pitcher Harry Howell also wrote a note to the St. Louis official scorer, promising him a tailored suit if he gave Lajoie the benefit of the doubt during his at-bats.[25]

Johnson publicly cleared Corriden, O'Connor and Howell of all wrongdoing and allowed Lajoie's eight hits to stand. Nevertheless, Cobb's final average ended up slightly higher (.384944 to Lajoie's .384084). But Hugh Chalmers, reveling in the publicity, decided to give each a new car. Meanwhile, O'Connor and Howell were quietly released by St. Louis in the off season and never worked for a major league team again. There was no doubt that Ban Johnson had a hand in O'Connor and Howell's departure.[26]

A few years later, it was Cobb's Tigers who were asked to "lay down" to help an opponent, in this case the Chicago White Sox. In September 1917, the first-place White Sox were in a close race for the American League pennant when they met the Tigers in a crucial series. The White Sox won all four games against Detroit and ran wild on the base paths, stealing 22 bases against catcher Oscar Stanage, who later sheepishly admitted, "That wasn't too unusual for me."[27]

Sometime afterward, each Chicago player contributed $45 to a pool for the Tigers pitchers, including the "Clean Sox" like Eddie Collins and Red Faber, who had not participated in throwing the 1919 World Series. (Buck Weaver, who was injured, didn't contribute any cash but did throw in a fancy handbag for his good friend Ossie Vitt, the Tigers' third baseman.) The money was given to Detroit's Bill James who distributed the cash to the rest of the staff. White Sox officials, including manager Pants Rowland, knew about the pool but said nothing. It was just business as usual in baseball.[28]

Two years later, in 1919, after the White Sox clinched their second American League pennant in three years, they were swept by the Tigers in the season's final series. Many believed that the White Sox eased up so that Detroit would have a chance to finish in third place and earn a share of the first-division money that went to the top three teams in each league. Some writers have suggested this was the White Sox players returning of the favor from 1917.

These two incidents would resurface many years later in Commissioner Landis's office at the end of December of 1926 and into January of 1927. Swede Risberg and Chick Gandil, (who were both thrown out for baseball in the Black Sox scandal) came forward to tell Landis about those 1917 and 1919 incidents between the White Sox and Tigers. Their motives were clear: they sought revenge on their fellow "Clean Sox" teammates (who were found innocent of any wrong doings in the 1919 World Series, and who did not get thrown out of the league for the Black Sox scandal) by showing they weren't entirely clean all of the time.

Risberg and Gandil came forward because they had heard about the Dutch Leonard Affair that was dominating the baseball headlines at the time, and both men saw their opportunity to throw more lighter fluid on an already roaring fire.

Endnotes

1. National Public Radio. *The "Secret History" of Baseball's Earliest Days.* Excerpted from *Baseball in the Garden of Eden,* by John Thorn. 2011. https://www.npr.org/2011/03/16/134570236/the-secret-history-of-baseballs-earliest-days. Accessed February 19, 2019.

2. Texas A&M University. (2013, April 8). *Baseball Gambling Was Common in Early Days*. www.sciencedaily.com/releases/2013/04/130408133025.htm. Accessed February 11, 2019.

3. Feldman, Aaron. *Baseball's Transition to Professionalism*. https://sabr.org/sites/default/files/feldman_2002.pdf. Accessed February 15, 2019.

4. ibid.

5. ibid.

6. ibid.

7. ibid.

8. ibid.

9. ibid.

10. ibid.

11. Longoria, Rico. *Baseball's Gambling Scandals*. ESPN Classic. Aired July 30, 2001. https://www.espn.com/classic/s/2001/0730/1233060.html. Accessed February 15, 2019.

12. ibid.

13. Pomrenke, Jacob. *The Whitewashing of Hal Chase*. https://jacobpomrenke.com/black-sox/the-whitewashing-of-hal-chase/. Accessed February 16, 2019.

14. ibid.

15. ibid.

16. ibid.

17. ibid.

18. ibid.

19. ibid.

20. Pomrenke, Jacob. *Gambling in the Dead Ball Era*. https://jacobpomrenke.com/black-sox/gambling-in-the-deadball-era/. Accessed February 15, 2019.

21. Longoria, op. cit.

22. Longoria, op. cit.

23. Pomrenke, op. cit.

24. ibid.

25. ibid.

26. ibid.

27. ibid.

28. ibid.

Ty Cobb and Tris Speaker, who played together for the Philadelphia Athletics in 1928, their last season in the big leagues.

CHAPTER 2

The Scandal Unfolds

One meaningless late-season game, ripe for tampering with, occurred on September 25, 1919. The Chicago White Sox had already locked up the American League pennant and were set to play in the 1919 World Series. Any games played at this point were merely to close up the books on another season. At windy and chilly Navin Field in Detroit on that day, the Detroit Tigers were hosting the Cleveland Indians. The Indians had clinched second place the day before, and so had nothing to play for either. The Tigers, however, were still in a battle for third place with the New York Yankees, so there was money on the line for Detroit's players. League rules in place for the 1919 season stipulated that every member on a 3rd place team would be rewarded with a $500 bonus, a significant amount of money for players whose salaries averaged $3,000 to $4,000 per season. The team that placed fourth in the league received nothing.[1]

When Dutch Leonard met with Tigers owner, Frank Navin, and American League President, Ban Johnson, in 1926, he indicated that Ty Cobb, Smoky Joe Wood, Tris Speaker, and he had met under the grandstand with Navin's field worker, Fred West, and agreed to bet on the game that day. According to Leonard, Cleveland Indian's manager Tris Speaker said the Tigers "didn't have to worry about tomorrow's game, because the Indians, since they were already assured of a second place finish, would be happy to lay down against the Tigers."[2] A win by the Tigers would keep Detroit's players in contention with the Yankees for the much desired $500 bonus for finishing third.

Leonard also claimed that Speaker's former teammate, Joe Wood, who was also his good friend since their days on the Red Sox, decided to join in on the plan. In addition, Leonard said the group decided that since they were playing a fixed game anyway, they might as well lay down some bets on the Tigers and make themselves a little extra money. Leonard said he would put up $1,500, while Speaker and Wood promised to wager $1,000 apiece on the game. Cobb allegedly said he was in for $2,000 and suggested that Navin Field worker, Fred West, place the bet according to Leonard.[3]

Essentially, Leonard was saying that Tris Speaker had agreed to throw the game. Speaker certainly seemed to have the influence to do it, as he was the manager as well as the best player on the Cleveland Indians. He could tell his players to lay down for the Tigers. More importantly to the story, Speaker had money on the game, which assured the bettors that he wasn't just in it as a favor to the Detroit Tigers, but to win money for himself as well.

All that said, Leonard's accusations were just words. Ban Johnson and Frank Navin knew that Leonard was likely still sore after being forced out of the major leagues over the previous winter and probably was seeking revenge on Cobb and Speaker. But to support his accusations Leonard also presented what appeared to be concrete evidence to substantiate his accusations—two letters sent to him in 1919, one from Cobb and the other from Smoky Joe Wood. Why Leonard had chosen to hold onto these letters for so many years was unknown.

Here is the text of the letter from Ty Cobb that Dutch Leonard produced:

Cobb's Letter[4]

Augusta Ga., October 23, 1919

Dear Dutch,

Well, old boy, guess you are out in California by this time and enjoying life.

I arrived home and found Mrs. Cobb only fair, but the baby girl was fine, and at this time Mrs. Cobb is very well, but I have been very busy getting acquainted with my family and have not tried to do any correspondence, hence my delay.

Wood and myself were considerably disappointed in our business proposition, as we had $2,000 to put into it, and the other side quoted us $1,400, and when we finally secured that much money it was about 2 o'clock and they refused to deal with us, as they had men in Chicago to take up the matter with and they had no time, so we completely fell down and of course we felt badly over it.

Everything was open to Wood and he can tell you about it when we get together. It was quite a responsibility and I don't care for it again, I can assure you.

Well, I hope you found everything in fine shape at home and all your troubles will be little ones. I have made this year's share of World Series in cotton and expect to make more.

I thought the White Sox should have won but I am satisfied they were too overconfident. Well old scout, drop me a line when you can. We have had some dandy fishing since I arrived home.

With kindest regards to Mrs. Leonard, I remain,

Sincerely,

Ty

Analyzing Cobb's letter, the $2,000 and $1,400 represent the amounts they intended to put on the game, and what the winnings would be given the gambling line, which was 7-10. The "men in Chicago" almost certainly refers to the money men behind the bookies. What Cobb was saying, and what Wood's letter would corroborate, was that the bookies simply did not have enough time to get the Chicago mob to take such an enormous bet.[5]

One other fascinating bit in Cobb's letter is the last paragraph about the White Sox, soon to be known as the Black Sox, and their losing of the 1919 World Series. Cobb would later admit to Commissioner Landis at his hearing to laying two baseball bets (the only two of his entire life, he said) on Chicago in Games 1 and 2 of the 1919 World Series. He testified that he lost $150 and never again bet on a baseball game.[6]

As for the bet on the Tigers and Indians game, while the participants all seemed to agree to make the wager, it appears they found out that it was easier to plan the scheme than to execute it. What seemed to have happened was that West's bookmaker got nervous with the amounts of cash being wagered and wanted the approval from his men in Chicago. Cobb may have gotten frustrated by the problems West's bookie had in placing the bet and eventually dropped out of the scheme. Cobb would later say that the letter connected him to the agreement to make the wager, but ultimately he had acted only as an intermediary, setting up Wood with West to place the bet.[7]

Even if Cobb's admission to wagering on Games 1 and 2 of the 1919 World Series were true, no evidence ever surfaced to substantiate it other than his testimony to Landis, and anything he ever mentioned to the press. Cobb had his faults like anyone else; however, gambling was not among them. He was also a man of means and power, which afforded him certain perks over the everyday ball player or common man. One example is that he played poker and sipped bootleg whiskey with the President of the United States, Warren G. Harding, at a private, all-men's club outside Augusta during Prohibition.[8]

It would not be inconsistent with Cobb's reputation and public behavior if his involvement with gambling were as limited as he claimed. One example of Cobb's view on gambling occurred in 1921, shortly after Landis became Commissioner of baseball. Landis's decision in the Black Sox scandal and his hard line stance against gambling put immense fear into ball players about gambling and the consequences they would face if caught. Shortly after Cobb became the player-manager of the Tigers in 1921, he walked by a Detroit billiards establishment just as three of his players were leaving. Cobb warned them to "get the hell away from such places."[9] They protested they were "just looking around." Cobb reiterated "Get away now and don't come back...or I'll turn you over to Frank Navin's cop. Or would you rather talk to Landis?"[10]

A later investigation by Ban Johnson into Cobb's personal life further affirmed that Cobb was not a gambler, as private detectives followed Cobb around and turned up nothing.

Cobb was wise with his money and became one of baseball's biggest philanthropists. Interestingly, long after he retired from baseball, Cobb established a private foundation to which he dedicated much of his time and resources in the last decade of his life. His foundation endures as a lasting legacy, and over the last 60 years has awarded more than $15 million in non-athletic scholarships to thousands of Georgia residents.[11]

Much of Cobb's letter was vague and subject to interpretation by the reader. Of course, Dutch Leonard tried fill in those gray areas with his account of the story.

The Wood letter, however, is more specific.

Wood's Letter[12]

Cleveland, Ohio, Friday.
Dear Friend Dutch,

Enclosed please find certified check for sixteen hundred and thirty dollars ($1,630.00).

The only bet West could get down was $600 against $400 (10 to 7). Cobb did not get up a cent. He told us that and I believed him. Could have put up some at 5 to 2 on Detroit but did not as that would make us put up $1,000 to win $400.

We won the $420. I gave West $30, leaving $390 or $130 for each of us. Would not have cashed your check at all, but West thought he could get it up at 10 to 7, and I was going to put it all up at those odds. We would have won $1,750 for the $2,500 if we could have placed it.

If we ever have another chance like this we will know enough to try to get down early.

Let me hear from you, Dutch. With all good wishes to Mrs. Leonard and yourself, I am,
JOE WOOD

Wood's letter appears to exonerate Cobb by claiming he did not put up a cent for the bet. It also seems to substantiate Leonard's story that Leonard had put up a $1,500 stake, which is why he got a $1,630 check (his $1,500 plus his $130 in winnings). Wood tried to get the whole amount down at those 7-10 odds, but West could only get the bookies to take $600 because of their reluctance to handle the larger sums the players originally wanted to bet. The $600 bet won $420, and after paying off West, it left $130 each for three people. Wood was one. Leonard was two.

But there is no mention of who the third person was, and it remains a mystery today.[13] Leonard claimed in his accusation to Navin and Johnson that the third person was Tris Speaker. Yet there is no mention of Speaker in the Wood letter, nor in the Cobb letter. In fact, there is no evidence connecting Speaker to the fixed game or the wager except for the word of Dutch Leonard.[14] As it turned out, that was enough to entangle Speaker with the rest of the parties in the scandal.

Endnotes

1. Posnanski, Joe. *The Dutch Leonard Affair.* http://joeposnanski.com/the-dutch-leonard-affair/. March 10, 2014. Accessed on April 13, 2019.
2. Thorn, John. *Cobb & Speaker & Landis. Closing the Books.* https://1927-the-diary-of-myles-thomas.espn.com/closing-the-books-cobb-speaker-landis-e7896605fbc1. Accessed April 13, 2019.
3. Posnanski, op. cit.
4. ibid.
5. ibid.
6. ibid.
7. Leerhsen, Charles. *Ty Cobb, A Terrible Beauty.* Simon and Schuster Publishers, New York, NY. 2013. p. 343.
8. ibid, p. 332.
9. Pietruza, David. *Judge and Jury: The Life and Times of Judge Kenesaw Mountain Landis.* (Kindle Edition). Location 7995.
10. ibid.
11. Moran, Mary C. *Ty Cobb: An Unlikely Philanthropist.* http://www.wealthmanagement.com/philanthropy/ty-cobb-unlikely-philanthropist. October 2, 2015. Accessed July 17, 2017.
12. Posnanski, op. cit.
13. ibid.
14. ibid.

CHAPTER 3

Dutch Leonard Grinds His Ax

When Dutch Leonard set off from his fruit farm in California in May of 1926 to go to Chicago and Detroit, he had revenge on his mind. Still stewing that Ty Cobb had released him the fall before, Leonard was determined to make Cobb pay, as well as Tris Speaker, who did not pick him up on waivers. Speaker was a teammate of Leonard's during Boston's glory years, and certainly knew of Leonard's talent. Leonard was bitter about having been forgotten by the baseball world after his release, and perhaps he also saw the opportunity to turn some knowledge into big money.

Leonard's first stop was Chicago and to Ban Johnson's office. At the time of Leonard's arrival, the American League President had become a shell of his former formidable self. Years of alcoholism and poor health clouded his mind and softened his iron will. It was a struggle for Johnson just to get up the energy and will to solve even routine problems.[1]

Nevertheless, Leonard indicated he had a highly incriminating story about Cobb and Speaker and had two letters to back up his accusation. Johnson likely sensed that Leonard was still angry about being canned by Ty Cobb and not picked up by Speaker, and that spite might be the real motivation for his visit. Johnson tried to ignore Leonard's efforts to talk with him.

According to author Charles Alexander, in his book, *Ty Cobb*, Leonard then went to the hotel where the Washington Senators were staying while in Chicago to play a series with the Chicago White Sox.[2] Leonard showed Cobb's and Wood's letters to Senators' manager, Bucky Harris, and club secretary, Edwin Eynon. Enyon, in turn, went to Ban Johnson's house with the news he had heard, prompting Johnson to track down Leonard to hear the story first-hand.[3]

In the meantime, when Leonard couldn't get a hold of Johnson, he went to Detroit to talk with his and Ty Cobb's boss, Frank Navin. The reasons he chose Navin were twofold: First, Navin had been involved with Leonard's release from the Tigers, and also Navin was one of the more influential owners in the American League. Navin, too, tried to stall Leonard, claiming he was too busy to talk to him. When the two finally did meet, Navin was impressed enough with Leonard's testimony and the two letters presented to him that he called up Johnson and told him that he must meet and talk with Leonard.[4]

Before meeting with Leonard, Johnson went to Cleveland to speak with Tris Speaker about the letters. From Cleveland, Johnson went to Detroit, where he met Frank Navin. There, Navin told Johnson that Leonard had not only talked to him, but also offered to sell copies of the letters to a local newspaper and had shown them to the Tigers' Harry Heilmann, who in turn notified Cobb what was going on.[5] When Johnson learned that Leonard had gone back to Chicago, he returned to his office and finally met with Leonard.

Ban Johnson knew what it could mean for his reputation and the reputation of the American League if this news got out to the public. He was scared and urgently wanted to stop Leonard. Even if the fixing of the game and wagering on it had happened seven years earlier, the story was certain to be a major scandal, particularly as two of the Gods of Baseball were allegedly involved.

Dutch Leonard's ploy worked. Even though the letters never mentioned a fix on the game and the claim came only from Leonard, Dutch hoped that submitting the letters to support his testimony (while implicating himself, too) would raise suspicion that the game had been fixed. Why would you pre-arrange a bet without pre-arranging the outcome of the game as well?

When Johnson sat down with Leonard to examine the two letters, he immediately saw they could be considered evidence to lend credibility to Leonard's story, but the evidence was especially incriminating due to the vagueness of the language. Leonard was more than willing to fill in the gaps. Even though the letters fell well short of hard proof and did not even

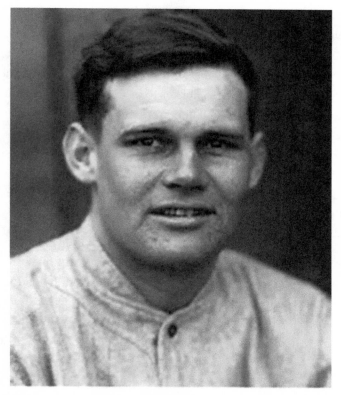

Dutch Leonard stirred up trouble for owners, managers, and teammates throughout his career, and even after his career had ended.

mention Speaker, Johnson was convinced that they must not see the light of day. So he took the option that most gilded-age strategists would opt for. He bought Leonard off. Navin and Johnson agreed to silence Leonard by throwing money at him. After negotiating with Ban Johnson's American League attorney, Henry Killilea, Leonard agreed to surrender the letters to Johnson for $20,000, which was the amount he claimed the Tigers owed him for his unconditional release the previous season.[6]

Later, when the story finally did become public, Killilea admitted his role in the negotiations:

> "Leonard came to Detroit last June and presented a claim
> against the Detroit club for ill treatment regarding a conspiracy
> to throw a ball game and names several players in the American

League. The matter was placed before Ban Johnson and I was called in on the case. I saw Leonard in Chicago in June and settled his claim.

Our agreement was that in the settlement of his grievance against the club he was to deliver to us the letters which would show conspiracy. These letters were delivered after the claim was settled and after that passed out of my hands.

I negotiated the transfer and acted as the representative of the Detroit club...Further than that I cannot go in the matter. All the papers relative to the case are on file in Judge Landis's office."[7]

But in the immediate aftermath of buying Leonard's silence about the release of the letters, Ban Johnson did not notify Commissioner Landis of the payoff to Leonard or the story behind it. Instead, he had Cobb and Speaker tailed by detectives to see if their behavior might shed light on their guilt or innocence. The detectives found no suspicious behavior by Cobb but saw that Speaker was a heavy gambler, at least with the horse races.

By the summer of 1926, only a dozen or so baseball men knew of Leonard's accusations against Cobb and Speaker. Leonard dropped out of sight and Johnson kept mum until he convened a closed-door meeting of the American League ownership in Chicago on September 9th. It was at this meeting that Johnson briefed the American League owners about Dutch Leonard's accusations. The American League owners in turn voted to turn the evidence over to Commissioner Landis, which Johnson did not want to do. Not only would the whole episode disgrace him and his oversight of the American League to the commissioner as the Black Sox scandal had, but his desperate attempt to hold onto some measure of power in the American League would be thwarted.[8]

Despite the owners' actions, Johnson continued to act as an independent authority. Shortly after the meeting, he met with Ty Cobb and Tris Speaker to inform them that they must resign their positions as player-manager and retire from baseball. At this point, we will probably never know what Johnson actually told Cobb and Speaker and why they both so quietly acquiesced to

Johnson's order. Johnson's version of it appeared in the press on January 13, 1927, two weeks before the matter had been settled:

"I gave Ty an interview just before he went on his hunting trip last fall. He talked to me for two hours.

He was heartbroken and maintained his innocence in that alleged betting deal which his letter tell about. I told him whether guilty or not he was through in the American League. I didn't think he played fair with his employers or me.

The actual facts which caused this whole explosion came to me early last summer.

Dutch Leonard had a claim against the Detroit Club. He threatened to sue for damages. He asserted that he had sworn statements of five men stating that Cobb had declared he would drive Leonard out of Baseball.

Ty always has been violent in his likes and dislikes. Those statements of his if carried to court, would have been damaging to the Detroit Club. Mr. Frank Navin, the owner, also faced the possibility that should he refuse to settle with Leonard the latter would sell the two letters."[9]

Upon hearing about the whole affair, Landis decided to ignore Johnson and his ruling and to conduct his own investigation, including visiting Dutch Leonard on his California fruit farm, on October 29th, after Leonard refused to come to Chicago. Leonard maintained his reason for not coming: "They bump people off once in a while there."[10] Of course, fear of being bumped off hadn't stopped Leonard from visiting Chicago months earlier to present his story and collect payment for the letters. Then, he took the money and ran.

After Landis got back to Chicago from his visit with Leonard in California, he decided to schedule a hearing to get everyone's testimony. Leonard was called repeatedly by Landis's office to attend the hearing to face Cobb, Speaker, and Wood, but Leonard ignored all requests. The hearings went on without Leonard, with the Commissioner taking the testimony of Cobb, Speaker and Joe Wood on December 20, 1926.

After the hearing, at the urging of Cobb and Speaker, the Commissioner released a statement by Leonard, as well as the letters written by Cobb and Wood about the incident on December 21, 1926. Leonard was represented only by his statement, which said the following:

> "After the first game (meaning the first one of two regularly scheduled games to be played between Detroit and Cleveland, at Detroit on September 24 and September 25, 1919), Cobb, Speaker, Wood and I happened to meet under the stands, and of course the talk was about baseball and that we (meaning Detroit) wanted to finish third. Speaker said, "Don't worry about tomorrow's game. We (meaning Cleveland) have got second place clinched and you will win tomorrow," and everybody then just agreed that if it was going to be a setup that we might as well get some money down on the game, that is, how to get up the dough and how much we would put up and Cobb said he would send West [a groundskeeper at Navins Field] down to us. I was to put up $1,500 and as I remember it Cobb $2,000 and Wood and Speaker $1,000 each...Several days later I received the Wood letter...with a check for $1,630. He wrote that West was only able to get down some of the money and that my share of the winnings was $130"[11]

Of course, the point of Leonard's claims wasn't that the September 25th game had been fixed to deny New York third place, but that it had been arranged so that he, Speaker, Wood, and Cobb could win some money betting on Detroit. The reason that Leonard gave for revealing the letters was because "by so doing, I was lending assistance in clearing up certain existing conditions which were detrimental to the good of baseball." In a less guarded and off-the-record moment he told writer Damon Runyon, "I've had my revenge."[12]

Endnotes

1. Leerhsen, Charles. *Ty Cobb, A Terrible Beauty.* Simon and Schuster Publishers, New York, NY. 2013, p. 340.

2. Alexander, Charles C. *Ty Cobb.* Oxford University Press, New York, NY. 1984. p. 187.
3. ibid.
4. Leerhsen, op. cit., p. 340.
5. Alexander, op. cit., p. 187.
6. Gay, Timothy. *Tris Speaker: The Rough and Tumble Life of a Baseball Legend.* University of Nebraska Press, Lincoln, NE. 2007. p. 230.
7. *Chicago Herald and Tribune,* December 23, 1926.
8. Gay, op. cit., p 230.
9. *Chicago Daily Tribune,* January 17, 1927.
10. Mark S. Halfon, *Tales From The Deadball Era: Ty Cobb, Home Run Baker, Shoeless Joe Jackson, and The Wildest Times in Baseball History.* University of Nebraska Press, Lincoln, NE. 2014. p. 100.
11. Halfon, op. cit., p. 101.
12. Pietrusza, David. *Judge and Jury: The Life and Times of Judge Kenesaw Mountain Landis.* Diamond Communications, South Bend, IN. 1998. p. 288.

Dutch Leonard was 2-0 in two career World Series starts, allowing only eight hits and two earned runs in two complete games performances.

CHAPTER 4

The Curious Case of Dutch Leonard

Dutch Leonard was a hard-throwing and very talented left-handed pitcher from 1913-1925. Though he had the tools for greatness as a pitcher, his at-times indifferent attitude and unwillingness to get along with his teammates kept him from reaching his potential over his career. Leonard's hot and cold attitude alienated him from every situation he was in while he was in the majors (and many during his minor league career, too), to the point where several times he quit to play in other outlaw leagues. The height of Leonard's on-field dominance came in 1914, when he posted an ERA of 0.96 in 224.2 innings for the Boston Red Sox, the best single-season earned run average in American League history. During his career, Leonard tossed 33 shutouts, including two no-hitters for the Boston Red Sox. Leonard and the legendary Cy Young are the only two pitchers in Red Sox history to toss two no-hitters.[1]

Dutch Leonard's given name was Hubert Benjamin Leonard. He was born on April 16, 1892, in Birmingham, Ohio, and was the youngest of six children of David and Ella Hershey Leonard. Leonard's father worked as a real estate agent in Toledo before moving the family to California in the early 1900s and finding work as a carpenter. While Hubert's older siblings became accomplished musicians (a brother, Cuyler, eventually made a name for himself as a composer and trumpet soloist), Hubert liked baseball and had a particular fondness for pitching. In 1911 at age 19, Hubert, who by then was known as "Dutch" due to his "looking like a Dutchman," pitched for the St. Mary's College team while attending classes there.[2] St. Mary's College was noted for having a great college baseball athletics program during those years. The college was located in Oakland, California, and baseball was the first sport played at the college. By the time Leonard pitched there, St. Mary's had built a reputation for cultivating young men for a career in baseball. Remarkably, five graduates from St. Mary's played in the 1915 World Series: Boston Red Sox left fielder Duffy Lewis, Philadelphia Phillies catcher Ed Burns, Phillies right fielder Gavvy Cravath, Hall of Famer Harry Hooper, the Red Sox right fielder, and Red Sox pitcher Dutch Leonard.[3]

Word of Leonard's exceptional ability as a pitcher spread quickly, and he was signed by the Philadelphia Athletics in 1911. As the Athletics' rotation was already loaded with great pitchers such as Jack Coombs, Eddie Plank, Chief Bender, and Cy Morgan, the services of young Dutch were not needed, and he did not appear in any games from them that season and was let go.

The following year, Leonard joined the Boston Red Sox for spring training, but had control issues due to problems with his arm and failed to make the team. Leonard was then sent to Worcester, Massachusetts of the New England League, where he similarly struggled. Shortly thereafter, Leonard abandoned the club and appeared at Boston team headquarters to complain to club president Jimmy McAleer that "I didn't get any support. It's a rotten league. I won't play there any more."[4] Leonard's selfish behavior would be indicative of what was to become a familiar pattern throughout his career. He always seemed to put himself before his club and was never shy about voicing his opinions and gripes, inevitably leading to his alienating himself from his teammates as well as management.

Because of Leonard's great potential, the Red Sox overlooked his bad attitude and sent him to Denver of the Western League, where he overcame a mid-season suspension for insubordination to win 22 games and strike out a remarkable 326 batters in 241 innings of work. The following spring, Leonard made the Red Sox squad out of spring training and joined the rotation.[5] Together with the young Babe Ruth, who joined the Red Sox the next year, the two formed the heart of a great Boston Red Sox staff during the mid-teen years.

Physically, Leonard was an imposing figure. He was built "more like a football player than a baseball player," according to F.C. Lane, editor and a prolific writer for *Baseball Magazine* from 1912 through 1937. Leonard was stocky at 5'10 ½," and because of his height and build, the lefty relied on the classic combination of an overpowering fastball and sharp-breaking curve. Later in his career he mixed in the spitball, and in 1920 became one of the few "grandfathered" pitchers who were allowed to continue throwing the spitball after it was made illegal.[6]

In his rookie season with the 1913 Red Sox, Leonard posted a 14-17 record and 2.39 ERA in 259.1 innings of work. Management was correct in seeing his great potential, though control remained an issue, as Leonard walked 94 that season to go along with 144 strikeouts. Those walks needed to be cut down. Overall, it was a solid rookie performance by the 21-year-old southpaw. However, Leonard's solid rookie performance that year gave little indication of the dominance he would achieve the following year.[7]

Leonard's historic 1914 campaign was indeed one of the best pitching performances by a pitcher in the history of major league baseball. Unfortunately, Leonard's season was cut short by a wrist injury in early September. In the 36 games in which he pitched, including 11 in relief, the left-hander posted an astounding 0.96 ERA. Leonard fanned 176 batters in his 224.2 innings pitched (giving him a league-best strikeout rate of 7.05 per nine innings) and lowered his walk total to 60, while hitting eight batters. For the season, he allowed just 24 earned runs (10 unearned) and won 19 games against five defeats.[8] The strikeout rate of more than 7 per nine innings is extraordinary for the Dead Ball Era, a level the great Walter Johnson only achieved twice in his amazing career.[9]

Leonard didn't win his first game of the 1914 season until his fourth start, a 9-1 victory on May 4 against Philadelphia. After dropping a game to Washington on May 30 to run his record to 5-3, Leonard did not lose another game until August 13, running off a 12-game winning streak during which he struck out 92 batters in 118 innings. Despite his microscopic ERA, Leonard did not enjoy any long scoreless inning streaks or periods of noteworthy invincibility. Rather, he remained thoroughly consistent throughout the season, shutting out his opponents in seven of his starts and allowing just one run in 10 other starts. He surrendered more than two runs in a game just four times all season, and never allowed more than four runs in any start.[10]

Because Leonard's season was curtailed by injury, he failed to win 20 games, which took a little luster off of and attention away from his performance, and as a result, Leonard's 1914 performance went somewhat unnoticed in the press. Even Leonard regarded his work that year as incomplete. As he later told F.C. Lane, "If I hadn't broken my wrist I think I would have done very well that year."[11]

Even with his wrist injury, Leonard's 1914 season did raise expectations for the 1915 campaign, as he had become perhaps the most dominant pitcher in the game. 1915 would prove to be a resounding success for the Boston franchise, but a turbulent year for Leonard. After receiving a raise in salary to $5,000 per year, Leonard reported to the team out of shape, and started only three games in the first six weeks of the season. To make matters worse, in late May, Leonard was suspended by the club for insubordination. According to newspaper reports, Leonard accused club owner Joseph Lannin of undermining manager Bill Carrigan's authority and generally mistreating his players. Leonard did not return to the starting rotation until early July, though he finished the season strong, posting a 15-7 record and 2.36 ERA. For the second consecutive year, Leonard led the American League in strikeouts per nine innings pitched, with 116 in 183.1 innings. He capped off that great season in impressive fashion, beating Philadelphia's Hall of Fame pitcher, Pete Alexander, in Game 3 of the World Series, 2-1. The Red Sox prevailed in the Series over the Phillies in five games.[12]

Leonard proved more durable over the next two seasons for the Red Sox, pitching a combined 568.2 innings, and posting 34 wins against 29 defeats. Although his strikeout rate dropped over time, Leonard did pitch his first no-hitter in 1916, a 4-0 win over the St. Louis Browns on August 30th. That autumn, Leonard also won his second and final World Series start, pitching Boston to a 6-2 victory over Brooklyn in Game 4, helping the Red Sox win another Series, in six games.[13]

On June 3, 1918, Leonard pitched a second no-hitter, a 5-0 shutout victory, this time over the Detroit Tigers. But for much of the season, he was distracted by the possibility of being called to war due to the United States' involvement in the first World War. Before the 1918 season, Leonard had considered doing something many of his Red Sox teammates had done, which was skipping out on baseball and joining a naval yard, which had very competitive baseball teams. Employment at the naval yards was considered war work, and could help keep a player from being drafted into the army. At the time, Leonard had been talked out of the naval yards by owner Harry Frazee. As 1918 went on, Leonard reconsidered. Originally, he was considered a Class 4 in the draft, which meant he was not likely to be called for duty because he had been married the previous fall, and because he was a farmer. But as the draft exemption rules changed, Leonard became a good candidate to be conscripted, as draft boards began to overlook the marriage exemption in cases in which there was enough money for the wife to live without the husband (like Dutch), plus marriages that happened after the draft was instituted (like Dutch). And non-full-time farmers (like Dutch) were losing their exemptions, too.[14]

On June 22, Leonard left the Red Sox, sensing urgency in avoiding the draft as the war heated up for the Americans in Europe. He signed with the Fore River shipyard team in Quincy, Massachusetts. It was good timing. Two days later, he was moved up to Class 1A for the draft by the government. He did not play again in the majors in 1918, finishing with an 8-6 record and a 2.72 ERA, his worst season to date.

Shortly after Dutch Leonard defected from Major League baseball, that July, baseball was formally declared a non-essential occupation by the government, meaning players were eligible to be drafted. The minor leagues shut down their operations. Major League Baseball shortened its season to end on Labor Day. More than 40 players defected to the steel mills and shipyards. However, professional baseball took notice and condemned the practice. "The American League does not approve of players trying to evade military service," league president Ban Johnson reportedly told the press. A *Baseball Magazine* article titled "A Rising Menace to the National Game" criticized the players' "slacker contracts" and called for government intervention.[15]

As a result, Leonard was nabbed by the army in September of 1918, as the War Department began cracking down on ballplayers who took refuge in shipyards. But Leonard was never sent to the front. Nor did he pitch for Boston again. Dutch won 90 games, losing 64 for Boston in the six years he was on the team.[16]

After the war ended and prior to the 1919 season, Leonard was included in a trade that also sent Ernie Shore and Duffy Lewis to the New York Yankees. Unlike Shore and Lewis, however, Leonard never appeared in a Yankees uniform, instead becoming a salary holdout. According to one report, Leonard demanded that his entire 1919 salary be deposited into a savings account, a demand that infuriated New York owner Jacob Ruppert. "No man who doesn't trust my word can pitch for my team," Ruppert declared.[17] Refusing to cave on his demands, Leonard went back to California to pitch for Fresno in the San Joaquin League.[18]

An exhibition match was played between Fresno and the Chicago Cubs in February of 1919. The game was documented in an article in the *Sun Maid Herald*. The article mentions that Leonard was the star player on the Fresno squad. Together with Bill Hall, another raisin grower in Madera, they defeated the major league Cubs' team 6 to 2.

The article also mentions an important detail about Dutch Leonard, that he was a farmer whose love for farming exceeded his love for baseball: "Hubert "Dutch" Leonard, who is prouder of his eighty-eight acre vineyard eight miles east of Fresno than of his great record with the big leagues..."[19] This view was likely discussed among the baseball teams and their owners, and suggested that perhaps Leonard did not give baseball a 100 percent effort because he was financially comfortable from the profits he reaped from his farm, rendering baseball as somewhat of a hobby for him.

In late May, the rights to the still-unsigned Leonard were sold to the Detroit Tigers for $12,000.[20] In his first season with the Tigers, Leonard led the club with 4 shutouts and 102 strikeouts. Now relying more on the spitball, Leonard spent the next three seasons with the Tigers, posting a modest 35-43 record.

When Leonard became a Tiger, he became a teammate of Ty Cobb's and soon began to clash with him. Their feud actually dated back to 1914, while Leonard was on the Red Sox, when the Georgia Peach accused the pitcher of cowardice after an incident at first base. Cobb dropped a bunt and Leonard rushed to cover first. Rather than risking a collision with Cobb, the pitcher gave him a wide berth, which infuriated Cobb. Rather than run to the bag, Cobb ran after Leonard, and the pitcher ran to the Boston dugout to safety.[21]

The two men coexisted as Tigers teammates until Cobb took over the managerial reigns in 1921. Cobb went out of his way to fine Leonard for breaking curfew, and to clamp down on Dutch's bending of the rules. The Tiger manager always seemed annoyed by Leonard, and seemed to like to torment him, too.[22] The relationship worsened when Cobb and Leonard fought over how to pitch to batters. After a heated exchange, Leonard quit the team, but the Tigers retained his rights. As a result, if Leonard ever wished to pitch in the majors again, it would have to be for Detroit, unless they traded him or gave him his release.

In addition to the problems with Cobb, prior to the 1922 season, Leonard again became tangled in a salary dispute, this time with Detroit owner Frank Navin, who refused to meet the pitcher's demands. Navin tried to make Leonard swallow a salary cut from the $9,000 he made in 1921.[23] Leonard, in turn, violated the reserve clause in his contract by jumping to Fresno of the independent San Joaquin League, an act that led to his suspension from organized baseball. After two years with Fresno, in which he compiled a 23-11 record, Leonard won his reinstatement and returned to the Tigers late in the 1924 season. Appearing in nine games for Detroit, Leonard went 3-3 with a 4.56 ERA.[24]

In 1925, Leonard started 18 games for the Tigers, posting a solid 11-4 record, despite a 4.51 ERA. It was Leonard's best season in years. However, the toxic relationship between him and Cobb resumed where it had left off a few years earlier. They constantly clashed. Despite Leonard's success that year, Cobb accused Leonard of not putting forth his best effort and scolded the pitcher in front of the team. Both men were getting older and Cobb's long dislike of Leonard grew to new levels of hatred. This hatred culminated in Cobb seemingly deliberately trying to push Leonard out of the league by getting him injured. According to Cobb biographer Charles Alexander, Cobb punished Leonard by deliberately overusing him, even after the team physician warned that the work could do permanent damage to the pitcher's arm. When Leonard protested that his arm hurt, Cobb castigated him in front of the entire team, exclaiming, "Don't you dare turn Bolshevik on me. I'm the boss here."[25]

Matters finally came to a head on July 14, when Leonard suffered the most brutal loss of his career, surrendering 12 runs and 20 hits to the

Philadelphia Athletics. Despite the pounding, Cobb kept Leonard in the game for the full nine innings. Even Connie Mack, the opposing manager, pleaded with Cobb to take Leonard out of the game, reportedly saying, "You're killing that boy." Cobb laughed at the suggestion. Cobb would later claim that Leonard was one of only two players he ever intentionally spiked during his career. As Cobb later explained, "Leonard played dirty—he deserved getting hurt."[26]

Later that month, Cobb placed Leonard on waivers and no other team picked him up. Leonard believed that Cobb notified the front offices of other teams in the league to stay away from him and not claim him off waivers. Leonard was particularly hurt that Tris Speaker, manager of the Cleveland Indians and a former Red Sox teammate, passed on him. Once Leonard had cleared waivers, Cobb traded him to Vernon of the Pacific Coast League, but Leonard characteristically refused to report.[27]

Even if Cobb tried to blackball Leonard and tried to convince other teams not to sign Leonard, it is doubtful any team would have picked him up anyway. His reputation as a complainer and sometime slacker was well known. Many in the American League questioned his integrity as a player. He routinely showed up for training camp overweight and was known for his late-night carousing. Not surprisingly, he turned to bending the rules to compensate for his shortcomings. In one instance, in 1918, in a start against Cleveland, the Indians complained that Leonard was using licorice spit to load up the baseballs. Indeed, Leonard did become a spitball pitcher as his talent dwindled.[28]

Leonard's behavior towards management did not help his chances to be signed by another team, either. Among his peers, he was regarded as a selfish, cowardly player who begged off tough assignments. As a professional baseball player, he was a mix of brilliance and indifference, with a me-first attitude that pervaded his whole career.

Despite all his troubles, Leonard was stubborn and refused to change his habits or attitude. "As a pitcher, he was gutless," Hall of Fame umpire Billy Evans once declared. "We umpires had no respect for Leonard, for he whined on every pitch called against him."[29] Leonard never did make it back onto the field after his release in 1926, but he did return to the big leagues and into the spotlight that winter with revenge on his mind.

For his post-baseball career, business and leisure seemed to encompass Leonard's life until his death. One striking detail on Leonard's character happened when Japanese-Americans, citizens and non-citizens alike, were removed from their homes and businesses in 1942 due to Executive Order 9022. They were sent to internment camps during World War II, due to the government fearing the 110,000 people of Japanese heritage might side with their native land against the United States, and as an act of revenge against Japan's attack on Pearl Harbor.

Leonard's home state of California was the state where most Japanese-Americans lived. Due to the deportation and internment in the camps, many of the Japanese-Americans lost their homes and businesses forever. Dutch Leonard, however, saved one farmer's home and vineyards during their deportation. Author, Richard Reeves, writing in his recent book *Infamy: The Shocking Story of the Japanese American Internment in World War II* documented Leonard's good deed:

> "A few white neighbors promised to look after homes and farms — some kept the promises, some did not. In Sacramento, a state agricultural inspector named Bob Fletcher agreed to take over the maintenance of three Japanese farms with ninety acres of vineyards. He paid the mortgage and taxes in exchange for 50 percent of the profits. When the war ended, the Nitto, Okamoto, and Tuskamoto families returned; their land and their profits were waiting for them. The same kind of thing happened in Fresno, where a prosperous local farmer, a retired major league baseball player named Hubert "Dutch" Leonard, who had won 139 games as a pitcher in the American League between 1913 and 1925, agreed to manage a Japanese farm and turned over $20,000 in profits after the war. But such stories were rare."[30]

Leonard seems to have been generous of spirit, and could afford to be generous of wealth due to his own prosperity. Dutch came through with his promise to the farmer, a rarity in a time when Japanese Americans businesses, farms, land and homes were typically pilfered or stolen.[31] It was an act of generosity rarely if ever exhibited by Leonard during his baseball career.

To the end of his life Leonard remained reluctant to discuss the details of his controversial career. As a nephew later told baseball researcher Joseph E. Simenic, "Many times we pleaded with him to sit down and put it on a recording—the highlights of his career—but he never felt in the mood and when he was not in the mood he was not about to do anything regardless of what it might be."[32]

Dutch Leonard died in Fresno of a cerebral hemorrhage on July 11, 1952 at the age of 60. He was buried in Mountain View Cemetery, in Fresno. Dutch was not in the best of health in his later years. It is believed that the cerebral hemorrhage was related due to complications from a stroke he had suffered in 1944. Leonard had also suffered a heart attack in 1942. A year after Leonard's death, an article appeared in the 1953 edition of The *Sporting News* called "Dutch Leonard Good Businessman." The article provided details of the estate left by Leonard when he died in 1952. An excerpt from that article suggested: "Many fans and others in baseball, who noted the extent of the estate of the late H.B. (Dutch) Leonard, wondered how a former ball player could accumulate so much money."[33]

The article noted that in 1910, "It was not generally known, but Ban Johnson, then president of the American League, paid Leonard $25,000 for a special service, presumably in assisting him in checking on reported gambling."[34] If this is true, then it could be inferred that Dutch was a spy for Johnson for a long time before the Cobb-Speaker affair. What is also noteworthy is that in 1910 Dutch Leonard was not a major league pitcher.

The article continued to detail how prosperous the pitcher had become in his post-baseball days around Fresno:

> "It may be that Dutch parlayed that 25 grand with other money he had accumulated as a star pitcher, to develop his fortune, appraised by the executors of his estate at $2,169,143.33. He operated a large ranch under the name of Leonard Bros., and owned one of the largest grape-growing, packing, shipping and storage businesses in San Joaquin Valley. His property holdings totaled 2,500 acres."[35]
>
> "The appraisal showed the estate included $133,385 worth of packing house materials, $96,329 in revolving funds of wineries,

about $65,000 in savings accounts, $55,000 in life insurance, $40,000 in accounts receivable and other farm equipment."[36]

Also reported by the The *Sporting News*, Leonard was "a collector of musical records . . . the estate also including more than $5,000 in records (reportedly as many as 15,000 discs), recorders, phonographs and other electronic equipment. There also was included 100 reels of educational film, three projection screens, and a 16 mm projector."[37]

In his leisure time, when not listening to his records or watching his educational films, Leonard was an avid golfer. Before he suffered heart attack in 1942, he was rated as among the best left-handed golfers in California.

According to an inflation calculator, the $2.17 million estate Leonard left in 1952 had a value equivalent to $18.3 million in today's dollars.

At the time of his death, Leonard was single. In 1917, he had married vaudeville performer Muriel Worth, who divorced him five years later (although SABR indicates that it was in 1931 that they officially divorced) The couple apparently had no children.

The terms of Leonard's will left his estate to his housekeeper, a sister-in-law and three nephews. It appears that a sister, another nephew, and a niece were not among his heirs.

His baseball cards are generally priced among the "commons," but for the length of his major league service, he appears on surprisingly few contemporary cards. He is shown on a 1979 Topps Record Holder card and has a similar card in one of the 1985 Topps "boxed" retail sets. He appears on several cards in the 1990s Conlon Collection series and a few other collectors' issues.[38]

Endnotes

1. Kiser, Brett, *Ghosts of Baseball's Past*, Iuniverse Publishers. Copyright 2016. Accessed January 26, 2006 on Google Books at https://books. google.com/books?id=g_3GEOSed0gC&pg=PA101&lpg=PA101&d-q=hubert+DUTCH+LEONARD+red+sox+and+tigers&source=bl&ots=e-HJUdRZmkq&sig=ACfU3U36RfWBnqtZ-DIOyLAJwCU3kzZQ-nA&hl=en&sa=X&ved=2ahUKEwjD3_K5_4TgAhWkllkKHWVH-BiQ4FBDoATACegQIChAB#v=onepage&q=hubert%20DUTCH%20LEONARD%20red%20sox%20and%20tigers&f=false.

2. Jones, David. *Dutch Leonard*. Society for American Baseball Research. http://sabr.org/bioproj/person/b37d9609. Accessed July 23, 2017.

3. Preston, J. G. *The Glory Days of St. Mary's College*. St Mary's College Magazine. https://www.stmarys-ca.edu/the-glory-days-of-saint-mary's-baseball. October 28, 2016. Accessed January 27, 2019.

4. Jones, op. cit.

5. ibid.

6. ibid.

7. ibid.

8. ibid.

9. ibid.

10. ibid.

11. ibid.

12. ibid.

13. ibid.

14. Fenway Park Diaries. *Fenway's Best Players: Pitchers, Dutch Leonard*. http://www.fenwayparkdiaries.com/best%20players/dutch%20leonard.htm. Accessed January 26, 2019.

15. Novak, Steve. For one controversial season, baseball's best fled the majors to play for Bethlehem Steel. *Lehigh Valley Live*. https://www.lehighvalleylive.com/news/index.ssf/2018/10/1918_bethlehem_steel_baseball.html. Accessed January 28, 2019.

16. Fenway Park Diaries, op. cit.

17. Jones, op. cit.

18. Lemke, Bob. Bob Lemke's Blog. *Dutch Leonard - a Wealthy Man*. http://boblemke.blogspot.com/2011/05/dutch-leonard-died-wealthy-man.html February 18, 2012. Accessed January 19, 2019.

19. Sun Maid Herald. *Raisins Leonard's Pride*. 1919;4(13). https://books.google.com/books?id=Ajk6AQAAMAAJ&pg=RA7-PA17&lpg=RA7-PA17&d-q=hubert+dutch+leonard&source=bl&ots=1cFuupCQKL&sig=ACfU3U-0wkW_50_iEwWXqm6ZQDT3lDGH2Ng&hl=en&sa=X&ved=2ahUKEw-j1gdGW14bgAhUCGt8KHfRCB4g4HhDoATAAegQICRAB#v=onep-age&q=hubert%20dutch%20leonard&f=false. Accessed January 26, 2019.

20. Jones, op. cit.

21. Jolt Left. *The Ty Cobb-Dutch Leonard Feud*. https://joltleft.com/the-ty-cobb-dutch-leonard-feud/. Accessed January 26, 2019.

22. ibid.

23. Lemke, op. cit.

24. Jones, op. cit.

25. ibid.

26. ibid.

27. ibid.

28. Fenway Park Diaries, op. cit.

29. ibid.

30. Fox Sports. *Dutch Leonard, American Hero.* October 21, 2015. https://www.foxsports.com/mlb/just-a-bit-outside/story/dutch-leonard-american-hero-102115. October 21, 2015. Accessed January 26, 2019.

31. ibid.

32. Jones op. cit.

33. Lemke op. cit.

34. ibid.

35. ibid.

36. ibid.

37. ibid.

38. ibid.

As a young man, Ty Cobb was unstoppable on the ball field. But even at age 38, his next-to-last season with the Tigers, Cobb hit .378 and led the AL in OPS.

CHAPTER 5

Ty Cobb: The Tiger Is Bitten

"I love Ty Cobb. I know he hasn't a crooked bone in his body,
but the situation is such that he has to go."- Ban Johnson

In 1926, the Tigers fell to sixth place in the American League, though
they had a respectable 79-75 record. Nevertheless, on November 3, 1926,
Ty Cobb caught the baseball world by utter surprise, announcing he was
stepping down as manager of the Tigers and retiring from baseball.[1] At the
time of Cobb's announcement, only a few baseball insiders knew the story
behind his decision.

The 1926 baseball season had been taxing on Cobb, both physically
and emotionally. He had been manager of the Tigers since 1921, and at
age 39, was still a solid player. Heading into the season, Cobb knew he had
an aging team that was mediocre compared with several other American
League baseball squads. The Tigers had strong hitting, but little in the
pitching department. Cobb also decided during Spring Training to focus
less on playing and more on his duties as manager, even though he was still
a huge asset on the field.

Cobb did play nearly every day through May and June, despite being
bothered by a bad back. His hitting was a big factor in keeping the team in
contention. However, Johnny Bassler, the Tigers hard-hitting catcher was
sidelined with a broken ankle, and the Tigers pitching staff just surrendered
too many runs to the opposition, which held the team back.[2]

As the Tigers sank in the standings, the fans got on Cobb. Henry P.
Edwards, *Cleveland Plain Dealer* sports editor even said "Ty Cobb has lost his
popularity in the city."[3] Edwards also wrote that "there are hundreds, yes,

even thousands of fans who attend the games at Navin Field in the hopes of having a chance to boo and jeer Cobb."[4] In an interview with Edwards, Cobb admitted to Edwards that "The last few years I played I was just tired, tired, tired."[5]

The Tigers finished the season strong, but they still landed in sixth place, twelve games behind the pennant-winning New York Yankees. Almost immediately, rumors began to fly whether Cobb would be back as manager or if Navin would even offer him a contract after the sixth place finish.

Cobb did not attend the World Series that year, and instead went home to Augusta, Georgia. From there he was off to the Grand Teton Mountains in Wyoming to hunt bears and moose in a party that included Tris Speaker. Both Cobb and Speaker went on this hunting trip knowing that when they returned they would be compelled to resign, a consequence of the secret meeting they had with Ban Johnson back in September.

After keeping mum on the situation for about four months after Dutch Leonard made the accusations, Ban Johnson called that secret meeting with the American League owners on September 9, 1926. Frank Navin, of course, knew what had happened, but the rest of the American League owners were still in the dark.

It is not clear why Ban Johnson called this meeting of American League owners. It is possible he felt that certain whispers and gossip were reaching a level that might leak into the press and that he sought a quick, quiet resolution.[6]

After Johnson disclosed the evidence to the American League owners, Cleveland Indians president, Ernest Barnard, made a motion to give all of Johnson's files pertaining to the charges of Dutch Leonard to Commissioner Landis. Yankees president, Jacob Ruppert, seconded the motion. The motion was passed unanimously. The owners wanted Commissioner Landis to conduct a hearing with Leonard, Cobb, Speaker, Wood, and West to investigate the charges.

Johnson, of course, was aghast by the resolution and extremely angered by it. He had wanted to settle the matter himself without any interference, especially from his rival Commissioner Kenesaw Mountain Landis.[7]

The day of the meeting, Attorney Killilea of the American League sent Landis copies of the 1919 letters from Cobb and Wood, and promised in writing the full cooperation of the American League President. However, the bulk of Johnson's information about the case seemed to stay in the American League's office for the next two months, if not more, as mentioned to the press by Johnson in an anonymous release to the press in mid-January 1927, when Landis was getting ready to meet with the American League owners and Johnson.

The previous September, Johnson had gone to see Cobb and Speaker at their homes to update them on the case (though they both knew about the charges already). When Johnson told Cobb that he planned to banish him from the American League forever, regardless of what happened at Landis's hearing, Cobb was "heart broken and maintained his innocence."[8]

When Cobb came back from his hunting trip, on November 3, 1926, he went to Detroit to hand over his letter of resignation to Frank Navin.

Despite being a controversial figure, many fans loved and admired Cobb and were stunned by his resignation. He was clearly one of the greatest ballplayers of all time, and he had earned some praise for his managerial skills, though others close to the Tigers and many fans were not as impressed. Not surprisingly, he was considered a harsh disciplinarian and a micro-manager of his players. According to author, Charles Leerhsen, one of the Tiger players who played for Cobb allegedly said "That man makes me so nervous I don't know if I am here or Peking."[9]

Public opinion about his managerial skills was divided. Cobb himself admitted to sports writer Fred Lieb: "Maybe I was not a managerial success, but just as surely I was not a managerial failure."[10] H. G. Salinger of The *Sporting News* wrote a very critical review of Cobb's performance as manager: "As a player, he was without peer, as a manager he became a man with a number of superiors...Cobb's natural nervousness did him in. It caused his various moods. He was rarely on an even keel. He was either too generous in his praise or too biting in his criticism. He left wounds that never healed."[11]

Cobb, in turn, claimed he was the victim of a conspiracy involving Frank Navin, Ban Johnson, and Kenesaw Mountain Landis. Cobb said those men wanted him out of the league, and in fact they may have, for reasons that hadn't yet surfaced publicly.[12]

Frank Navin denied the allegations of a conspiracy by Cobb. He knew better than to disclose information about the payoff of $20,000 to Leonard to keep him quiet about the two letters that Cobb and Wood wrote him. Navin remained cool and calm in his demeanor in order to quell the uproar of Cobb's resigning and poked holes in Ty Cobb's accusations publicly by telling the press:

"I don't know what he means when he talks about conspiracy. He was on a player's contract. The contract had expired. Therefore, it was unnecessary to engage in conspiracy to drop him."[13]

Countering this statement, Cobb had charged Navin for undermining the team with his penny-pinching ways. Navin also poked holes in this assertion by Cobb in an interview with the *Detroit News* by stating that he and his partners, Briggs and Kelsey, had let Cobb know that they were willing to go into their pockets "to buy and present to the ball club" any player that the Tigers as a corporation could not afford, but that Cobb failed to identify such a player who was on the market. Navin then continued his counter-assault by stating that "of the players they had acquired on their manager's recommendation, some were satisfactory but most were not." Navin then mentioned such names as Rip Collins, Del Pratt, Wilbur Cooper, among others, names he knew made Cobb look bad as an evaluator of talent as none had been successful in Detroit.[14]

Navin also went on the offensive against Cobb for failing to develop young players the way Joe McCarthy of the Chicago Cubs routinely did, and for causing unhappiness in the ranks. Navin also offered his assessment of the talent level that Cobb was in charge of managing:

"It is generally admitted that the Detroit club has in the last two years possessed the most promising material in either big league. We have always had promising material, but for some reason the players have not developed after they got here."[15]

In clear language to the public to not suspect anything in regards to letting Cobb go:

"I fired him, not because I thought he did anything wrong or dishonest, but because he failed as a manager. He couldn't win..."[16]

"It is true that I intended dropping Cobb at the end of the 1925 season because 11 or 12 players on the Detroit club demanded that I sell or trade them. They did not want it work under him. I explained this to Cobb so he would be able to handle the situation, and I had Harry Heilmann promise me that he would help me remedy the situation."[17]

When analyzing Cobb's performance as a manager, one has to look beyond his team's won-loss record and at the cards he was dealt. During the Cobb years, it is clear the frugal Navin did not give Cobb the necessary players to win a pennant. In fact, Navin had made only two sizable investments in the team since 1921. Cobb was playing with 6th and 7th place material and coming in 2nd once, 3rd twice in his 6 years managing.

So, Navin's attacks on Cobb could be seen as shifting the blame, a typical reaction by someone trying to do damage control. Some people believe a big reason for Cobb's firing was his salary of $50,000 per year. After Cobb was fired, the two were known to snarl "I made you rich!" at each other. Given Cobb's on-the-field success, his words ring far more true than Navin's.

The bombshell of Cobb's resignation as manager and the ensuing feud with owner Navin was still reverberating through the baseball world when a second explosion hit on November 29, 1926, when Tris Speaker resigned as player-manager of the Cleveland Indians. Bewilderment grew among the public as the reasons behind the resignations remained hidden and only a handful of inside baseball men knowing the story.

Commissioner Landis was ready to get down to the heart of the matter and make his own judgment. After he met with Dutch Leonard on his farm on October 29, 1926, he had his sights set on a series of hearings he would conduct in his office with Leonard, Cobb, Wood, and Speaker by the end of November. But Leonard was a no-show, thus forcing Landis to reschedule the date to December 20, 1926. On that day, everyone crowded into Commissioner Landis's office, everyone but Dutch Leonard, that is, who again did not come despite repeated requests by Landis's office.

At the hearing, Cobb and Speaker maintained their innocence. Joe Wood claimed he put money down on the game and corroborated what Cobb and Speaker had testified to: that they did not place any bets. Wood also let on that gambling was a routine thing in baseball at the time, citing that the entire Washington Senators once went broke from gambling on a game that he pitched against Washington's star pitcher, Walter Johnson. Cobb and Speaker said the idea of their fixing the game was ridiculous, and that Leonard, of questionable character anyway, was just out to make a buck by slandering them.[18]

The next day, on December 21, 1926, Landis went public with the scandal, providing Cobb's and Speaker's full testimonies. It was big news, reported on the front page of nearly every major newspaper in the United States.[19]

Endnotes

1. Ginsburg, Daniel. Society For American Baseball Research. *Ty Cobb*. https://sabr.org/bioproj/person/7551754a. Accessed July 24, 2017.
2. Alexander, Charles C. *Ty Cobb*. Oxford University Press, New York, NY. 1984. p. 181.
3. ibid.
4. ibid.
5. ibid.
6. ibid.
7. Leerhsen, Charles. *Ty Cobb, A Terrible Beauty.* Simon and Schuster, New York, NY. p. 346.
8. ibid
9. ibid.
10. ibid at page 336.
11. ibid.
12. ibid at page 338.
13. ibid.
14. ibid.
15. ibid.
16. Reynolds, Robert Grey. Jr. *The Ty Cobb & Tris Speaker Baseball Betting Scandal.* Kindle Edition. Locations 260-261.
17. Burgess, Bill. *Leonard, Cobb, Speaker Affair.* http://baseballguru.com/bburgess/analysisbburgess05.html. Accessed August 16, 2017.
18. Leerhsen, op. cit. p. 338-339.
19. ibid, p. 346-347.

CHAPTER 6

Cobb's Testimony

On December 20, 1926, in the offices of Judge Kenesaw Mountain Landis, Tyrus Raymond Cobb was called as a witness in the alleged game-fixing/gambling event from 1919, made public by Dutch Leonard. A number of preliminary questions were asked by Mr. Landis concerning Cobb's entry in baseball and his playing career. The main testimony, with questions posed by Judge Landis and responded to by Baseball God Cobb, was as follows[1]:

Landis: You became manager of the Detroit club when?
Cobb: 1921.
Landis: And managed the team from 1921 to 1926, both inclusive?
Cobb: Yes, sir.
Landis: I call your attention to the letter you have just identified as having been written by you and ask you if you recall the occasion of having written that letter?
Cobb: Yes, I wrote the letter.
Landis: And what was it about?
Cobb: It was a response to a request by Leonard that I ascertain from Wood, Joe Wood, the amount of money that was wagered on this game in question.

Talked on ball field

Landis: That is the game of September 25, 1919?
Cobb: Yes, sir. He stated—you want me to relate what he said?
Landis: Yes.

Cobb: He stated that he was having and he wanted to check up on the amount that had been wagered.

Landis: Do you recall where you were and where Leonard was at the time he made that request to you?

Cobb: On the ball field.

Landis: When was it that he made this request of you, as you say, with respect to the playing of that game, before or after the game?

Cobb: If my memory serves me right, it was the day of the game.

Landis: Well, before the game was played or after?

Cobb: Yes sir, before.

Landis: Give me the conversation, as near as you can remember it, just what was said.

Cobb: Well, he was leaving, could not be there after the game, and he wanted to find out as quickly after the game as possible—he wanted me to ascertain from Wood the amount that was paid. That is to the best of my knowledge.

Landis: When did you first hear a bet was to be put up on that ball same?

Cobb: Leonard came to me and wanted to know who would be a man they could trust. And that is where I figured that the—

Landis: What was your answer to him?

Cobb: I told him I would get a man for him.

Landis: And what did you do along that line?

Cobb: I pointed out West, a man that was employed around at the park.

Did speak of betting

Landis: Had you had any with him before about betting on ball games?

Cobb: No, sir.

Landis: Or about betting on anything else?

Cobb: No, sir.

Landis: Was there anything in his inquiry or statement to you about somebody that he could trust?

Cobb: Well, there might have been other conversations. I am only relating what I remember back, way back there, and there might have been other things. For instance, he talked about ascertaining what amount of money would be put up by Wood, see? He wanted me to inquire of Wood the amount of money that had been put up.

Landis: Well, that was, as I understand—

Cobb: And that would indicate to me what was going to be done. I also must have had knowledge of the fact.

Landis: When his request that you have told me about, that you would find out from Wood about the bet—

Cobb: His request?

Landis: And what happened, when did he make the request?

Cobb: My impression has been all along that it was the day of the game in question.

Landis: And was it before or after the game was played?

Cobb: It was before.

Landis: And was that at the same time that he asked you, in the same conversation in which he asked you for the name of somebody he could trust?

Cobb: It was.

Didn't talk to Speaker

Landis: Did you have any conversation with Wood about this bet?

Cobb: I did not. I did not until after the game. That is—wait a minute. I did not until I asked him concerning the amount of money that was bet.

Landis: Did you have any conversation with Speaker about this game?

Cobb: None whatever.

Landis: Betting on the game?

Cobb: No.

Landis: Did you bet any money on the game?

Cobb: Positively did not.

Landis: Did you intend to?

Cobb: I did not.

Landis: Did you have any conversation with anybody whatever about betting on the game, about your betting on the game?

Cobb: I did not.

Landis: You played in that game?

Cobb: I must have. I have never seen the box score yet.

Landis: I now hand you the box score taken from a Detroit paper of December 26th. Mr. O'Connor—pardon me, judge; that is a Chicago paper. *Chicago Tribune*, September 26, 1919.

Landis: Does that box score refresh your memory as to whether you played in that game?

Cobb: It indicates that I must have played in the game.

Landis: You have no recollection of the game?

Cobb: No.

Landis: I wish you would look at your letter, Exhibit No. 1, and calling your attention particularly to the language of that part of the letter starting with "Wood and I."

Cobb: Yes. "Wood and myself."

Tried to veil betting

Landis: "Wood and myself," and make any statement you desire to make respecting the language which you used in that letter to Leonard.

Cobb: You want me to explain it?

Landis: Yes.

Cobb: In writing this letter to Leonard it is apparent that I in a way tried to veil the betting end of it as a betting proposition. I wanted to convey the information that he had asked me for and that I had promised to give to him, and in so doing I used the expression of a "business proposition." Also in doing that I connected myself with the proposition, connected myself with Wood's name. In conveying to Leonard this information, I stated to him just what Wood had told me, the amounts of $2,000 to $1,400 quoted by the other side, was entirely different to the information that Wood conveyed to Leonard in his letter, which indicated that I was not in on the betting proposition, that Wood merely put me off by giving me the wrong information and a fictitious amount. In my letter I state: "The information gotten from Wood was that there was no money bet." If I was in on the proposition Wood most certainly would have given me the true information. I was giving Leonard merely the information that Wood had given me.

Landis: And what was the information, what was Wood's reply to you, to your inquiry that you say you made?

Cobb: That he had not got up a cent, that the other side refused to deal with him. It was at 2 o'clock, and the other side refused to deal with him.

Landis: Now, you say in that letter, "We completely fell down." What have you got to say about that expression, "We completely fell down?"

Cobb: That is just in keeping with the veiled manner that I tried to give Leonard the information that he had asked me to get.

Denies pact with Speaker

Landis: Now, in this statement that Leonard made to me in California, and which I have read into this record, he tells of a conversation under the stand after the game played the preceding day. Was there any such conversation between you and Wood and Speaker and Leonard?

Cobb: Positively no. If such a frame-up was true, why should we stop for a few minutes under the stand and arrange such an important matter? The players, both visiting and home players, come out from the field through a dugout to their respective clubhouses. Where would we have the time and where would we go for just a few minutes, as Leonard has stated, to frame up such an important matter?

Landis: Do you remember what the position of the Detroit club in the pennant race was at that time?

Cobb: From memory, no. Indications were it was third place.

Landis: Why was it you mentioned West to Leonard as a man that he could trust?

Cobb: He is the only man I knew or that was there handy, that I figured that he could trust.

Landis: What made you think West was familiar with this sort of thing?

Cobb: No other reason in the world except what I stated.

Landis: Had you ever had West place any bets for you on anything?

Cobb: Positively no.

Landis: Had you known or heard of his placing bets for other players or other persons on anything?

Cobb: Positively not.

Asked West about bets

Landis: Did you talk to West about taking care of this bet on this ball game?

Cobb: I did not. In fact, when this matter came up, sometime in the latter part of the season of 1926, I went to West and I says, "This is a very important matter, a lot is at stake, it must have happened several years ago, and I want you to tell me the truth. Do you know anything about the placing of a bet for Joe Wood or Leonard on a game?" At first he said no or declined to answer. I pressed him and told him to tell the truth because it meant a lot to me, and we tried to make the matter straight. He then went into the matter, told me he had taken some money down to post to bet and had gotten down six hundred and some odd dollars against four hundred and some odd - whatever the bet was - and that he said he'd taken the money to the train and given it to Joe Wood.

Wanted West's story

Landis: What do you understand he meant by his hesitation in telling you about this before?

Cobb: Well, at that time I did not really figure on why he hesitated. I merely continued to press him to tell the truth regardless, tell me the truth. I wanted to get right on it. I could not remember anything about it.

Landis: Well, what did he tell you?

Cobb: He then told me about it.

Landis: About putting up six hundred dollars against four hundred?

Cobb: Yes, and that he had gone to the train and given it to Wood. Now, this all happened this fall, 1926, after the—I guess it was after the letters had been—No, it was not after the letters, either. It was after it was known that certain charges had been made concerning this game. At the time I questioned West, I did not know whether I had gone to him in person or not; that was the reason I had pressed him to tell me what the truth was so I could get the thing straight.

Landis: You did not know whether you had gone to him in person when?

Cobb: In 1919, back when the game was played.

Landis: In connection with the game?

Cobb: Yes.

Landis: Have you now any recollection as to whether you went to West or had any talk with him at that time about that game?

Cobb: Well, I have not.

Landis: Or that bet?

Cobb: I haven't any recollection that I went to him or not. He put me right on that.

Wanted only to win

Landis: Now, getting back to the day of this game, or the day before the game, whenever it was that you had this talk with Leonard, did you and he, or either of you, say anything at that time about Detroit being in third place or having a chance for third place, or anything or that sort?

Cobb: The conversations back at that time were not impressed on my mind concerning the place we had or anything. I figured that I had knowledge of the fact that we were to win, that the Cleveland club had finished in second place, and had nothing to win, and we were fighting for third, and it had been a long season, 154 games, and the players were fagged out, and we had something to fight for, and the psychology was all in favor of us.

Landis: Just what do you mean by that?

Cobb: Well, I think the newspaper people, the club owners, the fans, all realize that the last few games of any season, where the clubs have nothing to win or lose, that they do not fight the games out like they do when they are battling earlier in the season, and a good indication of that is that such games played by teams who have nothing to win, the fans do not attend right at the end of the season as they do earlier.[1]

Cobb's responses were carefully crafted and left Landis with nothing to hang on him about the affair, instead shifting all the guilt on Wood whom Cobb asserted wanted to wager on the game. Cobb claimed to have been merely an intermediary to get Wood to West so that a bet could be placed. Cobb asserted he only put money on only two games in his life, losing $150 on the first two games in the 1919 World Series.

The box score of the fateful game from September 25, 1919 sheds little light either. Cobb had a single that day, Speaker ripped two triples, and Wood and Leonard did not pitch. As for the meeting under the stands to fix the game, it seems to be an unlikely thing to have happened. As Cobb points out in his testimony, "If such a frame-up was true, why should we stop for a few minutes under the stand and arrange such an important matter?"

Endnote

1. *Chicago Tribune*, December 22, 1926.

CHAPTER 7

Cobb: The Aftermath

The release of the evidence by Landis touched off a huge firestorm of publicity across the nation, almost comparable to what had followed when Joe Jackson and Eddie Cicotte admitted that they and others had thrown the 1919 World Series. Baseball writers and journalists across the United States analyzed and argued over the charges and denials. The news turned into a media frenzy, just as Ban Johnson had known would happen, as cries of "scandal" over the Dutch Leonard Affair rocked the public.

Now that the cat was out of the bag, Cobb was able to speak freely to the press. He described his anger and hurt over the whole thing by proclaiming, "Is there any decency left on earth? I am beginning to doubt it. I know there is no gratitude. Here I am, after a lifetime in the game of hard, desperate and honest work forced to stand accused without ever having a chance to face my accuser. It's enough to try one's faith."[1]

What added to Cobb's frustration was that Dutch Leonard never showed up at the hearing and that he (Cobb) was never able to confront Leonard face-to-face to rebut his accusations and vent some of his anger. Back out in California, Leonard instead stayed protected in his privacy, enjoying his revenge from afar.

In his interview with Chicago writer Harold Johnson on December 22, 1926, Cobb told Johnson that he had wanted to resign the previous spring spring but also wanted to win a pennant. Cobb tried to throw the press off by claiming that "my resignation had nothing to do with this investigation."[2] In addition, he took the opportunity to take another swing at Frank Navin by stating "I saw under the existing conditions in Detroit, that I wasn't to be allowed that privilege (to win the pennant in 1926)."[3]

Cobb then turned to the heart of the matter with Harold Johnson by declaring:

> "In the first place I want to say that I am innocent. The testimony of Mr. Wood and Mr. West will absolutely vindicate me. I did not in any manner participate in the betting.
>
> On September 25, 1919, at Detroit, the Cleveland club was in second place and the season was practically over. Cleveland could not advance in the standing, while Detroit was fighting for third place. Detroit had everything to win; Cleveland nothing.
>
> The Cleveland players had attained all they could, consequently they had let down. Leonard of Detroit, evidently seeing this opportunity, approached player Wood of Cleveland with a proposition to bet, inasmuch as pitcher Boland of Detroit had been announced for the next day. The latter had been a thorn in the side of the Cleveland club for years.
>
> These two boys (Leonard and Wood) bet $600 to $450. Before leaving Detroit for the coast Leonard asked me to check up on Wood and find out what he had bet and inform him by letter to Fresno. (Leonard had started for his California home before that game and Wood was not even in the line-up.) In the game in question, Speaker got two triples, while I managed to make only one hit in five times up, yet I was on the team favored to win, according to the stories told in the testimony.
>
> If Leonard could have been forced to face me before Commissioner Landis or the American League directors, I could have made him admit I had been falsely accused, but he refuses to meet me.
>
> I have been in baseball in the American League for twenty two years and have given the game everything humanly possible...and the accusations brought against me are terrible, after all these years of honest endeavor.

In all my career I made only two bets on the outcome of baseball games and those were placed during the World Series of 1919 between the Chicago White Sox and the Cincinnati Reds. After losing $150 on the White Sox in the first two games, I quit betting. I am most innocent of any wrongdoing in this affair as a newborn babe and I only hope the fans and public, who have been through my career will believe me."[4]

Of course, public opinion was everywhere about the scandal. Baseball was once again on trial for gambling, this time with two of its greatest Gods, in Cobb and Speaker, in the spotlight.

Among the many people inside and outside of baseball who rallied around Cobb and Speaker was Will Rogers (the famous stage and motion picture actor, vaudeville performer, American cowboy, humorist, newspaper columnist, and social commentator) who wrote: "If Cobb and Speaker had been selling out all these years, I would like to have seen them play when they wasn't selling."[5]

Even Umpire Billy Evans, who in September 1921 was involved in a bloody fistfight with Cobb, chimed in on the side of Cobb and Speaker. Evans called Leonard "gutless, a man the umpires had no respect for. It is a crime," declared Evans, that "men of the stature of Ty and Tris should be blackened by a man of this caliber with charges that every baseballer knows to be utterly false."[6]

Jack Graney, Charley Jamieson and Harry Lunte, who had played for Cleveland in the questionable game as well as Chuck Shorten, in right field for Detroit that day, all denied any knowledge of a fix. "It's all bunk," said Lunte.[7]

In late December 1926, evangelist and former major leaguer, William Ashley "Billy" Sunday chimed in with his own opinion of the Cobb-Speaker affair by proclaiming "If the charges made against Ty Cobb and Tris Speaker are true, the decent public may as well hang crepe on all baseball stands. Baseball has its crooks, but it will have to be crammed down my throat before I believe that Cobb or Speaker played such a part."[8] Sunday continued on stating that "both men are my friends: I know them well. They were leaders in the sport, men who made big money, and it is impossible to believe that they would toss everything to the winds for the sake of a small sum. If they wanted to be crooked they could have gone after big money."[9]

Another expression of support came from the Philadelphia Sports Writers association. In a telegram to Cobb, the association said:

> "Philadelphia, Pa., Dec. 23.--(AP)--"The Philadelphia Sports Writers association desires to express to you and Tris Speaker its utmost confidence in your honesty and integrity. The sporadic outbursts have in no way lowered you from the pedestal as the greatest ball player of all times. We deem it a privilege to invite you as a guest of honor to our annual banquet February 8 at the Hotel Adelphia."[10]

The message was signed by the officers of the association, Louis H. Jaffe, president; Robert T. Small, treasurer, and Larry McCrossan, secretary.

Another man who knew Cobb and Speaker weighed in. And his opinion was relevant because his career had been so similar to theirs. His name was Eddie Collins. Collins said:

> "Some more dirty linen. I don't believe it of Ty and Tris. Anybody who is acquainted with Cobb and Speaker know they are thoroughly honest men and above suspicion. I have known Ty and Tris for many years and will believe nothing that I read or hear that these men have been linked with a crooked angle of the game. These two men have been great assets to baseball. They have played the game fair and square, and this slush which is now being cast at them looks contemptible."[11]

Back in Augusta, Georgia, Cobb spoke on December 23rd, that "the scandal was a rotten business that was brought out by the vengeful nature of a man I fired from the team." Cobb also considered the American League officials equally guilty because they had paid Leonard to remain silent about the details of his story.[12]

That same night, the Augusta, Georgia City Council adopted a resolution that asserted complete confidence in the honesty, probity and integrity of Tyrus Raymond Cobb.

Meanwhile, also in Augusta, Cobb was presented with a floral wreath. The honor was intended to boost Cobb's confidence after Commissioner Landis had named him in the whole affair. In addition, some five hundred of Cobb's supporters gathered around the flag-draped Confederate monument on Broad Street to cheer him on. The dignitaries speaking on Cobb's behalf included Federal Judge William H, Barrett and Mayor William B. White. Cobb himself faced a banner that read TY IS STILL OUR IDOL AND THE IDOL OF AMERICA. Cobb indicated that he "was sad and happy both on this occasion." He took the opportunity to defend Speaker by saying that he "was as innocent as I," and will do anything to clear his name. Cobb also took the opportunity to cite Joe Wood's sworn testimony as exonerating him. His wife, Charlie Cobb, chimed in and proclaimed:

"Above all persons I should know that Ty Cobb is absolutely fair and square. We have been married 19 years and have five children. My husband may have his faults, but dishonesty is not one of them."[13]

As for Ban Johnson, who felt the matter should have been closed, Landis's release of the information shocked him. He thought he had disposed of the whole situation by paying Leonard off and banishing Cobb and Speaker. Johnson was further worried that Landis's actions would damage his own reputation by what this scandal would bring to baseball in general, and especially to his beloved American League. So Johnson backtracked his statements and tried to do damage control of the firestorm that had started in the press.

Not surprisingly, Johnson's statements to the press put himself in an unfailingly positive light. Johnson indicated that he was convinced that Cobb and Speaker did not fix the game back in 1919, but their actions still involved serious improprieties. Johnson was not convinced by Cobb's explanation of the letter that he wrote to Leonard in 1919. But at the same time, Johnson acknowledged Cobb's integrity as a competitive ballplayer and his legacy in the game of baseball:

"I love Ty Cobb," Johnson said. "I know Ty Cobb is not a crooked ball player. We let him go because he had written a peculiar letter about a betting deal that he could not explain and because I felt that he violated a position of trust."[14]

Johnson spoke about Speaker as "a different type of fellow...cute." Johnson knew Speaker had a long history of gambling, as verified by the Pinkerton detectives. Johnson knew that Speaker loved playing the horses, like many Americans did at the time in the 1920's, but insinuated that he may have also bet on baseball, given his propensity to gamble at a moment's notice. Either way, Johnson claimed the American League had wished to protect both Cobb and Speaker by keeping the charges against them secret.[15]

For Detroit owner Frank Navin, the report of the scandal to the public was another opportunity to throw a smoke screen on the whole sordid affair. When interviewed by the press, Navin was careful in his responses. He was not going to admit that he knew all along about the cover up of bribing Leonard for the letters, as well as covering it up to Landis and the press for a few months. Instead, Navin chose the middle ground, despite all of the attacks on Cobb he made to the newspapers. When pressed by the reporters on why the game that was allegedly thrown seven years earlier was allowed to smolder through the years, Navin replied in a statement to the press on December 22, 1926: "When I heard about the accusations then, I was dumbfounded...I did the only thing I could do. I took the matter to Ban Johnson."[16]

"Cobb says his resignation was in no way connected with the charges made by Leonard. That is agreeable to me. I will not contract him."[17]

Of course, this was a blatant lie by Navin. There was no way he would admit that he played a central role in bribing Leonard. He chose instead to claim it had all unfolded on the baseball diamond, and the firing of Leonard by Cobb was well beyond his control and would not interfere.

As for Commissioner Landis, besides this scandal, he found himself with another mess to clean up when ex-Chicago White Sox player Charles "Swede" Risberg contacted the commissioner's office (while the whole Speaker and Cobb affair was going on), and presented new and more widespread accusations about game-fixing he claimed had occurred. Cobb was even called to testify in that matter, which included claims by the Risberg (who was one of the eight banned Black Sox), that "the White Sox had contributed $45 or $50 apiece, $1,100 in all, to bribe the Detroit team to slough off (throw) consecutive doubleheaders at Chicago on September second and third."

The most dramatic moment of the Risberg hearings is when Cobb came to testify on the first day. Cobb was still seething over the whole Dutch Leonard affair and was angry at Landis for having questioned his integrity. Irving Vaughn, a local Chicago sports writer wrote "You could see by the expression on Cobb's face that he was bitter at Landis."[18] With his fate still hanging due to the Dutch Leonard Affair, Cobb now had to face another sordid accusation, compounding his anguish.

Cobb vigorously denied any knowledge of what Risberg claimed had taken place. Cobb stated "There has never been a baseball game in my life that I played in, that I knew was fixed."[19] When he finished his testimony he asked Landis sarcastically "Do you want to swear me in?" After his testimony, Cobb went back to Augusta and wired Landis to ask every witness in the Risberg case whether they knew of his ever being involved in crookedness. When Landis did pose the question to the witnesses, they all affirmed Cobb's honesty.[20]

Landis was shrewd in this matter and had his own cards to play due to an underlying motive from both the Cobb/Speaker and the Risberg cases. The underlying issue was Ban Johnson. The power struggle with Johnson that had gone on pretty much for the time Landis became commissioner was approaching a final showdown. Landis had been reelected to a new 7-year contract, with his salary increased from $50,000 to $65,000 a year. His motive for releasing the material, in addition to informing the public, was to publicly humiliate Johnson and expose his ineptness as the leader of the American League. In essence, Landis could both embarrass Johnson, who thought he had everything tidied up, and put himself in total control of the Dutch Leonard Affair. Landis had time on his side to decide the cases, during which he could let Johnson stew and lose credibility and become more vulnerable over time.

Cobb and Speaker were planning strategy to defend themselves, not only in the public eye, but legally as well. On December 26th, both Cobb and Speaker went to Washington D.C. and both were joined by Speaker's highly regarded Cleveland-based attorney, William H. Boyd.

In addition, Cobb wanted to use his political connections to put pressure on organized baseball. Senators William H. Harris of Georgia, Pat Harrison of Mississippi, and other congressional acquaintances of Cobb were sympathetic to the predicament of Cobb and Speaker. But sympathy alone could not muster any help for Cobb and Speaker by Congress, as there was no justification for government action against baseball in the area of anti-trust violations, because in the Federal League case four years earlier, the Supreme Court had ruled that anti-trust laws did not apply to baseball. The Justice Department told Cobb and Speaker the same thing regarding this matter.

Cobb used his connections to people in high places
and his wherewithal to build a strong defense against
Leonard's accusations.

From Washington, Cobb, Speaker, and attorney Boyd traveled back to Cleveland, arriving on the morning of December 28th. They went there to plot further strategy with Boyd, and spent the day going through law books in Boyd's office. Although Cobb and Speaker could not get help from the federal government, there was the distinct possibility that they could seek damages against those who publicized the incident. Boyd went to work on gathering evidence to clear his client, Speaker, on any game-fixing charges. As for suing organized baseball for damages, nothing about it was said.[21]

Cobb went back to Detroit with his admirer and friend, Edward S. Burke, who was the attorney that had represented the Detroit Tigers and Cobb in the Stanfield affair back in 1909. In that incident, Cobb had gotten into an altercation with George Stanfield, a bellhop at the Euclid hotel in Cleveland. History has distorted the whole incident, stating that Stanfield was African American to fit with Cobb's reputation as a racist. However, in Charles Leerhsen's book, *Ty Cobb: A Terrible Beauty*, the author's research showed that not only did Stanfield embellish the altercation with Cobb, but also that he was not African American. That detail was never being mentioned in the newspaper reports of the dispute, and on the 1910 federal census, Stanfield is listed as white.[22]

When Cobb arrived in Detroit, he retained attorney James Orin Murfin, Jr., a former Michigan circuit court judge, a regent at the University of Michigan, and one of Motor City's best known jurists.[23] When Cobb summoned reporters to talk to him about the situation, Joe Wood was there from Connecticut as well as Murfin. Cobb paced the hotel room as he spoke to the newsmen and told them he had been forced to resign and that stories about discontent on his teams were exaggerated. Cobb even said that most of the Tiger players had sent him telegrams indicating their condolences for him quitting. After the interview, Cobb went back to Augusta and Wood boarded a train back to Yale, as University authorities were deciding whether they wanted to keep him as their baseball coach.

No one knew when or where the Commissioner would render his decision, if it all. It seemed possible that Landis would do nothing, simply be content to let Cobb's and Speaker's careers end in a cloud of suspicion.

Landis ended speculation about what he would do by summoning the American League club presidents to an emergency meeting on

January 24, 1927, in part to inquire into press reports that the league had additional evidence on Cobb and Speaker that they had not turned over to the Commissioner. That information had been given to the press by an anonymous source who claimed to be part of baseball's power hierarchy. In the frenzy that occurred after Landis released the material and testimonies of Cobb and Speaker back in December, the press (for the most part) and the public (nearly unanimously) supported both the banished superstars. But Landis was boiling mad at the possibility that there was additional evidence that had not been produced by the American League officials.

By the time of the January 24th meeting, Ban Johnson had publicly admitted to being the anonymous source of the reports of blacklisting Cobb and Speaker to the press. Johnson was very sick at the time, suffering from chronic foot-and-mouth disease, and he had entered a perfect storm he knew he could not handle. After Johnson's physician certified that Johnson needed rest as he was suffering from a variety of serious ailments in addition to foot-and-mouth disease, the assembled baseball executives voted unanimously to give Johnson an indefinite leave of absence, and Tigers' owner Frank Navin was named acting American League President.

And so, after meeting with American League owners, and Ban Johnson out of the way, the Commissioner mulled over the evidence and pondered the fates of Cobb and Speaker. The decision finally came on January 27, 1927, in the form of a written statement by the Landis distributed by his secretary, Leslie O'Connor. Cobb and Speaker were exonerated.

> These players have not been, nor are they now, found guilty of fixing a ballgame. By no decent system of justice could such a finding be made. Therefore, they were not placed on the ineligible list. As thy desire to rescind their withdrawal from baseball, the releases which the Detroit and Cleveland clubs granted at their requests, in the circumstances detailed above, are canceled and these players names are restored to the reserve lists of those clubs.[24]

That same day as the judgment went to the press, Landis instructed Frank Navin to wire Cobb in Augusta that he was free to sign with any American

League team and that the Tigers would transfer his contract without cost. Cleveland similarly notified Speaker.[25]

To do further damage control on his own image in the eyes of the Detroit fans who loved Cobb, Frank Navin took further steps. To try to avert the outcry that would occur in Detroit upon the announcement that Cobb was a free agent, Navin ignored that part of Landis's instructions and instead said:

> "I am very happy in response to Cobb and Speaker being cleared by Landis. It was an unfortunate affair... I always said to anyone who asked me that I thought Cobb an honest ballplayer, who always did his best to win. I held the same about Speaker, though, of course I didn't know him so well as I did Cobb. We will take Cobb back on our reserve list."[26]

So with the proclamation by Landis, the nerve-racking wait was over for baseball fans, and most of them heard what they wanted: Baseball Gods Cobb and Speaker were innocent and free to continue their careers in the game.

Cobb, however, didn't believe that the favorable decision came from Landis's impartial judgment, as reported to the public by his secretary. Cobb believed that his lawyer, James O. Murfin, who was "an exalted man, tough had forced Landis's decision."[27] Cobb added that Murfin and Speaker's counsel had forced the acquittal from Landis, as the attorneys had gathered enough evidence of still additional scandals that would be forthcoming to the public if Landis did not decide in their favor. If Cobb was going down, he would take all of baseball with him. He threatened a lawsuit against the game. "I could say a few things about fake turnstile counts and juggled ticket-counting practices by major league owners," Cobb said later. Despite Cobb ultimately prevailing in the case, he was boiling mad that Ban Johnson had given credence to Dutch Leonard's charges and that Kenesaw Mountain Landis took two months to render his decision. Speaker may have felt the same way, but never made his feelings known after the verdict was delivered.

What both these men may have never considered is that their reputations and careers had became part of the power struggle between Johnson and Landis and that they had been used as pawns in a continuing chess match between the two Czars of baseball. The *Philadelphia Daily News* framed the scandal in this way:

> "Landis and Ban Johnson wanted to make a grandstand play in which the two veteran stars were to be ruthlessly sacrificed to prove that baseball is honest. It was expected that this pure and holy stand would elicit tumultuous applause from the fans, whole interest for publication, at least were being guarded. But the dear old public, instead of cheering baseball's nobility of character, found its sense of common justice so outraged that it clamored for the blood of the accusers instead, both of the direct accusers and those whose failure to defend the players implies a belief in their guilt and a concurrence in the apparent banishment from Organized Baseball."[28]

The whole affair left Cobb bitter. After the verdict was handed down by Landis, Cobb remarked with venomous sarcasm:

"Very decent of the judge. For weeks, I had been agonized by the scandal, sick of heart and convinced that my baseball bow-out would always be tainted with a question."[29]

Cobb wanted some sort of retribution for his good reputation having been dragged through the mud, and for being forced to resign by Ban Johnson. Cobb went on:

> "Well, we won. The verdict of guiltlessness and my full reinstatement left me in a position to file suit for any sum I cared to name, and to collect. And baseball was frightened out of its shoes that I would take that step. From all sides, owners and managers of National and American League teams came at me with offers calculated to get me back in uniform, and to circumvent a legal disaster."[30]

In Congress, a group of Senators (Pat Harrison of Mississippi, George Wharton Pepper of Pennsylvania, James E. Watson of Indiana, James Couzens of Michigan, and William J Harris of Georgia) issued this statement:

> "We find the action of Judge Landis and Ban Johnson outrageous, the act of publicity-seekers who were not only

unjust, but dishonest. This country is not going to be satisfied with baseball's plea that is a mistake about Ty Cobb and Tris Speaker, and kindly pardon its travesty of justice. They are entitled to legal redress for the great wrong done them, and we urge them to take this step."[31]

Legal experts advised Cobb that any defamation suit against baseball for the whole affair would succeed. And succeed with a nice payoff for Cobb. Cobb's friend, attorney Edmund Burke, was in touch with former Secretary of State and former Supreme Court Justice, Charles Evans Hughes, to see if he would handle Cobb's case against Major League baseball. Cobb later claimed that Evans had accepted the case, and would have charged $100,000 in attorney's fees to bring suit against Major League Baseball. A few years later, in 1930, Evans was appointed to the Supreme Court again, this time as Chief Justice. He is the only Supreme Court justice to serve non-consecutive terms on the court (1910–1916, 1930–1941).

Even with legal minds telling Cobb that winning a defamation of character suit was a good possibility, in reality, it may have been a long shot for Cobb, Speaker, and Wood. Commissioner Landis was a crafty lawyer and judge and if he wasn't "morally or legally sure of his ground he would not think of laying himself and organized baseball open to libel (or defamation) suits that would ruin the institution and the Commissioner."[32]

History was on the side of Landis as well. The *Chicago Tribune* reported that:

> "Somehow, libel suits against Judge Landis seldom even blossom much less bear fruit. He was threatened with all sorts of suits by the Chicago Black Sox who threw the 1919 World Series to the Cincinnati Reds. He was threatened two years ago with libel suits by Cozy Dolan and Jimmy O'Connell of the New York Giants, who were accused of offering $500.00 to Heinie Sand of the Phillies to "ease up" at shortstop in an important game.
>
> Thus far no one has so much as out the Judge to the expense of hiring a lawyer by threats of libel suits, for he acts as his own lawyer and as the lawyer of organized baseball."[33]

Underneath all the bitterness and embarrassment from the Dutch Leonard Affair, Cobb had a change of his heart to sue due to his love of the sport:

"What you've given your life to, you don't tear down. I could not sue baseball, maliciously wronged as I had been. But I gave no clue to the American League of my intentions. The owners could only mitigate their mistake, and show regret by luring me back into uniform. And so they came at me from all sides with apologies and checkbooks in hand."[34]

When he resigned the previous fall, Cobb indicated he wanted to retire and spend time with his family. He had lost his ambitions to set more records. He had thought about leaving in 1925 when he saw how little Navin cared about bringing quality players into Detroit. But now that the affair was over, what he wanted was vindication. He did not want to leave the sport with any doubt or cloud over his good name. At 40, Cobb knew he had lost some of the greatness he had exhibited for two decades in Detroit. He also knew he had something left in his tank.

The Georgia Peach Moves On

The influence on Landis by Cobb and Speaker's attorneys on their acquittal will never be known, but one thing was certain: The Dutch Leonard Affair was over. Now what? Cobb was still a player without a home. So Cobb went back to Augusta, picked up his dogs, and went hunting. One of those dogs was named Connie Mack, which might have clued people in on what Cobb would do next, but only a few within Cobb's inner circle had that information.

Despite his burning desire to prove himself yet again and the alleged great interest in him, Cobb had to wonder if there were also doubts due to his age and perhaps the damage done to his reputation. Could he play for a team other than the Tigers after all these years? Cobb certainly did not want to go out under a cloud of suspicion and negative attention, nor did he want to finish his career playing for just anybody—for any run-of-the-mill skipper. He had earned his place in history as one of baseball's finest, and wanted to go out calling his own shots.

Cobb would soon learn the answer to his fate shortly. Back in November, a month before the public knew about the whole scandal, the New York Giants' legendary manager, John McGraw, made it clear there was room for

Cobb on his Giants team, after Cobb had announced his resignation from the Tigers. Landis, however, slapped down McGraw and instructed him to "lay off Cobb." Landis felt it was too soon after Cobb's resignation, with the public still processing such seismic news. Furthermore, Cobb would have had to clear waivers from the American League to play in the rival National League. With the politics and rivalry between the leagues, it is highly unlikely Cobb would have made it through.[35]

Interest was also shown by the St. Louis Browns, New York Yankees, Philadelphia Athletics, and the minor league Baltimore Orioles, who offered Cobb $25,000 to join their team.

To a veteran like Cobb, Philadelphia may have had an edge. If there was ever an old chestnut with a great baseball mind and reputation it was Cornelius Alexander McGillicuddy, aka Connie Mack. Mack managed the Philadelphia Athletics for the club's first 50 seasons of play, starting in 1901, before retiring at age 87 following the 1950 season, and was at least part-owner of the team from 1901 to 1954. He was the first manager to win the World Series three times, and was the first manager to win consecutive Series on separate occasions (1910–11, 1929–30); his five Series titles remain the third most by any manager, and his nine American League pennants rank second in league history.[36]

Cobb clashed with Mack at Philadelphia's Baker Bowl in 1909 after Cobb spiked Frank "Home Run" Baker, possibly accidentally, on a slide into third. The next day, Mack issued a fiery speech to the papers about Cobb and how his "second nature to act mean on the ballfield"...and that Mack would never have him on his team. Eighteen years later, the opportunity presented itself, and although playing in the Baker Bowl required a major adjustment for Cobb, over the years he had grown to admire Mack.[37]

As Cobb matured in baseball over the years, he noticed the genius of Mack and how he analyzed every detail in a game. Cobb also liked the way Mack employed psychology in the game at every opportunity he could get. "If you get the other fellow worried, the battle is half won," closely resembled Cobb's own philosophy.[38]

And so, on February 4, 1927, Connie Mack went down to Augusta, Georgia by train to try to sign Cobb to be a Philadelphia Athletic. Cobb met him at the train station and drove him to the swanky Bon-Air Vanderbilt

Hotel. They bumped into Dan Howley, once a coach under Cobb with the Tigers and now manager of the St, Louis Browns, who also tried to woo Cobb by coming to Augusta. Having two managers making their pitch to the superstar Cobb was rather awkward, but must have been good for Cobb's ego. Mack was so excited to be down in Augusta to meet Cobb that he told a reporter "You can't overemphasize my eagerness to sign Cobb." Awkward or not, both men had dinner at Cobb's house that evening, and the next morning posed for a photographer from the *Augusta Chronicle* before all getting on a train bound for New York City. When Mack had Cobb to himself in a private compartment of that northbound train, he presented Cobb with a contract with the salary left blank. "Put down any amount you want Ty," Mack told the Georgia peach. Cobb mulled it over and knew it would be the last contract he would ever sign due to his age. But he wanted to do it with a bit of flair and have a ceremony in his new ballclub's hometown of Philadelphia.[39]

Before Mack and Cobb traveled to Philadelphia to tell the world that Cobb would be signing with the Athletics, on February 6, 1927, both Cobb and Mack first attended the fourth annual Baseball Writer's dinner held in the East ballroom of the Commodore Hotel in the heart of Manhattan. When Bozeman Bulger, who was the Dean of New York sports writers, reached Cobb's name while reading the list of ballplayers who were at the meeting, the whole gathering rose to their feet and cheered Cobb until he was forced to give a small speech. Cobb was flabbergasted and the emotions of his gratitude could be heard in his voice.

Two days later, in Philadelphia, Cobb announced he was joining the Philadelphia Athletics. The crowd went wild, shouting to Cobb "You still have plenty left." Mack, who sat in the crowd, smiled gleefully, knowing that Cobb still did have plenty left him.[40]

Cobb would have two very good seasons with Mack and his Athletics, batting .357 in 1927 and .323 in 1928. The man who was dragged in with him on the Dutch Leonard affair, Tris Speaker, joined Cobb as his teammate in the 1928 season after spending the 1927 season with the Washington Senators.

So two Gods of Baseball would come full circle in their careers and play out their last days for a manager who was a Baseball God himself and on an Athletics team that was getting better every year. The Dutch Leonard Affair had indeed passed, and Cobb got what he wanted: Vindication.

Even near the end of his life, Cobb still remained guarded about the whole affair. In a letter to his good friend J. Taylor Spink, Cobb indicated:

"Taylor, even to the most wonderful friend I have in the world, which you are...my lips are still sealed on this matter. This is an honor thing with me... It is just too distasteful to talk about. I think it is too late now to stir up things. Most of the people involved are now dead. It almost killed me to suffer such dishonor in a game which I loved so much and to which I think I gave so much. I admit the whole thing rankles me and I talk too much. Some day I'll tell the story which has some twists which would intrigue even your reportorial heart, but not now."[41]

In 1961, Spink shared his thoughts on the matter with the public:

"That was enough for me. I never pressed the issue. Had Ty maintained his health, I'm sure he would have talked, but even then, he was going downhill. That letter, written December 27, 1958, was in wavering handwriting."[42]

Endnotes

1. Alexander, Charles C. *Ty Cobb*. 1984. Oxford University Press, New York, NY. p. 188.
2. *Chicago Tribune*, December 22, 1926.
3. ibid.
4. ibid.
5. Ward, Geoffrey C., Burns, Ken. *Baseball, An Illustrated History*. 1994. Harper Collins Publishers, New York, NY. p. 182.
6. Alexander, op. cit., p 189.
7. ibid.
8. Reynolds, Robert Grey. Jr. The Ty Cobb & Tris Speaker baseball betting scandal. Kindle Edition. Locations 13-20.
9. Baseball Fever website. *The Leonard, Cobb, Speaker, Baseball Affair*. https://www. baseball-fever.com/forum/general-baseball/history-of-the-game/62702-the-leonard-cobb-speaker-affair. Accessed on October 2, 2017.
10. ibid.
11. ibid.
12. Reynolds, op. cit., Location 190.
13. Alexander, op. cit., p. 189.

14. Leerhsen, Charles. *Ty Cobb, A Terrible Beauty.* Simon and Schuster, New York, NY. p. 348.
15. ibid.
16. *Chicago Tribune*, December 22, 1926.
17. Ward and Burns op. cit., p. 183.
18. ibid.
19. Alexander, op. cit., p. 193.
20. ibid.
21. Reynolds, op. cit., Location 237.
22. Leerhsen, op. cit., p. 220.
23. Alexander, op. cit., p 191.
24. ibid.
25. ibid, p. 194.
26. Reynolds, op. cit., Locations 307-311.
27. Alexander, op. cit., p. 194.
28. Cobb, Ty with Stump, Al. *My Life In Baseball...The True Record.* 1961. Doubleday & Company, New York, NY. p. 246.
29. ibid.
30. ibid, p. 248.
31. *Chicago Tribune*, December 23, 1926
32. ibid.
33. Cobb with Stump, op. cit., p248.
34. Leerhsen, op. cit., p. 353.
35. ibid.
36. Baseball Reference. *Baseball Hall of Fame Online.* http://baseballhall.org/hof/mack-connie. https://www.baseball-reference.com/managers/mackco01.shtml Accessed September 20, 2017.
37. Leerhsen, op. cit., p 353.
38. ibid., p. 354
39. ibid. p. 355-356
40. ibid. at p. 356.
41. Baseball Fever website, op. cit. Accessed October 2, 2017.
42. ibid.

CHAPTER 8

Tris Speaker: The Gray Eagle Soars

"Despite spending most of his career in Ty Cobb's considerable shadow, Tris Speaker's .345 lifetime batting average and revolutionary defensive play made him one of Cobb's few rivals as the greatest player of the 1910s."
- National Baseball Hall of Fame

The hoopla that surrounded Cobb's resignation was met with additional shock when the Gray Eagle, Tris Speaker, handed in his resignation on November 29, 1926. However, the announcement did not cause as much of an uproar as Cobb's perhaps because Speaker said he was joining a company outside of baseball, or because people thought he was through with baseball anyway, with his batting average having dropped from .389 in 1925 to .304 in 1926. Nevertheless, Speaker's retirement was still big news, as despite his having been overshadowed by Cobb and more recently Babe Ruth, Speaker was one of the most dominant players in the game during his long career, along with being a successful manager. Nearly 100 years since his retirement, Speaker's 3,514 hits are still good for fifth all time and his dominating play in center field left him with numerous records that still stand today.

To some extent, Speaker's achievements have been forgotten after he left the game, and he knew it. Near the end of his life, Speaker admitted "When we were young and good...the writers were kind enough to say of me that I was the closest thing to Cobb. Now let's be immodest about this. I was good and I knew it...But as good as I was, I never was close to Cobb and neither was Ruth or anybody else."[1]

Author Timothy Gay, in his well-researched book on the Gray Eagle, *Tris Speaker: The Rough and Tumble Life of a Baseball Player*, explains that

Speaker was a player who is often unjustly overlooked. Gay points out that unlike other Deadball Era stars, Speaker's legacy has significantly faded: "Movies are produced about Shoeless Joe Jackson and Ty Cobb. Novels are written about Christy Mathewson and Honus Wagner. Cy Young and Walter Johnson make virtually everyone's short list of best pitchers ever. But Tris Speaker has fallen through the cracks. He's the forgotten superstar from baseball's dead-ball epoch."[2]

Gay's book shows that in addition to Speaker being a gifted athlete, he was also a complicated person. Some of the complexities of his character and some of his off-the-field activities were known to the Czars of baseball, and that reputation factored in to how Speaker was perceived in the whole Dutch Leonard Affair.

Tris Speaker was known as a tough guy on and off the field and as one who was fond of gambling—on horses, and maybe beyond that. As a member of the Cleveland Indians, on August 27, 1918, Speaker was involved in an altercation with home plate umpire, Tommy Connolly, in which he threw a punch at Connolly over a disputed call at home place at Shibe Park in Philadelphia. Speaker took great offense at being called out at home after his teammate, "Tioga" George Burns, hit a shallow single. For the punch, Speaker was suspended for the rest of the shortened season, which ended in early September due to the United States' entry into the war in Europe.[3]

In his book, *Baseball As I Have Known It,* Fred Lieb wrote that Speaker once told him that he was a member of the Ku Klux Klan. Although the Klan kept its membership rolls secret, Speaker's alleged membership would not be a major surprise given that the Klan experienced a nationwide revival beginning in 1915, gaining much popularity with its anti-Catholic rhetoric. In addition, the Klan's national leader from 1922 to 1939, Imperial Wizard Hiram W. Evans, lived near Speaker in Hubbard, Texas. Former Player's Union Chief, Marvin Miller, asked that Speaker should be removed from the Hall of Fame due to his membership in the Ku Klux Klan.[4]

Gambling was also part of Speaker's past for years. When Speaker went to spring training in Hot Springs, Arkansas in 1909, he was exposed to the vices and pleasures that the city offered to its patrons. Besides the hot springs, which allowed men to enjoy the warm natural waters that soothed the body and spirit, brothels, racetracks, speakeasies, cockfights and all manner of gambling dens were rampart in the city and area known as the "Valley of The Vapors."[5]

Speaker was what used to be called a "man's man." Preferring the company of other men who shared his interests and values, he didn't marry until he was in his mid-thirties. He was a skilled horseback rider, calf roper, marksman, and all-around outdoorsman who loved to hunt and fish in remote areas of the United States and Canada, sleeping on the ground and preparing his own sparse meals.

Speaker never got far from his Texas roots. Sportswriters often characterized him as a product of the arid and barely tamed West, as did William A. "Bill" Phelon of the *Chicago Inter-Ocean*, newspaper who called Speaker "the bounding cowboy of the Texas plains, the bad man of the lariat and revolver." The fact that Hubbard was a well-settled little town of about 1,600 residents—with stores, schools, and even a bank, in an area where rainfall was generally adequate for the cotton cultivation that dominated the eastern half of Texas—usually escaped people from the East who wrote about Speaker.

Speaker was on the Boston Red Sox roster during that whole Game Six fiasco in the 1912 World Series, when Wood was replaced by lesser starter Buck O'Brien. There is speculation that the Red Sox bet on themselves in that Game 6 thinking they would win it with Wood pitching.

It was suspected throughout the baseball world that Speaker gambled. In the summer of 1926, Ban Johnson's detectives followed Speaker as a result of Dutch Leonard's accusations about his and Cobb's gambling. What the detectives found was that Cobb was not interested in wagering, but that Speaker... "liked to put action down on everything." Tris routinely lost a bundle at the track, the detectives told Johnson. It did not surprise Johnson. It wasn't the first time he utilized private detectives to follow Speaker.[6]

In addition, Clay Folger, who was still the head of security at Dunn Park in Cleveland, confirmed the rumors that Speaker had gambled, and he indicated that a park employee had placed bets for Cleveland players. Folger further noted that Speaker had frequently bet on the horses, putting down around ten dollars a bet. He did state also, however, that Speaker had stopped gambling two years earlier.[7]

Contrary to Folger's belief that Speaker had given up gambling *Sporting News* correspondent Henry P. Edwards, recalled another bet that Speaker had made in 1925, shortly before the Dutch Leonard Affair occurred. Edwards reported that that the Indians received a hot tip about a horse and a pool of $300 was created, with Speaker contributing $200 to the pool. The horse had a 15 to 1 odds to win and when it did come in, they had won $4,200. As for Speaker, he took his $3,000 winnings and put it into a bank and claimed to never gamble again.[8]

The Life and Legacy of Tris Speaker

Tristram E. Speaker was born on April 4, 1888, in Hubbard, Texas, south of Dallas. His family had relocated from Ohio just prior to the Civil War. Speaker's father, Archie, died when Tris was 10. Tris's mother, Nancy Jane, whose brother fought for the South during the Civil War as had two of Speaker's father's brothers, owned a boarding house business.

Speaker was born right-handed. However, when he was a young child, he taught himself to throw left-handed after twice breaking his right arm from being thrown off a bronco. Soon Speaker began to bat left-handed as well. Speaker also loved football and was a successful athlete in both sports; he played football in high school and was captain and pitcher on his high school baseball team. In 1905, Speaker entered the Fort Worth Polytechnic Institute (now Texas Wesleyan University), where he pitched, doing the same for a nearby semipro team. Tris also worked as a telegraph lineman and cowpuncher.[9]

In 1906, Speaker wrote to several professional teams asking for a tryout and was signed by Cleburne of the Texas League for $65 per month. Tris did not do well as a pitcher. However, when he was put in the outfield, where he hit .268 and stole 33 bases in 84 games. When the North Texas League and South Texas League merged in 1907, Speaker moved to Houston and hit a league-leading .314 with 36 steals in 118 games.[10]

The Red Sox purchased Speaker's contract near the end of the 1907 season. In the minors, Speaker sharpened his skills and became a more reliable player. He led the Southern Association in hitting in 1908 with

Tris Speaker excelled defensively for the Red Sox and Indians, despite appearing to be fielding off the wrong foot in this iconic photograph.

a .350 average, stole 28 bases, and drew raves for his outfield play. In a spring exhibition game against the Giants, sportswriter Sid Mercer recalled, Speaker "scooped up a grounder and threw out one of the fastest Giants on one of those automatic attempts to score from second on a single. It happened again the next day. That time he doubled a runner trying to score on a fly."[11]

Despite interest from the Pittsburgh Pirates, the Brooklyn Superbas, the Washington Senators, and, at last, the Giants, the Travelers sold Speaker back to Boston because Speaker had become a good enough ballplayer to benefit the New England ball club. After a cup of coffee with Boston in

1907, Speaker played in 31 games in 1908, batting .224. His fielding was exceptional, however, aided in part by none other than Red Sox pitcher Cy Young. "When I was a rookie," Speaker later recalled, Young "used to hit me flies to sharpen my abilities to judge in advance the direction and distance of an outfield ball."[12]

From there, Speaker developed into one of the best players in the game—and, in fact, in baseball history. Speaker was a passionate and fiery competitor. No one could argue that point, given his statistics, the respect his peers had for him, and testimony of those who wrote about him and those who watched his performance day in and day out. Speaker was a complete player. In his book, Timothy Gay writes: "[Nearly] eight decades after Tris's retirement, he still holds American League records among outfielders for most career chances, most put-outs, most assists, most double plays, and—here's a statistic not often associated with center fielders-most unassisted double plays." Unassisted double plays! Speaker, Gay reminds us, "played so shallow and with such energy and enthusiasm that perhaps as many as six times in his career he caught line drives and out-hustled the runner to get a force-out at second." His fielding glove was known as the place "where triples go to die."[13]

Speaker was a three-time World Series winner and an early inductee into the Hall of Fame. Babe Ruth called Speaker the finest defensive outfielder he ever saw. Gay further argues that Speaker was "the best all-around player in the history of not one but two franchises."[14]

Many baseball fans think of Willie Mays as the quintessential center fielder, cemented in history by his iconic catch in the 1954 World Series against the Cleveland Indians that was documented on film. Film never captured the essence of Tris Speaker and his outfield play, but considering the amazing numbers he put up, he also has to be regarded as one of the best ever to play center field as well.

In addition to being a great fielder, Speaker was also one of the best hitters ever in Major League Baseball. He compiled a career batting average of .345 (sixth all-time), and among his 3,514 hits were 792 doubles (1st all time) and 222 triples (6th all time), and compiled a lifetime OBA of .428.[15]

Two of the championships Speaker helped win were with the Red Sox, in the 1912 and 1915, for whom he hit above .300 every year (1909-1915) he was on the team, while regularly ranking among American League leaders in several offensive and most defensive categories. Along with teammates Harry Hooper and Duffy Lewis, Speaker formed one of the best fielding outfields in history. During this period, Speaker led AL center fielders in putouts five times and in double plays four times. Twice he had 35 assists, the American League record. In 1912, Speaker, playing in every game but one, won the Chalmers Award as the league's Most Valuable Player. He batted .383, third in the league behind Cobb and Joe Jackson, and led the league in doubles, home runs (tied), and on-base percentage. ("Spoke," one of Speaker's nicknames, came, ironically, from Speaker's teammate and rival Bill Carrigan, who would yell, "Speaker spoke!" when Tris got a hit.) To cap it off, in the World Series against the New York Giants, Speaker got a key hit in the 10th inning of the decisive eighth game after his harmless foul popup fell untouched between first baseman Fred Merkle and catcher Chief Meyers. Given a second chance, Speaker singled in the tying run.[16]

The Boston fans loved him. Speaker received $50 each time he hit the Bull Durham sign, first at the Huntington Avenue Grounds and later at Fenway Park. He endorsed the Boston Garters products, had a $2 straw hat named in his honor, and received free mackinaws and heavy sweaters. Hassan cigarettes created popular trading cards of Speaker depicting him running the bases.[17]

Despite the team's success on the field, tensions were often high in the clubhouse. Speaker and catcher Bill Carrigan never got along and had several brawls. Speaker was often not on speaking terms with Duffy Lewis, who, like Carrigan, was an Irish Catholic. (Religious differences had created cliques on the club, with Speaker siding with other Protestants, including Joe Wood and Larry Gardner). The atmosphere grew more complicated with the arrival of Babe Ruth in 1915. Ruth crossed Speaker's good friend Joe Wood and Speaker never fully forgave him.

Relations between the Grey Eagle and Red Sox, team president, Joe Lannin, were turbulent throughout Speaker's time with the Boston Red Sox. After the Red Sox won the World Series in 1915, Lannin angered Speaker by proposing that the outfielder's salary be cut from about $18,000 – higher at the time than that of Ty Cobb – to $9,000, since Speaker's batting average had declined three years in a row (1913: .363, 1914: .338 and 1915: .322; [he batted .383 in 1912]). Many owners raised salaries when the rival Federal League challenged Major League Baseball in the 1914 and 1915 seasons, to keep them from jumping to the new league, which offered higher salaries and did not have the reserve clause in place. He succumbed to the pressure from the Federal League and raised Speaker's salary in 1914 to keep him from jumping to the Federal League's Brooklyn Club, which had offered Speaker a three-year contract for $100,000 to be its player-manager). When Speaker held out a year later, Lannin traded him to Cleveland for Sad Sam Jones, Fred Thomas, and $55,000.[17]

Red Sox fans were devastated over losing Speaker. He had helped guide the team to two World Series victories and was one of the best players in the league. When he did return as an Indian to play the Red Sox at Fenway Park in the on May 9, 1916, Speaker received a massive outpouring of affection from the fans in Boston even though he was wearing a Cleveland uniform. In an awkward moment, Speaker mistakenly headed toward the Red Sox dugout at the end of one inning. Boston pitchers, meanwhile, complained that without Speaker in center field, they could no longer groove fastballs when behind in the count, being certain that he would catch everything hit his way. The Red Sox, however, even with the loss of Speaker to the Indians, won the World Series again.

As for Speaker, he became the idol of Indians fans and hit even better with his new club than he had in Boston. Overall, 1916 may have been Speaker's best season. He hit .386, to finally break Cobb's lock on the batting title, and led the American League in hits, doubles (tied), slugging, and on-base percentage. Speaker's 35 stolen bases ranked fifth in the league.[18]

Speaker's physique was tall and solid, 6 feet tall and a sturdy 193 pounds. He batted from a left-handed crouch and stood deep in the batter's box. He held his bat low, moving it up and down slowly, "like the lazy twitching of a cat's tail," according to an admirer, and took a full stride. "I don't find any particular ball easy to hit," he said. "I have no rule for batting. I keep my eye on the ball and when it nears me make ready to swing." Nevertheless, "I cut my drives between the first baseman and the line and that is my favorite alley for my doubles." He was a remarkably consistent batter. In

1912, Speaker set a major-league record with three separate hitting streaks of 20 or more games, while his 11 consecutive hits in 1920 set a mark that went unsurpassed for 18 years.[19]

Speaker spent 11 seasons with the Indians, averaging over .350 during that time. He paced the American League in doubles four straight seasons. As late as 1925, the year he married the former Mary Frances Cuddihy of Buffalo, New York, the 37-year-old outfielder hit .389 in 117 games. The following year, his final season with Cleveland, he hit .304 in 150 games.[20]

Endnotes

1. Alexander, Charles. *Spoke: The Biography of Tris Speaker*. McFarland & Company, Inc. Jefferson, NC. Kindle Edition, Location 52.
2. Boyle, William. University of Texas at Arlington website. *Tris Speaker*. http://www.uta.edu/english/sla/br060418.html. April 10, 2006. Accessed July 27, 2017.
3. Gay, Timothy. *Tris Speaker: The Rough and Tumble Life of a Baseball Legend*. University of Nebraska Press, Lincoln, NE. 2007. p. 180.
4. Jensen Don. Society for American Baseball Research. *Tris Speaker*. http://sabr.org/bioproj/person/6d9f34bd. 2006. Accessed July 17, 2017.
5. Gay, op. cit., p. 73.
6. Alexander, op. cit., Locations 986-989.
7. Alexander, op. cit., Location 4200.
8. ibid.
9. Jensen, op. cit.
10. ibid.
11. ibid.
12. ibid.
13. Alexander, op. cit., Locations 4200-4204.
14. ibid.
15. Gay, op. cit, p. 130.
16. Jensen, op. cit.
17. ibid.
18. ibid.
19. ibid.
20. ibid.

CHAPTER 9

Tris Speaker the Manager

As player-manager of the Cleveland Indians, Speaker compiled a 617-520 record (.543) between 1919 and 1926. The Indians club he took to the World Series in 1920 had been demoralized and shocked by the midseason death of shortstop Ray Chapman when he was beaned by New York Yankees' pitcher Carl Mays. Speaker helped to rally the team after the awful incident, winning the American League pennant and going on to win the World Series five games to two over Brooklyn. Speaker was one of the first skippers to platoon extensively. In the Indians' championship year, he loaded up his batting order with right-handed hitters when a left-hander pitched, and vice versa. Speaker himself was the only left-handed hitter who faced left-handed pitchers. In pre-game warm ups, he did not believe his team should warm up in a batting cage, preferring his hitters to practice under real circumstances with a catcher behind the plate.[1]

After the 1926 season, when Speaker was forced to resign because of the meeting with Ban Johnson, The *Cleveland Plain Dealer* wrote "Baseball in Cleveland and Tris Speaker have been synonymous for so long that a Speaker-less team will seem contrary to natural law." What Mathewson was to New York, what Cobb was to Detroit, what Johnson was to Washington, Tris Speaker has been to Cleveland."[2]

While Speaker is recognized as one of the all-time great players (even though overshadowed by Cobb), his excellence as a manager is rarely recognized. Speaker's high point as manager was the Indians' world championship in 1920, particularly after the tragic mid-season death of shortstop Ray Chapman. His performance in 1921 was also quite remarkable, keeping the Indians in the pennant race against the mighty New York Yankees, ultimately finishing just 4.5 games back. How those teams were assembled and how Speaker ran them reveal a special managerial and leadership skill set that is important to document.[3]

Speaker, who took over as manager of the Indians on July 19, 1919, and guided them to a very strong 40–21 mark for the rest of that season. He had a superb eye for talent and a special ability to motivate and get the best in his men. Grantland Rice called him "an alert, hustling, magnetic leader, who can get 100 per cent out of his material." Equally important is that he secured that "material" by seeing potential where others did not. In a *Cleveland Plain Dealer* article headlined "Spoke Converts Discards into Valuable Assets," Henry P. Edwards noted that Speaker should be known as the "Miracle Man."[4]

Speaker, perhaps in contrast to Cobb, was able to develop players and get the most out of them. There are a number of examples from his years as Indians' manager.

Ray Caldwell is one example of Speaker's "potential" philosophy. Caldwell, who was an alcoholic, was traded away by the Yankees after the 1918 season, and waived by the struggling Red Sox the following August and appeared to be finished. Speaker signed him later that month, shortly after taking over as Indians manager. As Franklin Lewis related in his history of the Indians, Speaker inserted a customized training regimen into Caldwell's contract: "After each game he pitches, Ray Caldwell must get drunk. He is not to report to the clubhouse the next day. The second day he is to report to Manager Speaker and run around the ball park as many times as Manager Speaker stipulates. The third day he is to pitch batting practice, and the fourth day he is to pitch in a championship game."[5]

Caldwell thrived under Speaker, going 5–1 with a 1.71 earned run average for the Tribe in 1919. One of those wins was a no-hitter against his old team, the Yankees. Another was a game in which he was struck by lightning in the ninth inning; he recovered and finished the game. In 1920, he continued his spectacular comeback when he fashioned a 20–10 record. Under Speaker's tutelage, Caldwell was able to keep his drinking under control.

A year after picking up Caldwell, Speaker acquired minor league pitcher Duster Mails from Sacramento of the Pacific Coast League. After pitching for the Brooklyn Robins in 1915 and 1916, Mails had spent three seasons in the minors. "I didn't deliberately try to dust them off," he explained. "I couldn't make the ball go where I wanted it to go." (He had an 0–2 record with 14 walks and 16 strikeouts in 21 1/3 innings with Brooklyn.) Speaker, however, saw the potential that Mails had, as he had been following Mails's progress in the Coast League, where he won 37 games in 1919–20. Speaker proclaimed "I have been trying to get Mails for a year past.... I have had Mails in mind for some time and he came to us when he did only after long bargaining and planning." Mails joined the Indians for the late-season stretch, and he won seven games—including two shutouts—against no losses with a 1.85 earned run average. In the 1920 World Series, he pitched 15 2/3 scoreless innings and won one game.[6]

Speaker also was able to work youngsters into the lineup in the midst of the fierce pennant races in 1920 and 1921, When given a chance by Speaker, these youngsters performed very well from the start. After the death of shortstop Ray Chapman in August 1920, 21-year-old Joe Sewell was purchased from New Orleans. A recent team captain at the University of Alabama, Sewell took batting practice each morning against the left handed pitcher Mails. Speaker wanted the left-handed-hitting rookie to build up his confidence against left-handed pitching. Sewell hit .329 in those final weeks of the season and, in his first full season, 1921, Sewell hit .318 with 36 doubles.[7]

Speaker reclaimed the careers of position players as well, not only pitchers. Detroit sportswriter H. G. Salsinger recognized Speaker's personnel skills. "He [Speaker] has proved himself one of the greatest base ball leaders of all time... [and is noted for his] dextrous [sic] handling of players."[8]

A key transaction that paved the way for the Indians' success was their trade, on March 1, 1919, of the difficult and temperamental Braggo Roth to the Philadelphia Athletics for Larry Gardner, Charlie Jamieson, and Elmer Myers. Speaker was not the manager of the Indians at the time, but he pushed for the deal. Franklin Lewis goes further and describes Speaker's presence in the trade talks. In his history of the Indians, Lewis describes Speaker's role with the Indians before he took over as the team's manager, replacing Lee Fohl. "The Fohl–Speaker combination was formed almost immediately upon the arrival of the Texan in Cleveland. Spoke was the natural field leader, and Fohl recognized his strength and adaptability promptly."[9]

Steve O'Neill was a fine defensive catcher but, before Speaker took over the helm of the Indians, a weak hitter. O'Neill had hit above .253 only once, and his on-base percentage had never reached .350, when he hit .289 in 1919. He hit between .311 and .322 the next three seasons, and his on-base percentage was above .400. Speaker gave O'Neill three specific tips to help him at bat[10]:

1. Go to the plate thinking you'll get a hit.
2. Out-think the pitcher.
3. Don't swing at bad balls.

Speaker converted third baseman Joe Evans to an outfielder. He had never played in the outfield until 1920. A .214 hitter before 1920, he hit .342 the next two seasons.

On February 24, 1917, Smoky Joe Wood joined his former Red Sox roommate and friend on the Indians. "Undoubtedly," Franklin Lewis wrote, "Wood came to the Indians on Tris's recommendation." Charles Alexander notes that the $15,000 James Dunn paid Boston to acquire Wood was far above his "market value" at the time. With his arm "gone" and his career as a pitcher over, Wood made a solid comeback as an everyday player. Speaker had seen Wood's potential as a hitter years before when he was on Boston and noticed Wood was a decent hitter as a pitcher. In four years: from 1910 through 1913, Wood hit .273 (92 hits in 337 at bats), including four home runs, four triples, and 24 doubles.[11]

Speaker was also far ahead of his time in how he used his players. He was an early advocate of platooning, long before the word even existed in baseball. John McGraw of the New York Giants employed some of the same techniques at the time, and decades later, Casey Stengel of the New York Yankees would be labeled a managerial genius for his use of platooning that the early pioneers had introduced in the 1920s.

The concept of playing left-handed hitters to face right-handed pitchers and vice versa had awkward names at the time, including "double-batting shift," "interchangeable players," "switch-around players," and "reversible outfield." Speaker himself called it his "triple shift" because he employed the tactic at three positions: first base and two outfielders.[12]

Speaker's ability to identify and develop talent and then get the most of it on the field earned him great respect in the game at the time (even if those skills have been largely forgotten). "He was," wrote veteran sportswriter Gordon Cobbledick, "proving himself a warm and understanding handler of the varied temperaments, dispositions and talents under his command. There was never any doubt among the players that instructions from him were orders to be obeyed, but he didn't place himself on a pedestal. While the ball game was in progress, he was the boss. When it was over, he was one of the gang."[13]

At the close of the 1921 season, Heywood Broun wrote in *Vanity Fair*: "He is a leader who never gives up and never allows his team to give up in spite of the circumstances of a game. It seems to me that he is by far the finest manager in professional baseball."[14]

Tris Speaker managed the Indians for five more seasons, before being forced to resign due to the accusations of the Dutch Leonard Affair. During those seasons, the Indians won more games than they lost, but were never a serious challenger for the American League pennant, with the exception of a spectacular late-season rush in 1926. Of course, the emergence of Babe Ruth and his superb Yankees teams were difficult to keep up with.

Endnotes

1. Jensen Don. Society for American Baseball Research. *Tris Speaker*. http://sabr.org/bioproj/person/6d9f34bd. 2006. Accessed July 27, 2017.
2. ibid.
3. Steinberg, Steve. Society for American Baseball Research. *Manager Speaker*. http://sabr.org/research/manager-speaker. Accessed July 27, 2017.
4. ibid.
5. ibid.
6. ibid.
7. ibid.
8. ibid.
9. ibid.
10. ibid.
11. ibid.
12. ibid.
13. ibid.
14. ibid.

Speaker's slashing style at the plate gave him extra-base-hit power while maintaining bat control. In his 11 seasons for Cleveland, he led the AL in doubles 6 times, while fanning only about once every 40 plate appearances.

CHAPTER 10

Speaker: The Aftermath

Like Cobb, Speaker went on that hunting trip to Wyoming knowing he would be resigning from baseball after meeting with Ban Johnson. It appears that the dates that Cobb and Speaker chose to resign were not dictated by Johnson, whose only requirement may have been that they occur weeks apart to make it appear that they were, unrelated events. Speaker resigned on November 29, 1926 while Cobb made his announcement about four weeks earlier, on November 3, 1926.

At the time of his resignation, Speaker had not signed his contract for 1927. To put Indians' fans at ease over the Speaker situation, Cleveland Indians team president, Ernest Barnard, had remarked that contracts would not be sent out until the stockholders' meeting in January, and that there was no basis for "the silly rumors" that Speaker wouldn't be back.[1] Barnard, of course, remained quiet about the September 9th meeting, where American League Owners first learned about the Dutch Leonard Affair. From an outsider's perspective, Speaker seemed to be exploring his options.

On November 19, Speaker drove to Detroit "on business" in the company of his close friend Dave R. Jones, who had become wealthy operating an auto parts plant in Cleveland. Asked in Detroit about rumors that he and Cobb were interested in buying the Boston Red Sox or some other team, Speaker replied, "I'm too busy thinking about the Indians and the 1927 race."[2] That would all change in a week.

Outwardly, Speaker did not seem worried about his forced resignation by Ban Johnson. He and his wife, Fran, traveled down to Columbus to be among the 90,000 people who filled the new Ohio Stadium for the Ohio State-Michigan football game, and a couple of weeks later, they visited

Cleveland Indians owner Edith Dunn in Chicago and took in the annual Army-Navy game as part of an even bigger throng at Soldier Field.

Regarding rumors that the Indians' owner might want to reduce his salary, Speaker was curt: "I'll quit the game first."[3] About to leave for the winter in California, Indians' owner Edith Dunn wouldn't comment on Speaker's salary or whether he would be rehired. As was the practice of that time, the exact amount of his contracts had never been made public; but for the past few seasons his salaries had been in the $30,000–$35,000 range, which made him one of the five or six highest-salaried non-executives in baseball.

Upon his return to Cleveland, at noon on Monday, November 29, Speaker called local sportswriters together. Nattily attired in bow tie and gray suit, he announced his resignation as Indians manager. He said he had considered quitting after the 1925 season, but "I made up my mind to stick with the team until we made a respectable showing in the championship race and then retire." Besides, he knew his legs were going. Sometimes it had become "just plain hell trying to scamper over the ground to pull down a long fly." He was "taking a vacation from baseball that I expect will last the remainder of my life."[4]

Speaker bid the newsmen goodbye and returned to the home at 8014 Carnegie Avenue he and his wife shared with her mother. The next day, Barnard announced that Jack McCallister, long associated with the Cleveland franchise as a scout and coach, would succeed Speaker as manager. Speaker's explanation for why he quit was plausible—but also untrue.

With Motor City still reeling not only from Cobb's resignation, but also his very public battle with Frank Navin, Speaker took a different approach. When asked by the media what he would do next, Speaker indicated that he was leaving the Cleveland Indians to pursue professional opportunities in the trucking business. "I considered quitting last year, but the Indians were in sixth place and I didn't want it said that I was leaving a rudderless ship. So I stuck it out another season." This was reported by the *Washington Post*.[5]

It was reasonable that Speaker would be retiring as a player. In November of 1926, he was thirty eight years old. He had no doubt lost a step or two and his batting average had dropped from .389 in 1925 to "only" .304 in 1926. But it was his retirement as a manager that made people think something else might be going on. The 1926 season was successful for the Indians, as

Speaker's team had finished only three game out of first place. To give up his life's passion to work at a company called Geometric Stamping Co. was both shocking and perplexing.

The *Cleveland Plain Dealer* tried to give their readers some sort of answer in the editorial section:

> "Baseball in Cleveland and Tris Speaker have been synonymous for so long that a Speaker-less team will seem contrary to natural law. What Mathewson was to New York, Cobb was to Detroit, what Johnson was to Washington, Tris Speaker has been to Cleveland, This year, Speaker took a team that was scheduled by all the wise birds to finish a submerged seventh and led it to a final position within two or three hair breadth of the championship. This achievement is hailed as a little short of a baseball miracle. We are still a little bewildered, but we feel that no fair objection can be advanced against Speaker's decision. And so, as he goes out, into a new field, we join with all the rest of Cleveland in wishing him good luck, long life and every happiness."[6]

The holidays were rapidly approaching and Cobb and Speaker's resignations still were a mystery to the public, despite the explanations the baseball Gods had provided. However, the *New York Times* and other newspapers were starting to learn what was really going on and were on the verge of breaking the story.

Before that could happen, Commissioner Landis released details of the affair to the public along with Cobb's and Speaker's testimonies, the day after the hearings in his office had been held.

Speaker's testimony follows, as published by the newspapers on that date:

Landis: Did you remain with Cleveland from 1918 to 1926, both inclusive.
Speaker: Inclusive, yes, sir.
Landis: What do you know about this transaction I have been inquiring about?
Speaker: I only know that sometime in July of 1926 or June that Leonard had been back east from California and was accusing us of entering into an

agreement to fix a bill game in 1919. I got what details I could to find out who was in any ball game or mixed up in any betting and I was told that Joe Wood had written Leonard a letter stating that a bet had been made an a ball game in 1919 and that this was the game that he was trying to connect me with.

Denies knowledge of bets

Landis: Prior to that had you any knowledge of this transaction?
Speaker: None whatever.
Landis: Did you have any conversation with Leonard, Wood or Cobb before or after this ball game played in 1919, any conversation back there at that time?
Speaker: No, no conversation at all.
Landis: When had you become manager of the Cleveland club?
Speaker: I think in August of 1919, very recently anyway.
Landis: In this statement, which I have read here, that Leonard made to me in California, he says that you and Cobb, Wood, and Leonard happened to get together the stand after the game of September 24 and that at that time you made the statement that Detroit would win the day's game, that Cleveland had cinched second place; what have you got to say about that?
Speaker: I had no such conversation.
Landis: He also says that at the same time and place there was talk about "Our" meaning Detroit, wanting to win third; did you have any such conversation as that?
Speaker: No such conversation at all.
Landis: Who were you rooming with during that time?
Speaker: Joe Wood.
Cobb: Did Wood never say anything to you about this ball game?
Speaker: Wood never mentioned this ball game to me at any time until I called him to ask him what he had written in the letter, last June or July.

Knew of Leonard's letter

Landis: What occasioned you to call him to ask him that what he had written in the letter?
Speaker: I was told that Leonard was here trying to implicate me with these letters and in a ball game that was fixed in 1919.

Mr. O'Connor: By "here" do you mean the commissioner's office, Mr. Speaker?

Speaker: I mean he was east, he was from California. No, I don't mean the commissioner's office. I can explain that a little better by saying that Mr. Johnson came to Cleveland and told me that Leonard had some such letter from Wood and asked me if I knew anything about it, and I told him that I did not, and he said, "Well, you had better get in touch with Wood and see what is in this letter if possible; see if he remembers what he had written," and at this suggestion I called Joe Wood.

Landis: Well, now there has been something said here about that mere fact occasioning the shifting of odds so that the professional gamblers in laying odds would make the club lower in the race the favorite over the club that was above that club in the race as the race stood at that time. What do you say about that?

Speaker: Well, the only answer we have for that is that it is a well-known fact among baseball men and newspaper men and possibly among the fans that when a club at the tail end of the season has no place to go, that they automatically let down. They just say "well we must go through and play the schedule," and the managers very often switch their entire ball club and put in rocky ball players or ball players they are trying out to see whether or not they will be major league ball players.

Knew West by sight

Landis: The statement has been made here that Wood and West had a conversation at the Cadillac hotel in Detroit on the morning of this September 25th game. Did your team stop at the Cadillac hotel?

Speaker: We did.

Landis: Do you remember anything about whether were around that hotel that day?

Speaker: Well, I must have been around there that morning. I don't know how long I was around there. I most always go out to the ball park rather early.

Landis: Now that morning around the hotel was there any sort of intimation to you of any kind of nature. Do you know West?

Speaker: Yes, sir, I know him.

Landis: Did you know him then?

Speaker: Well, I didn't know him by name; I knew him by sight as an employee of the ball club.

Landis: Did you see West when he came down to the Michigan Central depot that evening when Wood says West turned over this money to him?

Speaker: I did not.

Landis: I wish you would take this box score of that game and look at it. You are an expert and I am not, and tell me whether there is anything that appears in that box score that is worthy of comment one way or the other?

Speaker: Yes, sir; there is quite a little worthy of comment in this box score that is in regard to this ball game. In the first place I have used my regular lineup with the exception of short-stop, and Lunte played shortstop in this ball game.

Had regulars in game

Landis: In place of whom?

Speaker: In place of Ray Chapman. Now, whether Chapman was injured or whether I had permitted him to go home, or whether he was sick, I don't recall. But it is the only change in my entire lineup that I played all season or since I had the management of the ball club, trying to win every ball game. I notice in this box score that I personally made three hits. In the numbers down below two of those hits are cited in this box score as being three-base hits. If I had known anything about the ball game being fixed, or if I was in on a ball game that was fixed up and had money placed on the ball game, I certainly would not have been out there making that kind of a result in the ball game, and I would not have permitted Wood to have to have remained out of the ball game.

Landis: You say you would not have let Wood out if you were going to fix It. What do you mean by that?

Speaker: I mean that I played Wood against left hand pitching. I alternated Wood, being a right hand batter against left hand pitching, with Graney in left field and with Smith in right field, and had I been fixing a ball game, and any club being in the position it was not to go up or down, there would have been no criticism I would have had in fear of keeping Wood in there, had I had young ballplayers on the bench, so that I could have made an entire switch in my ball club.

Cobb held to one hit

Speaker: I also notice that Cobb was up four times and only made one base hit; they don't credit it for being an extra base hit, but he is credited with having one stolen base. If we were working with Cobb, we would certainly try to fix it so he could have some hits.

I look at the score of the ball game and I find that the Cleveland was never out of the game until at least the eighth inning, when they scored two runs and are only two runs behind. There is many a ball game when four runs are scored in an inning.

The score is Detroit 2 in the first, 2 in the second; we scored 2 in the third, we also scored another one in the fifth; that put us only one run behind them. They came back and scored 2 of their own in the fifth. We scored another run in the sixth, they scored 1 in the sixth, we scored 1 in our half of the seventh and the score then would be 7 to 5. In the seventh inning, they scored two runs in the eighth inning making it 9 to 5, and we did not score in our half and they didn't play their half.

Landis: Now, in one of the newspaper accounts of that game the statement was made that the game was played in an hour and six minutes, and it seems to have been a heavy hitting game. What have you got to say, if anything, about that?

Speaker: The only thing that I can say about that judge is that that ball game was played quickly because there was a six o clock or a 6:15 train that would get the Cleveland club back home on the night of this game. The players hustled from the bench to their positions and back in order to save as much time as possible.

Wood withholds name

Landis: [From the questioning of Joe Wood] Mr. Wood, can't you give me the name you spoke about this Cleveland friend of yours that was in on this bet, who had one-third of this bet? Can you give me any information at all about what his business or his occupation is?

Wood: He is a man who has never been in baseball in any way. I wouldn't mention his name to you.

Landis: May I ask Mr. Speaker that during the fall when the teams are out of the game, did you ever know of different teams playing these games where the players exchanged positions, playing one position for two innings and switching and playing another position?

Speaker: Yes, I have known of that condition to exist.

Landis: Knowing Leonard as you did and about his trouble back in Boston and knowing his temperament and so forth, would you enter into any sort of an agreement with him to fix a ball game?

Speaker: Well, I wouldn't have to know him to do that; I wouldn't enter into any agreement with anybody to fix a ball game; you wouldn't have to know him.[7]

From the onset of Leonard's accusations, Speaker proclaimed his innocence and pointed to the fact that he wasn't even mentioned in the letters. One can speculate that it was possible Speaker dropped out and was replaced by a "man from Cleveland," as Joe Wood alluded to Landis, who could have been another friend of Wood's. Or it could have been Speaker. No one knew and Wood wasn't letting on by admitting anything that would give any credibility to Leonard's accusations.

Unlike Tigers owner Frank Navin, who was very combative with Cobb in the press back in Detroit about justifying Cobb's resignation, Indians President E.S. Barnard was more civil, but still gave credence to the idea that the players had gambled. In a statement to the press on December 22, 1926, two days after the hearings in Landis's office, Barnard indicated to the press:

> "Everyone who has admired the work of Tris Speaker and Ty Cobb on the ball field during the past fifteen or twenty years will regret to see these men implicated in an incident of this character.
>
> Both Speaker and Cobb from the inception of the charge have denied their personal participation in the matter there is conclusive evidence to prove that there was something wrong with this game in question.
>
> I did not ask for Speaker's resignation. I knew that this case would be settled in the proper time by the proper persons.

The whole thing is merely additional evidence of the looseness that existed in the game just previous to the 1919 World Series.

The ball player of the present day is fully awake to the fact that his business has a wicked past to live down and is determined to do everything in his power to restore public confidence in the integrity of his works. I personally feel that at no previous time has the game been as clean as it is at the present time."[8]

One gets the sense that Barnard's statement was connected to his going along with the collusion that had taken place on September 9th of that year when the American League owners handed the Dutch Leonard files over to Commissioner Landis and promised to keep this whole thing quiet.

His statement shows his loyalty to the other owners and offers absolutely no support for the character or innocence of Cobb or Speaker. If anything, Barnard created a false narrative by implying that major league baseball in 1926 was clean, as opposed to the pre-Landis era. In essence, it was a statement of support for Landis and whatever decision he may come to regarding the fates of Cobb and Speaker.

As for Fred West, still employed at Navin Field, all he could add to the proceedings was that he had placed a bet for Joe Wood without knowing part of the money was Leonard's. He had never placed bets for Speaker or Cobb, had never heard of their betting on any baseball game.[9]

In his testimony to Landis, West indicated:

"I took a sealed envelope from one place to another on the date mentioned. The following day I called at the second place. Got another sealed envelope. I am not in the habit of opening them."[10]

When the hearing was over, Cobb and Speaker demanded that Landis make public all the evidence he had, including what they had testified to that day.

On Tuesday afternoon, December 21, with Landis absent, his secretary Leslie O'Connor gave out a 100,000-word collection of materials. What was released included the transcripts of the hearing held the previous day and Landis's October 29th interview with Leonard, together with the two letters to Leonard concerning the game of September 25, 1919. Landis's appended statement read in part:

"These men being out of baseball, no decision will be made, unless changed conditions in the future require it."[11]

The commissioner's action created a nationwide sensation and left most people dumbfounded. Bozeman Bulger of the *New York Evening World* later observed that when newspapers across the country printed everything Landis released, they were "paying telegraph tolls on more than eight solid columns of matter. It drew the same prominence and space as a President's message."[12]

It seemed everyone had something to say about the whole ordeal. For Speaker it would be inevitable that Indians President Barnard would chime in on the whole affair. But Barnard didn't defend Speaker, who had worked for him for the last 11 years.[13]

For the *Brooklyn Daily Eagle*'s Thomas S. Rice, that Landis had gone public with Leonard's charges was "already appalling, but I am convinced that if the expose had come from another source, the consequences would have been absolutely ruinous. Darn the whole mess. It has had the same effect as if a lifelong friend had suddenly died."[14]

The *Boston American*'s Nick Flatley felt about the same way:

"It makes us feel like a three-year-old kid would if asked to prove that there is no Santa Claus."[15]

Tommy Holmes, Rice's Brooklyn Eagle colleague, saw it differently. Instead of fighting the charges, observed Holmes, Speaker and Cobb "took the easiest way out, which apparently speaks volumes for their inability to prove a darned thing."

On December 20th, after the Landis hearings were over and before boarding his train for Cleveland a few days later, Speaker described himself as the "goat" of the whole affair, adding that "The only thing they have against me is the word of a man who is behind this flare-up, Leonard," and that he had been told Leonard had been out to get him ever since he waived on the pitcher in 1925.[16]

When Speaker arrived in Cleveland that night, he was met by camera flashes and a barrage of reporters' questions. "Boys," he said, "I'm going home... I told Judge Landis and I say now that I never bet a dime on a game and that I never had anything to do with a game being 'thrown' or know of a game being 'thrown.'"[17]

The front page of the next day's *Cleveland Press* carried a photo of Speaker giving an exclusive interview to Joe Williams at the Press office at "a late hour" on the first. "Joe," Williams quoted Speaker as saying, "You can tell the world, and be right about it, that I love baseball too much to throw a game. It's just too bad that a fellow like Leonard who happens to dislike me is able to provoke such a mean situation."[18]

Speaker also personally distributed a typewritten statement to the local *Plain Dealer and News*, again pointing out that he wasn't even mentioned in the two notorious letters. Terming Leonard "a veritable Judas," he explained that he didn't claim him on waivers because "I knew in my heart he had run his race as a major league pitcher."[19]

Speaker further noted that Leonard threatened to get him when he refused to pick him up after Cobb put him on waivers. Speaker was hoping for Leonard to come, so that the Gray Eagle could clear his name. Speaker further maintained that "The testimony on file with the Commissioner, together with the explanations given to him by Cobb and Wood, proves beyond doubt that there was no thought of wrongdoing on the part of either man, and there is absolutely nothing to show that the game was fixed."[20]

In his own words as quoted from the *Chicago Tribune* on December 22, 1926, Speaker said the following:

> "I have been made the goat of the game. I want the people to know and believe me when I say I am entirely innocent of any wrongdoing in connection with the alleged throwing of that game or of placing a bet on the result. I didn't know any bets had been made on the game until last June, when the matter was called to my attention by Ban Johnson, President of the League.
>
> The testimony on file in the office of Commissioner Landis will vindicate me. I am not mentioned in the letters written to

"Dutch" Leonard and by either Ty Cobb or Joe Wood. The reason is plain. I knew nothing of any wagers or of any "fixing." The only thing they say they have against me is the word of the man who is behind this entire flare-up, Leonard. I have requested repeatedly that Leonard be brought in to face me, but he has positively refused to come in to a meeting.

Leonard has deliberately falsified in any statement he has made that implicates me. I never bet a single penny on that or any other game and I was entirely ignorant of any bets being made until as I said before in June. It seems strange the powers that be of baseball should take the word of a man of Leonard's caliber when my name does not appear in the case.

I have been told when Leonard was waived out of the American League that he made the statement that I was a fine kind of a friend to have and that he would "get me." I must say he took a fine way to make good on his threat, He should have taken into consideration that I was only the manager, not the owner of a ball club, and that I had an obligation to my employer, the late James. C. Dunn, to protect his interests by not adding a man to his club roster I knew in my heart had run his race as a major league pitcher.

It has been a terrible strain and trying ordeal for me, but there is real satisfaction in knowing that my name is not connected with the case in any manner except by word of mouth of veritable Judas. I feel confident the day will come when Leonard, if he has a spark of manhood in him, will agree to appear before Landis to clear my name. I am absolutely guiltless.

In conclusion, I want to say that the testimony together with the explanation given by both Wood and Cobb proves there was no though of wrong doing on the part of either man, and there is absolutely nothing to show the ball game was fixed."[21]

The holidays couldn't have been more dismal for Cobb and Speaker, with the public now informed of the whole ordeal. In between Christmas and New Year's Day there were a flurry of public denials by those ball players that played in that now infamous September 25th game. Some of these players included: Steve O'Neil, Charles "Chick" Shorten (right fielder for the Tigers that day), Elmer Myers, Harry Lunte (who substituted for Ray Chapman that day as Chapman was making wedding arrangements) and umpire Dick Nallin were quoted as indicating they didn't see anything that would give rise to the notion of cheating. Jack Graney noted that O'Neill threw out two Detroit runners and tagged out another. Speaker himself had two triples, and pitcher Bernie Boland, who was on the mound that day for Detroit insisted that he "never gave Speaker anything in my life."[22] Charlie Jamieson was quoted as the whole affair "seemed rather silly...One player who obviously was playing good ball and another who sat on the bench are accused of giving a game away. It's ridiculous."[23]

Polls were conducted across the United States on what folks thought of the whole thing. The Cleveland press and Scripp-Howard newspapers in other cities had statistics drawn from these polls that indicated an 800 to 12 endorsement for Speaker and Cobb in Cleveland and 1,275 to 44 in their favor elsewhere.[24]

Baseball Magazine ran an editorial in favor of both Cobb and Speaker and asserted that it all came down to "the unsupported testimony of a self-confessed conspirator who refused to meet the accused before a formal tribunal."[25]

One source was willing to confirm Leonard's story. His name was George Barris who was the megaphone announcer at Navin Field in 1926, but he was the scoreboard operator back in 1919. Barris had interviewed with a Chicago newspaper and admitted that the Tigers, Chick Shorten told him Cleveland was going to throw the game, and gave him $60 to bet on Detroit about 2 o'clock that afternoon. In addition, Barris indicated that he also bet his own money, which was $20 at odds at 4 to 5. Landis ignored this accusation by Barris, because he also admitted he had a grudge against Cobb due to a fight back in 1920 over a craps game in the dressing room.

If the evidence and accusations were not confusing enough, Fred West who made that bet for Wood that day, contradicted his own testimony and changed his story. He now claimed that it was not baseball that he and

Wood bet on, but rather a horse race. Originally, the plan was to bet on the game but the participants changed their minds when West got a tip about a racing horse named Panaman, who was running at the Windsor track. In West's new story, he bet $400, with three different Detroit bookies and won $680, then hurried to the Michigan train station to deliver the money before the Indians train pulled out late that afternoon. West's story change was a rather blatant attempt to help Speaker, Cobb, and Wood. They all denied it anyhow.

What might have given credibility to West's horse racing assertion was the fact that a few weeks later when Johnson publicly denounced Speaker with his "cute" speech to the press. Part of the evidence Johnson had procured by Pinkerton detectives two years earlier, reported that Speaker had gambled included horse racing.

On the outside, Speaker remained stoical, but the whole ordeal seemed to be taking a toll on him. A report surfaced by sports columnist, Francis S. Powers, that Speaker "was suffering from extreme nervousness upon his return from Chicago and was under a physician's care for several days."[26] Even with the reports indicating that he was sick, on December 22, 1926, Speaker got dressed and went downtown. He was constantly stopped by people telling him they were behind him. That night he gave out a statement of thanks through the media by stating "To tell the truth, the public never will know how much I have taken this to heart. I may smile and grin but down in my heart there are no smiles."[27]

On New Year's Eve, Speaker addressed the public by stating:

"I wish everyone a Happy New Year. As 1927 is about to greet us, baseball is uppermost in my mind. May no scandal ever interfere with the greatest of all American sports. To all my friends, to all baseball fans and particularly to the hundreds of thousands of baseball kids, I send my honest, loyal greetings."[28]

Sports writer Joe Williams believed Ban Johnson had it out for Speaker because of an incident back in the 1921 season, when Speaker as Cleveland manager protested two games, both of which ended in critical losses to the New York Yankees. Johnson disallowed the first protest which had to do with the refusal of plate umpire Frank Wilson to change his no strike call on Frank Baker, even though the base umpires agreed that Baker had gone through with his swing.[29] The other protest dealt with Speaker claiming that when New York runners were on first and third base, Roger Peckinpaugh laid down a bunt, blocked Cleveland's Steve O'Neil from getting to the ball as Peckinpaugh reached first before the throw, thus loading the bases. A rally then ensued by the Yankees. Johnson ruled against that protest too. Cleveland owner Jim Dunn accused Johnson of being unfair to Cleveland, and their friendship was soured over the whole incident. Johnson always blamed Speaker for shattering his friendship with Dunn.[30]

Nevertheless, when Cobb, Speaker, and Wood employed powerful attorneys to defend themselves in the incident, it reinforced public opinion that the men were innocent of any wrongdoing and now were going to war against baseball to clear their names. Speaker retained William H. Boyd, the prestigious Cleveland attorney, while Cobb hired James O. Murfin, the former Michigan circuit court judge and a current regent of the University of Michigan, who was an experienced litigator in baseball litigation. Both attorneys gave an aura of confidence not only to their famous clients but to the public as well.

In early January of 1927, Murfin told the media that "it's a cinch."[31] Speaker's attorney Boyd backed up Murfin's assertion by stating "If Murfin thinks Cobb's case is a cinch, you can get a fair idea of what I think about Tris Speaker's case. For Tris is only implicated...through Leonard's charges. He (Speaker) wrote no letters and is not referred to in the letters written by Cobb and Wood."[32]

Attorney Boyd also combatted Johnson's assault on Speaker's character:

"Speaker never fixed a game, never participated in fixing a game and never played a crooked game.

Tris Speaker, never bet on a baseball game in his life, with one exception. And that was on a World Series game in which he was not playing. And he then bet on the American League team merely out of sentiment.

I won't say whether Speaker ever bet on horse races or not, but I will say that is none of Johnson's or the American

League's business. Such charges are silly. We are ready for the showdown.

Tris Speaker quit baseball because he loved baseball more than himself. He quit to prevent a scandal. But he is fighting now and won't quit until he is cleared."[33]

Another weapon in the Cobb-Speaker arsenal in addition to powerful lawyers was the fact that they had the option to leave Major League Baseball and jump to another league. Word had it that some prominent sportsmen were said to be building another league to rival major league baseball. The cities that were mentioned as possible franchises were: Cleveland, Pittsburgh, Cincinnati, Detroit, Milwaukee, Kansas City, and Minneapolis or Indianapolis.[34] With Cobb and Speaker still being stars with something left in the tank, they would be an asset to any new league on the field, as well as drawing crowds, thereby increasing revenues for the owners.

In the midst of the controversy over the past months, Speaker had said that although he had no interest in managing anywhere, in reality, he still wanted to play baseball. But he hid his feelings from the public. Asked where he might play, he said, "I am willing to take an oath I have received no offers."[35]

To make matters worse for Speaker, while waiting for the decision from Landis, Ban Johnson issued statements to the press about Cobb and Speaker. Johnson's actions added fuel to the fire of his battle with Landis, as Johnson was trying to do damage control that he started to begin with. Towards Cobb, Johnson sounded sympathetic and almost reasonable:

> "I don't believe Ty Cobb ever played a dishonest game in his life. If that's the exoneration he seeks I gladly give it to him... We let him go because he had written a peculiar letter about a betting deal that he couldn't explain and because I felt that he had violated a position of trust.[36]
>
> "I love Ty Cobb. I never knew a finer player. I don't think he's been a good manager, and I have had to strap him as a father straps an unruly boy. But I know Ty Cobb is not a crooked player... He was heartbroken and maintained his

innocence in that alleged betting deal which his letter tells about. I told him that whether guilty or not he was through in the American League. I did not think he played fair with his employers or with me."[37]

When it came to Speaker, however, it was clear that Johnson had lost any sense of balance or comportment. Johnson had known and worked with Speaker for many years; he had been a part-owner of the Cleveland Indians:

"Tris Speaker is a different type of fellow. For want of a better word I'd call Tris 'cute.' He knows why he was forced out of the management of the Cleveland club. If he wants me to tell him I'll meet him in a court of law and tell the facts under oath.

"I have men working for me, on my personal payroll, whose business it is to report on the conduct of our ballplayers. We don't want players betting on horse races or ball games while they are playing. We don't want players who are willing to lay down to another team either for friendship or money. That's why I get these reports. ... This data belongs to me and not to Landis. The American League gave Landis enough to show why Cobb and Speaker were no longer wanted by us. That's all we needed to give him. I have reports on Speaker which Landis will never get unless we go to court.

"I sent a detective to watch the conduct of the Cleveland club two years ago. I learned from him when and by whom bets were made on horse races and ballgames. I learned who was taking the money for the bets. I learned the names of the bookmakers who accepted the wagers and how much the betters made. I was gathering evidence. ... Speaker was implicated in the deal by statement of Leonard. Also I had the data of my detectives."[38]

On the afternoon of January 23, 1927, a few hours before the American League owners' decisive meeting with Landis, and four days before Landis issued his statement clearing Cobb and Speaker, newsmen observed

121

Speaker talking in the Blackstone Hotel lobby, first with Clark Griffith and later with Connie Mack.[39] Rumors began to swirl about Speaker's return to baseball. "Tris has a cheerful time of it these days," quipped the *New York Herald Tribune's* W. O. McGeehan, "as he wanders about bargaining for himself. His shrill cry resounds through the market place: 'old ivory for sale, but not cheap.'"[40] Actually, Speaker wasn't shopping around his aging skills as much as McGeehan had assumed.

It was during the week of Landis's decision, sometime between January 23 and 27, Speaker tentatively committed himself to sign with Washington. When Speaker was exonerated by Landis and the decision was handed down on the 27th, that same day, the ball began rolling for Speaker's new future in baseball. At the Washington Senators Spring Training site in Tampa Bay, Florida, Clark Griffith acknowledged that Speaker was going to join the team. That night Griffith telephoned Speaker a firm offer, later confirmed by wire. Accompanied by his wife Fran, Speaker then took a train for Philadelphia, ostensibly to attend the Penn Athletic Club's dinner honoring veteran athletes, but actually to meet with Connie Mack and inform the Athletics' manager and part-owner that he intended to accept Griffith's offer.[41]

From Philadelphia, Speaker proceeded to New York, where he had agreed to listen to an overture from the Yankees. Believing Speaker was still available, Miller Huggins made the train trip up from St. Petersburg, the Yankees' training site, arriving thirty-six hours ahead of schedule. The Speakers checked into the Hotel Roosevelt on the evening of January 30, and the next morning Speaker met with Huggins at the Broadway Central. After they parted, Speaker smilingly told reporters he had already agreed to play for Washington, which meant Huggins had made a round-trip of some two thousand miles for nothing. "It was a mean trick to play on Huggins," wrote Joe Vila, "but no tears should be spilled."[42]

Later that day, Speaker met with Washington club secretary Eddie Eynon, who came up to New York for the occasion, and signed his contract for a sum that was never made public. Guesses then ranged as high as a $50,000 salary plus a $10,000 signing bonus. Shirley Povich, the *Washington Post's* sports editor for nearly half a century, probably came closest to the actual figure, which he put at $25,000.[43] That would have matched Walter

Johnson's current salary, most in the history of the Washington franchise. Speaker denied playing competing offers against each other. He wanted to play regularly, something neither Mack nor Huggins could promise him. Bucky Harris affirmed that Speaker would be his regular center fielder.

Although Griffith claimed to have outbid everybody for Speaker's services, Connie Mack told a luncheon gathering of the Tampa Rotary Club that he had offered Speaker more money than Griffith. It was a sign of Speaker's professional integrity that he turned down Mack's proposition because he already had Griffith's offer. "This cost Speaker considerable money, I am sure," said Mack, "but it testifies to the honesty of the man. You can't make me believe that a man who would be that square could be guilty of any crookedness in baseball or anywhere else."[44]

What makes Speaker's signing so significant with Washington, plus the fact that other American League teams lobbied for his services, was that Ban Johnson had banned him from the American League. Johnson asserted that the ban would stand no matter how Landis ruled. Clearly aware of this, when Landis gave his ruling that both Cobb and Speaker were cleared of any charges, he made sure to rescind the ban on them. Landis bucked Johnson and made sure that Cobb and Speaker were to remain in the American League by nixing inquiries from the Giants' John McGraw and Pittsburgh's owner Barney Dreyfuss, both in the National League. Landis asserted his authority and clamped down on any power Johnson thought he had on Cobb's and Speaker's future. With the ruling, Johnson had lost the war with Landis he fought for baseball's supreme Czar.

The Dutch Leonard Affair had ended for Speaker, and a new beginning was dawning for the Grey Eagle.

Endnotes

1. Alexander, Charles. *Spoke: The Biography of Tris Speaker*. McFarland & Company, Inc. Jefferson, NC. Kindle Edition, Locations 3974-3978.
2. ibid., Locations 3969-3974.
3. ibid.
4. Gay, Timothy. *Tris Speaker: The Rough and Tumble Life of a Baseball Legend*. University of Nebraska Press, Lincoln, NE. 2007. p. 231.
5. ibid.

6. ibid.

7. *Chicago Tribune*, December 22, 1926

8. ibid.

9. Alexander, op. cit., Location 4065.

10. *Chicago Tribune*, December 22, 1926

11. Alexander, op cit., Locations, 4071-4074.

12. ibid.

13. ibid., Location 4085.

14. ibid.

15. ibid., Locations 4085-4090.

16. ibid., Locations 4090-4094.

17. ibid., Locations 4094-4099.

18. ibid., Location 4099.

19. ibid., Locations 4099-4104.

20. Posnanski, Joe. *The Dutch Leonard Affair*. http://joeposnanski.com/the-dutch-leonard-affair/. Accessed April 15, 2019.

21. *Chicago Tribune*, December 22, 1926

22. Alexander, op. cit., Locations 4121-4126.

23. ibid., Location 4126.

24. ibid., Locations, 4126-4130.

25. ibid., Locations 4130-4135.

26. ibid.

27. ibid.

28. Pietrusza, op. cit., Locations, 7509-7516.

29. Alexander, op. cit., Location 4202.

30. ibid.

31. Pietrusza, op. cit., Location 7516.

32. ibid.

33. *Chicago Tribune*, December 30, 1926

34. ibid.

35. ibid.

36. Spink, J. G. Taylor. *Judge Landis and 25 Years of Baseball: The Story of America's First Commissioner of Baseball*. NightHawk Books, Taos, NM. Kindle Edition. Locations 2834-2839.

37. ibid., Locations 2839-2844.

38. ibid., Locations 2844-2856.

39. Alexander, op. cit., Location 4261.

40. ibid., Locations 4274-4278.
41. ibid.
42. ibid.
43. ibid.
44. ibid., Locations 4314-4318.

CHAPTER 11

Joe Wood: The Man in the Middle

"See, I kept charge of all the money. About $12,000 involved you know...We'd bet on ourselves."- Smoky Joe Wood

In 1985, A. Bartlett Giamatti, then president of Yale University, bestowed an honorary doctorate on ninety-five-year-old Smoky Joe Wood, former Boston Red Sox pitcher (1908–1915) and Cleveland Indians utility player (1917–1922). That such a prestigious university would confer such an honor to a high school dropout from Kansas City might seem strange enough (even if he was Yale's baseball coach for twenty years). Giamatti would become National League President in 1986, and in 1989, commissioner of baseball. Although Giamatti served as commissioner for only a few months due to his untimely death, his decision to ban Pete Rose permanently for gambling on baseball lives on as a monumental judgement in the annals of baseball history. Giamatti's gesture to Wood was all the more ironic given that Joe Wood had been involved in the Dutch Leonard Affair 60 years before.

By 1926, Wood had been away from Major League Baseball for four years and was coaching the Yale College baseball team. To him, the whole scandal must have been a nuisance, as he was being called to testify in Chicago on incidents that happened years ago. Wood could not be punished by Landis because the Commissioner's powers did not reach beyond Major League Baseball. However, his credibility at Yale was questioned due to the scandal and its repercussions on the reputations of those involved.

In his interview with Lawrence Ritter for the book *The Glory of Their Times*, Wood expressed shock that Dutch Leonard had saved his letter from 1919 regarding the bet. Wood also explained that he was the trusting type and had written to Dutch Leonard in the same manner he would write to his brother Pete. He never dreamed it would come back to bite him.

Wood himself had a history of gambling, which made his testimony seem credible to Landis. The biggest incident may have been something that happened in Game 6 of the 1912 World Series, between the Red Sox and the New York Giants.

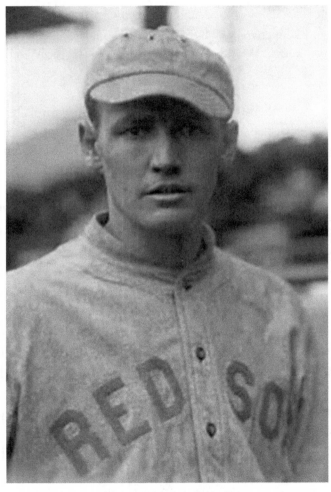

"Smoky" Joe Wood is one of the rare big league ballplayers who was successful both as a pitcher and a position player. He finished his career with an ERA of 2.03 in more than 1400 IP and a batting average of .283 in nearly 2000 ABs.

The 1912 World Series Betting Scandal

Certain shady events during the 1912 World Series are a prime illustration of Joe Wood's propensity to bet, and also of how gambling during the Dead Ball Era involved both the players and management. It also shows Ban Johnson at the peak of his power as Czar of Baseball, and his determination to stamp out gambling in baseball.

Before Game 6 of the Series, Wood (who that year had one of the great pitching seasons of all time for the Red Sox, compiling a record of 34-5), advised his friends and family to bet on Boston before his scheduled start. With the Red Sox ahead three games to one (darkness had caused one game to end in a tie) and Wood ready to take the mound for the Red Sox in Game 6, it seemed likely that the Sox would win the World Series then and there, given that the American League's top pitcher had already beaten the Giants twice in the Series.[1]

Instead, Red Sox manager Jake Stahl was ordered by owner James McAleer to start Buck O'Brien, who was not as lethal as Wood, in Game 6. The Red Sox lost that game, and Wood was embarrassed and angered at having wrongly advised his family and friends to bet on it. Wood would start in Game 7, and ended up losing that one, too. Sixty-five years later, Fred Lieb, a highly prominent sports writer, would remember the carnival atmosphere aboard the Boston-to-New York train on that fateful Sunday in 1912.

> "The Red Sox had taken a three-games-to-one lead over the Giants in the World Series (Game 2 had been a darkness-induced tie), and the next day their ace, Smokey Joe Wood — 34-5 for the season, 2-0 in the Series — would take the mound for the clincher. It was like traveling to a coronation, with the players already weighing the value of their soon-to-be-won crowns. Little did they realize that their seemingly inevitable investiture was about to be challenged, and not so much by the McGrawite pretenders as by their own potentate, majority owner Jimmy McAleer."[2]

Unlike other owners who were wealthy and had bought baseball teams besides for the love of the sport, McAleer's passion was baseball and baseball only.[3] McAleer had played center field for Cleveland throughout the 1890's, then managed in the American League for eleven years. McAleer's wealth was not great enough to buy the Red Sox, but he had gained control of the franchise with the help of American League President Ban Johnson, who put up most of the money on his behalf. This would later prove to be a toxic situation for McAleer, as his reliance and indebtedness to Johnson would later come back to haunt him.[4]

McAleer let his greed get the best of him with his desire to fill the newly built Fenway Park one more time during the 1912 season. But that could happen only if his club lost Game 6 to the Giants, and how likely was that with Joe Wood on the hill? "So McAleer conferred with manager Jake Stahl, and persuaded (or maybe ordered; accounts differ) Stahl to hold back Wood and instead start Buck O'Brien, a twenty-game winner during the season and hard-luck loser of Game 3 a few days earlier."[5]

It was not unreasonable for the Red Sox to wait on pitching Wood, as they held a 3-1 lead in games and Wood would have been coming back on two day's rest. Like all Dead Ball Era aces, Wood's workload had been back-breaking. He had already pitched more than 360 innings that year. Plus, O'Brien was no slouch.

As it turned out, O'Brien pitched miserably, giving up five runs (three earned) on six hits, and contributing a run-scoring balk in his only inning of work. That was all the Giants got, and it was all they needed for a 5-2 victory. The Series would indeed return to Boston to generate additional revenue from paying customers.

The Red Sox's overconfidence and their loss in Game 6 had further consequences. Game 7 was never planned for at Fenway, but with it now on the schedule, seats for the game had to be sold on a first come first serve basis as advance sales had not been made.

To compound the problem, the Red Sox failed to inform its most passionate fans, the Royal Rooters, of the fact that there was no reserved seating. The Rooters were a group of five hundred die-hard fans, who were led by Mayor John "Honey Fitz" Fitzgerald. They were famous for arriving at games in Fenway Park very dramatically—in parade formation—marching onto the field and into their reserved seats. But on this day, the Rooters were herded into a standing room area.

This did not sit well with the passionate Rooters, whose regular seats were being occupied by "ordinary" fans. Soon, the Rooters got rowdy and a riot broke out over the seating arrangements. Mounted police were eventually summoned to contain the infuriated cranks. Wood was warming up at the time the riot broke out and he stopped and retreated to the dugout, resuming his preparation half an hour later. Fred Lieb would claim that Wood's arm stiffened in the interval. Given Wood's terrible performance in Game 7 (6 runs in the first inning), the claim could be true. Horrible pitching by Wood coincided with awful fielding by the Red Sox, who blundered plays and looked like the Keystone Cops. Like O'Brien in Game Six, Wood lasted one inning. Now there would be a game eight, and a coin flip determined that it would be at Fenway Park. Another game meant more revenue for the owners and players.[5]

Jimmy McAleer's deeds had made a black mark on the game of baseball for the Boston fans: he alienated not only his players but the team's most passionate fans in the Royal Rooters. The next morning's papers were full of complaints of the Red Sox brass. The Royal Rooters wanted no part of game eight, and neither did many others. A "crowd" of only half of the seating showed up to see if the Sox would lose three in a row and hand the series to the Giants. Thanks to the Red Sox's incredible good fortune in the bottom of the tenth (Fred Snodgrass's error, the foul pop hit by Speaker that fell at Merkle's feet). McAleer was spared the ultimate humiliation, as the Red Sox eked out a tense World Series riddled with question marks by the fans and the media alike.

American League President Ban Johnson had watched the whole debacle play out and was livid. The next season, in 1913, the Red Sox struggled, and McAleer fired manager Stahl, who happened to be a close friend of Johnson. This did not sit well with the baseball Czar, who ran the American league like a feudal lord. If an owner displeased him (and was not filthy rich), he was gone. McAleer was forced to sell the team.

Wood first learned of Dutch Leonard coming east to make his accusations about the September 25, 1919 incident in a phone call from Tris Speaker in either late June or early July 1926, after the college baseball season had come to an end. Wood had known Leonard for years when they played on Boston together and even loaned money to Leonard so he could buy his first motorcycle. Wood was not in the loop when the controversy first unfolded. He had been out of professional baseball for three years, putting all the focus on Cobb and Speaker.

After a quiet summer, the dam broke on September 9, 1926, when the American League handed the evidence to Commissioner Landis as a "courtesy," to make him aware of what was happening. But instead of Landis just passively accepting the information obtained from Johnson's office, he got to work immediately, sending a telegram and phoning Dutch Leonard the next day to meet either in Los Angeles or Chicago.[6] Leonard demurred, making several excuses, including running his wine business and his wife being too sick to be left unattended.

Landis became fed up with Leonard's excuses for not meeting in person about the matter and went to see him on October 29th at his home in Sanger, California. There, Leonard told Landis the whole story about the betting incident.

The conversation with Leonard motivated Landis to call a meeting between Leonard, Cobb, Speaker, Wood, and West, which was to happen on November 29th. However, Leonard again refused to attend. Instead, Cobb, Speaker, and Landis met at the Commissioner's office in Chicago on November 27th.

By this time, Landis had fully taken over the investigation of the matter. He summoned Joe Wood to Chicago and again called Leonard to attend a meeting scheduled for December 20th at the People's Bank Building in Chicago. But again Leonard refused.

Meanwhile, Wood had arrived in Chicago and was speaking with Cobb, Speaker and their lawyers. When December 20th came and Leonard didn't show, Cobb, Speaker, and Wood declared that the proceedings would be prejudicial as they would not be able to face their accuser.[7]

The meeting, however, went on anyway in front of the press, and as noted, at Cobb's and Speaker's urging, the transcript was published in the newspapers around the United States the next day. Wood soon left by train back to Yale.

On the afternoon of December 23rd, Wood met with Business Manager of the Yale Athletics Association, Harold F. Woodcock, and Burnside Winslow, Chairman of the Yale Baseball Advisory Committee, for two hours regarding the Dutch Leonard Affair. It was decided that Wood's fate at Yale as its coach would be decided in January after the holidays were over.

Local papers in Connecticut got wind of the news and threw their support behind Wood. Mainly, they focused on Wood's firm stand against gambling in the collegiate levels of baseball as a redeeming factor. However, the papers also reported that Clyde Engle, a former Red Sox teammate of Wood, would replace him if let go.

Meanwhile, Wood traveled back to Cleveland to meet with Cobb, Speaker, and their attorneys on strategy, while Landis mulled his decision on the Dutch Leonard Affair.

On January 4, 1927, weeks before Landis's verdict, the Yale Athletic Board of Control met in the trophy room of the gymnasium from 8:00 pm till after midnight regarding the fate of Joe Wood. The next day, Wood was exonerated. Professor Nettleton, Chairman of the Board, made the announcement:

> "No action has been taken or is now contemplated by the Board of Control of the Yale University Athletic Association to alter its existing relationship with Joe Wood. During his terms of service at Yale, he has confirmed in character and conduct the definite endorsements which led to his appointment as athletic coach, The board of control possesses no evidence which, in its judgment, discredits the honesty and integrity of his past record."[8]

Wood stayed silent to the press regarding the decision, and in the end, the whole episode did not hurt Wood's reputation at Yale. The following letter was published in the local newspaper on Saturday, January 8, 1927:

"We always had a leaning towards Yale and this leaning hasn't been straightened back any by the action of the Yale athletic officials in standing by Joe Wood, former major league leaguer accused of betting on a game by "Dutch Leonard. It seems that Old Eli has taken the view that, if Wood did do what Leonard says he did, it wasn't so terribly terrible and that, anyway, they don't believe it and that Joe, since becoming a coach at Yale, has been a fine gentleman, a successful coach and a wonderful influence on the young athletes over whom he has had supervision."[9]

On January 27, 1927, when Landis finally released his decision, he sensed that Wood's situation at Yale might have been put in jeopardy[10]; Landis told him that if he had any problems at Yale over the Dutch Leonard Affair, the Commissioner would help him out. Wood states this to Ritter as follows:

"I was at a World Series, with Landis down in NY and he says, 'We gonna have any trouble over this thing, Joe?', I said, 'I don't think so.' 'You let me know and if ya do, I'll come make a trip up to New Haven.'"[11]

After many years away from baseball and his coaching position at Yale, Wood surfaced on the baseball scene again in the book *The Glory of Their Times*. As noted, only parts of the interviews were published, as some of the transcript about the Dutch Leonard Affair was too explosive to be made public. Ritter promised Wood he would destroy the tapes of that part of the interview. He didn't, but they did not see the light of day, either. Instead, the full transcript was archived at Notre Dame University with other interview content that was not published. Wood also interviewed with Eugene C. Murdock on April 19, 1975 and disclosed more about the Dutch Leonard Affair in another set of tapes which are housed in the Cleveland Public Library.

Wood interviewed with Ritter on October 15, 1963 and October 1, 1965. The former pitcher substantiated speculation that the Dead Ball Era was saturated with gambling and fixing games. Corruption and game-fixing were not spoken about, but were aspects of the game that were familiar to all who played. In addition, gambling among ballplayers extended beyond the ball field. Card games, horse racing, dog racing, boxing and, of course, baseball were some of the activities which were popular with players and bookies.

In the interviews, Wood also stated that the 1920 White Sox were not playing their best to win the American League title. In a conversation Wood had with Eddie Cicotte at the Winton Hotel in Cleveland near the end of the 1920 season, Cicotte said to Wood that the Sox "didn't dare win."[12] In addition, he claimed, the Tigers were willing to take it easy on Cleveland to ensure them a championship.

In the published Ritter interviews Wood claims he merely helped with the transaction and did not himself bet, which is quite different than how he testified before Landis, where he more or less took the fall for the other alleged participants.

Overall, in the Ritter interviews, Wood leaves the reader wondering if there might have been more to the Dutch Leonard Affair than was made public. He asserts that Ban Johnson received information about betting prior to and during the 1920 World Series. This suggests that the Dutch Leonard Affair was not the only focus of the investigation by Ban Johnson and Kenesaw Mountain Landis. Wood indicated that their inquiries also involved betting during the 1920 World Series, in which he and Tris Speaker had participated. Wood did state, though, that the players had bet on their own team, which to him seemed to not be a problem, because the Indians would have had no reason to throw a game if they had bet on themselves. Wood and others, if they did wager, probably felt they would have been absolved of guilt had their wagers ever become public.

Essentially, in the Ritter interviews, Wood admitted that he took the fall for Speaker and Cobb, having claimed to Landis that he had wagered on the game but the others hadn't. Wood had been able to say that because he was out of baseball, he was beyond the wrath of Commissioner Landis, while and Cobb and Speaker were not. Wood was safe, but the legacies of Cobb and Speaker could have been tarnished forever.

The interviews also spotlight Landis and the fact that he dropped his usual role of authoritarian during the inquiries. Wood documents that Landis was very passive in his orchestration of the hearings with Cobb, Speaker, and Wood. Instead of being a hard-bitten lawyer going for the kill on cross examination, Landis conducted the hearings like a sideshow presented for the benefit of the reporters.

Landis's questions served the purpose of amplifying his own successes and achievements as commissioner. He asked both players if there were betting and easing up by teams (to have other teams in a pennant race stay competitive in order to win the pennant) since he became commissioner, to which, of course, they said no. Landis played the media to get them to present a version of the reality of baseball in which gambling and game-fixing had become a thing of the past since he had become commissioner.

Further diminishing the validity of the hearings, Landis let them go on without the presence of the central character in the affair, the accuser himself, Dutch Leonard. This let the Cobb, Speaker, and Wood attacks on Leonard's credibility go unchecked. All three players asserted that Dutch Leonard was merely fishing for money by reporting the whole affair, and that he was being vengeful for having been thrown out of baseball and forgotten. Landis did not interrupt any of the players' attacks on Leonard and their testimonies went into the record as unchallenged evidence.

Furthermore, Landis overlooked blatant misinformation by Cobb, Wood, and Speaker. One example Landis not questioning Cobb's explanation that he was merely following Wood's instructions and that Cobb had given him the wrong information and a fictitious amount of money that was involved. Landis also let stand unchecked Wood's testimony that the affair was none of Cobb's business, even though the alleged events took place in Detroit on Cobb's own turf and Cobb had written a letter to Leonard about it. In addition, Landis also did not challenge Wood's proclamation that he and Speaker had not discussed betting on this particular ball game over the past six years, even though he had information that betting by both Wood and Speaker had taken place in the 1920 World Series.

The interviews with Wood also documented his relationship with Speaker. We learn from the tapes that Wood admitted he was a "loyal person" and said "My religion is to help anybody that needs my help, do a favor for someone who wants a favor."[11] This undying loyalty to people was applied to Speaker by Wood. Hugh Fullerton, the celebrated sports writer who helped found the Baseball Writers Association of America, and who broke the story in the press about the gambling scheme at the 1919 World Series, suggested that Speaker was like a father figure to Joe Wood. In Wood's own words: "Speaker and me...we'd do anything for one another; I'd have gone to hell [for Tris] and he'd have gone to hell for me."[13] Wood seems to have displayed that loyalty in taking the fall for Speaker.

Additional revelations by Wood that were not part of his testimony to Landis contained information that was so lethal that Wood didn't even tell his brother Pete. It also lends credence to Cobb's assertions that he and his lawyers had enough information to destroy baseball if he was found guilty by Landis and kicked out of baseball.

What is clear is that the Landis and Johnson investigations went further than the one game played on September 25, 1919. It also shows that materials were given to Ban Johnson about bets that were made prior to and during the 1920 World Series. Johnson, of course, did not want the public to know this and never released the information, which would have hurt the game much more than what was published by Landis. Wood corroborates Cobb's story in Cobb's autobiography that there was information stored in that Cleveland Bank's vault that contained information to destroy baseball if released.

Wood also insinuates that Cobb was more of a gambler than people suspected. He assumes that Cobb and Leonard had more interactions involving gambling than just the one game, and that Cobb had stiffed him on several occasions, propelling Leonard to say to Damon Runyan:

"I have evidence to show that baseball is a game only for suckers to bet on...They don't get a chance unless they are in on the know. Baseball is a trust of the worst sort. It is a closed corporation."[14]

Wood's remarks, and his directness towards both Ritter and Eugene Murdoch a decade later, painted a very different picture than the one that Landis had relied upon to exonerate Cobb and Speaker.

Endnotes

1. Wood, Gerald C. *Smoky Joe Wood*. University of Nebraska Press, Lincoln, NE. 2013. p. 347, Note 10. Citing Michael Hartley from, *Christy Mathewson, A Biography* (McFarland Publishers, Inc. Jefferson, North Carolina 2004. p. 98: "It was later said that Joe Wood, expecting himself to pitch, had bet a large sum on the game." Mike Vacarro (without documentation) asserts that Joe's brother bet one thousand dollars.

2. Kopf, Mike. *Big Book of Baseball Blunders*. http://robneyer.com/baseball-books/big-book-of-baseball-blunders/red-sox-mcaleer-1912-series/. Accessed April 15, 2019.

3. One example is Jacob Ruppert, owner of the New York Yankees. He was interested in baseball, but he owned a brewing business.

4. Kopf, op. cit.

5. ibid.

6. Wood, op. cit., p. 250.

7. ibid., p. 253.

8. ibid.

9. ibid.

10. ibid., p. 254.

11. Burgess III, Bill. The Baseball Guru website. *Leonard Cobb Speaker Affair*. http://baseballguru.com/bburgess/analysisbburgess05.html. Accessed April 15, 2019.

12. Wood, op. cit., p. 291.

13. ibid.

14. ibid., p. 289.

CHAPTER 12

The Czar of Baseball and the Judge

"His contribution to the game, is not closely equaled by any other
single person or group of persons."
–Branch Rickey on Ban Johnson

Before Judge Landis became commissioner of baseball, Ban Johnson was
the most powerful man in America's national past time. His power would
be severely curtailed by the elevation of Landis on November 12, 1920
as Baseball's first commissioner after the whole "Black Sox" scandal in
the 1919 World Series. It was a watershed time for baseball, with Landis
chosen to lead baseball after acting swiftly and strongly to cleanse the sport
of corruption and scandal. As a condition for taking the job, Landis insisted
that both the National League and the American League owners to give him
unlimited and sole power to rule over the sport as its chief enforcer, and he
got it. This put Johnson and his power in the American League in the back
corner; the title of "President" of the American League became a title only.
He became little more than a figurehead.

The Early Life of Ban Johnson and the
Foundations of the American League

Byron Bancroft Johnson was born in Norwalk, Ohio, on January 5, 1864.
He was the fifth of six children of Alexander Byron and Eunice C. Fox
Johnson. Shortly after Ban's birth, the Johnsons moved to Avondale, Ohio,
then a Cincinnati suburb, though today it is part of the city. Johnson's dad,
Alexander Johnson, served as a prominent school administrator. Alexander
hoped his son would continue the family tradition in picking a career in

education or going into the clergy. Alexander was severely disappointed and became irritated with his son because Ban ignored his studies to run off to play baseball. After graduating from preparatory school, Ban Johnson showed a lack of focus in his studies, transferring from Oberlin College to Marietta College to the University of Cincinnati Law School, where he would remain for less than two years. At Marietta, Johnson gained a reputation as a fearless catcher on the school baseball team by playing the position without a glove, mask, or chest protector. When Johnson started playing for the semipro Ironton, Ohio team while on vacation from school, a thumb injury soon ended his career.

Johnson dropped out of law school midway through his sophomore year in 1886. He took a job as sportswriter at the Cincinnati *Commercial Gazette* at $25 a week. His father was furious. The paper's highly-respected editor, Murat Halstead, had to convince Johnson's father that journalism was an honorable profession. When sports editor, O. P. Caylor, left the Cincinnati paper to take a similar position in New York, Halstead named Johnson to the job.[1]

Johnson soon earned a reputation for having a great knowledge of sports, as well as one who did not shy away from a fight and who spoke his mind. Johnson would get involved in the most volatile topics of the day and never backed down from a challenge. For example, when the Players League was formed in 1890 to break the monopoly that the National League held over the sport, Johnson backed the Players League. His stance alienated many powerful men in the sport, including American Association of Baseball's Indianapolis Hoosiers' owner, John Brush (who would later own the New York Giants in the National League and challenge Johnson in the Baseball War of 1901-1903. He would also refuse to let the Giants play in the 1904 World Series, which ultimately led to no series being played that year). Even with his strong and controversial opinions, Johnson's perseverance won him the admiration of others, such as star first baseman Charles Comiskey, who had joined the Players League.[2]

In 1892, Ban Johnson first became acquainted with Charles Comiskey, the new manager of the Cincinnati Reds, and they soon became close friends. The roots of the future American League was actually born in the "Ten Minute Club," a friendly Cincinnati bar which Johnson and

Comiskey frequented.[3] The tavern derived its name from a rule requiring at least one person at each table to order a drink every ten minutes.[4] With Comiskey's urging, Johnson applied for the presidency of the Western League in 1894.

The Western League began in 1892, when the Players League folded after 1890 and the American Association was absorbed by the National League the following year. The Western League had financial problems from its inception, and owner Jimmy Williams was forced to close down the league in July, 1892. Then, in the fall of 1893, the former members of the defunct league sought to give it another try and restart the league. Williams did not want to participate in resurrecting the league, claiming he could no longer take charge of keeping the league afloat financially. Through the lobbying of Comiskey to committee members Denny Long of Toledo and James Manning of Kansas City, in November of 1894, Ban Johnson was named President-Secretary-Treasurer of the Western League and given a salary of $2,500 a year. This was Ban Johnson's first taste of real power.[5]

Under Johnson's presidency, the Western League became more profitable for the rest of the 19th century. In six years as president, besides cracking down on rowdy behavior and curtailing the use of profane language by players, he declared war on gamblers. In those days, baseball and baseball players had a poor reputation in the eyes of the public. The whole sport was seen as something that was seedy, rampant with gamblers and cheaters. This negativity, along with the frequent violence at the games, kept down attendance, which in turn cut into the owners' profits. Johnson was determined to change that image and make the Western League a reputable and successful organization. His success was evident by 1897, when the league drew nearly one million fans, with the top clubs in Kansas City, Milwaukee, and St. Paul drawing better than some National League franchises.[6]

Johnson's ambition for the league league was to put the Western League on the same footing as the National League as a "major" league, rather than being just a thriving "minor" league. When the National League voted to reduce their size from twelve to eight teams prior to the 1900 season, Johnson saw a great opportunity to take further steps to elevate his league to a "major" status. Johnson shifted the St. Paul club to Chicago and the Columbus franchise to Cleveland, to compete with the National League teams directly, and he even changed the Western League's name to the "American League." The following year, Johnson declared his organization a "major league," and abandoned the circuit's western roots, moving franchises into National League territories in Boston and Philadelphia, as well as Baltimore and Washington (which the National League had abandoned the year before).[7]

Also during this time, Adrian "Cap" Anson was attempting a reorganization of the old American Association, which had gone out of business after the 1891 season. Although the project eventually collapsed, fear that it might interfere with or destroy his own big league ambitions spurred Johnson on with his goals. In addition, the five-year Western League Agreement expired at the close of the 1900 season, which made it a convenient time to try to move the league to the next level. The stars further aligned for Johnson in June of 1900, when a group of National League players, unhappy over low salaries and being trapped by the reserve clause, formed a union: the Players Protective Association.[8] The new American League hence became a viable and possibly lucrative alternative for the disgruntled players, while those players offered an opportunity for Johnson to strengthen his own league.

The Great Baseball War of 1900 to 1903

In the final years of the 19th Century and early 20th Century there were three so-called "Baseball Wars." Ban Johnson was involved in all three, though he played a different role in each battle. The first was the Brotherhood War of 1890, in which Johnson was an observer of the fighting as sports editor at the *Commercial Gazette*. He had no personal stake in the outcome. In the last of the three wars, the Federal League challenged both the National League and Ban's American League from 1913 to 1915. In this case, Johnson was in the role of the establishment being challenged by outsiders. In the second war, Johnson was on the other side of that relationship—the outsider challenging the establishment—his league battling for legitimacy and equal standing with the entrenched and powerful National League. This battle would later be known as the Great Baseball War of 1900 to 1903.

With his newly named American League, Johnson took notice of some of the faults of the National League and tried to exploit them. One big step he took was to not follow the National League's $2,400 salary cap. As a result, 111 players from the National League jumped to the new venture, including top stars such as Cy Young, Napoleon Lajoie, and John McGraw.[9] In addition, before the 1902 season, Johnson transferred the Milwaukee club to St. Louis to compete head-to-head with the Cardinals, and continued his raid on National League rosters, coming away with more big name players, including sluggers Ed Delahanty, Jesse Burkett, and Elmer Flick.

The results were impressive. In 1902, the American League outdrew the National League by more than 500,000 fans. In the four cities home to franchises in both leagues, the upstart American League outdrew the National League in all of them by a wide margin. In Boston, the American League Americans drew a total of 348,567 compared to 116,960 in the National League for the Beaneaters. In Chicago, 337,898 fans turned out for the White Stockings in comparison with their cross town rivals in the National League, the Orphans, who drew 263,700. In Philadelphia, the Athletics outshined the Phillies by a huge margin of 420,078 to 112,066, and finally, in St. Louis, the Browns topped the National League Cardinals, 272,283 to 243,826.[10]

Originally, Johnson hoped to make the transition with the full approval and support of the National League, but if the NL owners opposed him, he was prepared to fight. In preparing for the 1901 season, the American League established franchises in three unoccupied eastern cities—Baltimore, Washington, and Buffalo—and in one National League city, Philadelphia. In defending his eastward expansion, Johnson said, "While we wish to work in harmony with the major league, we have grown large and strong enough not to be dictated to, and will choose our own grounds and infringe on National League territory, even without its consent, if our wishes are not respected."[11]

When the National League owners met for their annual meeting in New York in December, 1900, two matters demanded immediate attention: recognition of the Players Protective Association and recognition of the American League. Both of these matters were turned down. The National League owners told Johnson, in particular, that he could wait for recognition "until hell froze over."[12] Johnson responded by transferring the Buffalo franchise to Boston, challenging the National League head-to-head in one of its major city strongholds. Next, Johnson compiled a list of 46 top-flight National League players, and sent a band of "raiders" into action to steal them away from the older league.[13]

These raids on National League players were very successful, as 45 of the players were signed to American League contracts. Following the 1901 season, Johnson's agents secured 37 more National League players. In response the National League went to court to win back its lost players, and although it secured several apparent victories in the courtroom, it never regained its greatest players.

The American League was winning the battle for fans, too, due in part to the many excellent players who jumped to its side, and also due to the fan experience at the ballpark. Just as he had done in the Western League, Johnson's crackdown on rowdyism, brawling, drunkenness and profanity on the field and in the stands was transforming baseball into family entertainment. His sound, business-savvy leadership had set the American League distinctively apart from the strife-torn National League.

In August, 1902, one reporter observed:

> "The National League is unquestionably conducting a losing fight...By continuing the old methods now being carried on, the old league is getting more and more the worst of it...The American League has the call--by a great percentage--with the public, and will continue to retain it, because of its superior management and the popular methods in vogue."[14]

Seeing the writing on the wall, the National League owners decided to quit the battle with their rival at the close of the 1902 season. The so-called "peace conference" took place at the St. Nicholas Hotel in Cincinnati, on January 9-10, 1903. Most of the disputed players were awarded to Johnson's teams and the American League was granted the right to move into New York City, an important point of contention. "It was an American League victory," proclaimed sportswriter, Irving Sanborn, "and those principles for which 'Ban Johnson and Company' began the fight two years ago are established."[15]

Although John Brush, owner of the New York Giants, still tried to prevent the American League from building a park in New York City, and although a few player disputes arose to threaten the peace, the American League had now firmly established itself as a second major league.[16]

Out of the peace conference emerged a new governing agency for Organized Baseball, the National Commission. The commission was composed of the presidents of the two major leagues and a third member to be chosen by the first two. The third member and chairman of the Commission was August "Garry" Herrmann, owner of the Cincinnati Reds. In reality, however, to a large degree Johnson had control of Herrmann's vote, which made Johnson the dominant force in the National Commission.[17] Herrmann was accused of being "Ban's man," and was charged with siding with Johnson and against the National League in player disputes. These allegations were probably exaggerated, especially considering that Herrmann was a National League owner, but nevertheless Johnson soon became the most powerful force in the National Commission, and soon was the acknowledged "czar" of baseball.[18] Moreover, the next fifteen years, 1903-1918, was a period of increased popularity and profit for the sport, and Johnson became intimately associated with the game's burgeoning success.

More importantly, the agreement between the two leagues included a reaffirmation of the principle of the reserve clause and the sanctity of contracts. Once again, the players' inability to negotiate with different teams would render them little more than paid slaves on the plantation. They were powerless pawns in the business of baseball. The hope and expectation of higher wages and a voice in contract negotiations, seemingly made possible by Johnson's moves to establish the American League, were gone, as Johnson cemented his American League on the same owner-friendly footing as the once-rival National League was on.

The Feud With John McGraw

Ban Johnson's policy of containing rowdyism and bad behavior applied not only to fans at the games, but also to the men who played and managed the games as well. Johnson swiftly punished players and managers who crossed the line. Unfortunately, Johnson's tactics were not always successful, as seen in his battle with John McGraw.

At five feet, seven inches, 155 pounds, John McGraw was not an intimidating figure, not likely to instill fear from the way he looked. But few men packed more fury than McGraw. He more than made up for his diminutive structure with a fiery and intimidating disposition.

Ban Johnson, on the other hand, made a very different first impression. His large frame and booming voice made him an intimidating figure that struck fear into people's hearts.

Both of these men had, in a few short years, ascended to the upper rungs of baseball's power ladder. McGraw had taken a terrible New York Giants ball club and turned it into a powerhouse, while Johnson had gone from an enemy of the major league baseball establishment to the most powerful man in the game.

McGraw and Johnson had crossed paths in the 1890s and quickly realized that their personalities did not mesh. As a player for the Baltimore Orioles, McGraw had developed the reputation as a bullying, ill-tempered, and at times violent ballplayer. Appropriately positioned at the hot corner—third base—McGraw was an outstanding player, batting .336 with 436 stolen bases through nine years in Baltimore. He got his first chance to manage in 1899, proving leadership abilities at age 26 that brought the Orioles to a fourth-place finish in the then 12-team National League.[19]

The Orioles folded after 1899 and McGraw was out of a job, without any team to manage, until Ban Johnson came along with the American League in 1901. Johnson offered McGraw a player-manager post with an American League version of the Orioles. It was another chance for McGraw to lead a team, and in a way, he would be going back home.

McGraw brought all his know-how to the new league, including a harsh style of umpire-baiting that Johnson was trying to suppress. Even with Johnson's stance on umpire harassment, McGraw's bullying continued. Johnson responded with numerous fines and suspensions. McGraw's dream opportunity was rapidly turning to frustration. In response, McGraw packed up and left Baltimore midway through his second season there, taking many of his star players with him, to the National League and the New York Giants. In retaliation, after the 1902 season, Johnson moved the Orioles to New York to compete with McGraw's Giants. This Orioles team would eventually be known as the New York Yankees.

Johnson continued his battle with McGraw by helping to engineer trades and player purchases to help make his new Gotham entry, the New York Highlanders, more competitive. After a last-place showing at Baltimore in 1902 as the Orioles, the revamped Highlanders of New York hopped to fourth in 1903, ten games over the .500 mark.

The personal animosity between McGraw and Ban Johnson came to a head in 1904 when the NL champion New York Giants declined to meet the champions of the "junior" American League, the Boston Red Sox (led by 26-game winner, 37-year-old Cy Young). McGraw said his Giants were already the world champions because they were the champions of the "only real major league."[20]

As early as July 5, 1904, as reported in *Sporting Life*, Giants owner John T. Brush (who didn't like Johnson since the days when he was the sports editor of the Cincinnati *Commercial Gazette* in the early 1890's) had stated publicly, and in contradiction of a preseason agreement for a championship series between the leagues, that his National League club would not play the winner of the American League "if each wins the pennant in its respective league."[21] At that point in the season, the Giants were comfortably on top of the NL standings, and the New York Highlanders were just games behind the Boston Americans. The American League race went down to the wire, and the Highlanders temporarily took over first place on October 7, when they defeated Boston. But the Americans won three of their four remaining games to clinch the American League pennant. The Giants, who had won the NL by a wide margin, stuck to, and broadened their plan, refusing to play any AL club, either the champion Boston or the crosstown New York team, in the proposed "exhibition" series (as they considered it).

Stung by criticism from fans and writers over not having a World Series in 1904, in January 1905, Giants' owner Brush drafted rules that both leagues adopted that winter. The rules compelled the two winning clubs to participate and governed the annual determination of sites, dates, ticket prices and division of receipts. These new rules essentially made the World Series the premier annual Major League Baseball event.

Johnson reigns supreme as the Czar of Baseball

As the American League grew and prospered under Johnson's leadership, so did his power as league president. If problems occurred, Johnson dealt with them quickly and firmly. Whether it was the Tigers striking over Ty Cobb's suspension in 1912, or floating loans to teams to strengthen the league, the persistent Johnson usually got his way. He became so powerful that he even changed the outcome of the 1910 American League batting race between Ty Cobb and Nap Lajoie when the results did not suit him. Johnson left no doubt in anyone's mind who was in charge.

Ban Johnson enjoying a smoke with his league's number one revenue-generator, Babe Ruth.

To further cement his power over the American League as baseball's Czar, Johnson held 51% of the stock of each American League club in the vault in his Chicago office. This power had been given him by league owners back in 1901 on the eve of the Great Baseball War, when it was feared that internal subversion might weaken the league in its fight against the National League.[22] By transferring stock control to the president, no such defections could occur. Armed with such great authority, Johnson arranged for the sale of clubs, hired and fired managers, negotiated trades between clubs, and blacklisted players, managers, and umpires. With such immense power came some resentment and resistance, as anti-Johnson factions began to develop and to look for ways to bring him down.[23]

Examples of the unchallenged power that Johnson wielded are well documented in the baseball archives. One example occurred in 1909, when at its annual meeting the National League was compelled to choose a successor to president Harry Pulliam, who had committed suicide the previous summer. Among the contenders for the position was John Montgomery Ward, former baseball star and now a prosperous New York attorney. Johnson was opposed to Ward's election because he held Ward responsible for shortstop George Davis's jumping a Chicago American League contract and re-joining the New York Giants during the Great Baseball War.[24] Johnson denounced Ward in the newspapers, and asserted that he would not sit on the National Commission with Ward if the latter should become the National League president. Whether Johnson's opposition to Ward tipped the scales against him is difficult to determine, but it was taken into serious consideration. After four days of discussions, the deadlock ended when Thomas Lynch was picked instead as a compromise choice to be President of the National League.

The following year, Larry "Nap" Lajoie of Cleveland and Ty Cobb of Detroit engaged in a close race for the American League batting championship. Interest was intensified when the Chalmers Automobile Company offered an automobile to the player who ended with the highest average. On the last day of the 1910 season, as recounted earlier in the book, Cobb had a nice cushion, but since many players did not like Cobb, a small conspiracy was hatched to try to help Lajoie win the batting title. Cleveland played the St. Louis Browns in a double-header, and with the cooperation of the Browns' manager, coaches, third baseman, and the official scorer, Lajoie came up with 8 hits in 8 at bats, nearly all bunts down the third base line.[25]

When Johnson heard that Lajoie, not known to be a fast runner, had beaten out six bunts in one day, he wanted to know why. As a result of his investigation, he fired Browns' manager, Jack O'Connor, and forever barred him from baseball, and ordered that Howell their pitching coach, be dismissed. Howell later returned as a minor league umpire, but never returned to the big leagues as a player.[26] St. Louis third baseman, Red Corrigan, was exonerated because of his youth and innocence, and because he acted under O'Connor's orders. Although Cobb won the batting title despite Lajoie's eight hits, the Chalmers company gave a car to both players.

In 1912, Johnson would have his own showdown with superstar Ty Cobb and the whole Tigers organization. On May 15, 1912, the Tigers were playing the New York Highlanders (later named the Yankees) at Hilltop Park, when throughout the game Cobb was trading insults with a fan named Claude Lucker who, the year before, had lost one hand and three fingers of the other hand in a printing press accident, a fact that Cobb very likely was not aware of.

The abuse from the fan was relentless, and Cobb tried to get the police to remove the abusive spectator, but to no avail. At the end of the third inning, Cobb launched insult about Lucker's sister, to which Lucker countered by calling the Georgia Peach "a half-nigger."

After a teammate (we don't know who said it, although some accounts point to Sam Crawford) asked Cobb if the was going to take that. Ty jumped over the railing and into the stands and pounded and kicked Lucker until Cobb was finally restrained by the police.

During the beating, a fan screamed "he has no hands." Cobb yelled back "I don't care if he has no feet." If such an incident were to happen today, you would have a line of lawyers ready to sue Cobb, as well as public outrage demanding that he be suspended for a year or thrown out of baseball altogether. But this was 1912, and amazingly, many players, other fans, and the press thought Cobb was justified in his response to the incessant taunting.

When Ban Johnson heard of the incident the next day, he promptly suspended Cobb indefinitely. Cobb was outraged that he was suspended without a hearing or a gathering of the facts. Cobb said "I should at least have had an opportunity to state my case."[27]

Cobb's Tigers teammates agreed with Cobb, and on May 17 announced they would not play until Cobb's suspension was lifted.

What resulted on May 18th, was the first player's strike in baseball history. Rather than forfeit the game due to having no players, Hughie Jennings, the Tigers manager, recruited some amateur players in case the team carried out their threat not to play. When Cobb walked onto the field of Shibe Park in Philadelphia at 2:30 PM with the rest of his teammates to start the game, the umpires informed him he could not play. The rest of the Tigers left the field with him, and the substitute Tigers played instead, and were annihilated by the Athletics 24-2.[28]

Even with this embarrassing loss, and even though they were putting their own careers in jeopardy, Cobb's teammates stood by him and refused to play in any upcoming games. In addition, the Tiger players began contacting players on other teams, urging their fellow players to strike as well. They even considered joining another baseball league called the United States League. This action, which could have led to the players organizing a union, made the owners nervous. Although not the most popular player among his peers, many of them sympathized with Cobb and agreed it was wrong for him to be suspended without due process.

Ban Johnson was furious at the other Tigers players for refusing to play and was forced to cancel the next day's game of May 19th between the Tigers and the Athletics, saying the Tigers had to field a competitive team. A meeting of American League team owners in Philadelphia on May 20th resulted in fining each Tiger player $100 for striking; Cobb's suspension remained indefinite. Meanwhile, the rest of the Tigers team returned to action on May 21st.

On May 25th, Cobb's status changed. Johnson approved the reinstatement of Cobb and issued a $50 fine. An investigation led Johnson to state:

- Cobb used "vicious language in replying to a taunting remark of the spectator"
- Cobb's suspension of 10 days and a $50 fine was a "lesson to the accused and a warning of all players"
- Cobb did not "appeal to the umpire, but took the law into his own hands"[29]

Further, Johnson underscored the league's policy regarding abuse by fans going forward:

- Issuing "sure and severe punishment" for those players who "assume to act as judge and avenger of real or fancied wrongs while on duty"
- Boosting the number of police officers at ballparks
- Removal of fans who engage in "actions or comments [that] are offensive to players and fellow patrons"[30]

Cobb returned to the line-up on May 26th, after what turned out to be a 10-day suspension. The Tigers played against the Chicago White Sox that day. Cobb went 1 for 4 in a 6-2 Tigers victory. The verdict on Johnson's power in the case was mixed. Cobb was forced to the sidelines for 10 days, but the fine of $50 was a mere slap on the wrist. Though it was clear Johnson held a lot of power, the same could be said of Cobb, especially among his fellow ball players. The dynamic between the two giants of the game would be tested again many years later in the Dutch Leonard Affair.

Endnotes

1. Santry, Joe, Thomson, Cindy. Society for American Baseball Research. *Ban Johnson*. http://sabr.org/bioproj/person/dabf79f8. Accessed August 3, 2017.
2. Murdock, Eugene C. *The Tragedy of Ban Johnson*. http://library.la84.org/SportsLibrary/JSH/JSH1974/JSH0101/jsh0101c.pdf. Accessed August 3, 2017.
3. ibid.
5. Santry and Thomson, op. cit.
6. ibid.
7. ibid.
8. ibid.

9. ibid.

10. Baseball-reference.com. 1902 American League and National League attendance records. https://www.baseball-reference.com/leagues/NL/1902-misc.
shtml; https://www.baseball-reference.com/leagues/AL/1902-misc.shtml.
Accessed February 8, 2019.

11. Murdock, op. cit.

12. ibid.

13. ibid.

14. ibid.

15. ibid.

16. ibid.

17. ibid.

18. ibid.

19. This Great Game: The Online Book of Baseball. *1904: McGraw v. Johnson.*
http://www.thisgreatgame.com/1904-baseball-history.html. Accessed August
4, 2017.

20. ibid.

21. ibid.

22. Murdock, op. cit.

23. ibid.

24. ibid.

25. ibid.

26. Controvince, Anthony. MLB Network. *Author Says Cobb's Reputation Built
on Tales.* https://www.mlb.com/news/ty-cobb-history-built-on-inaccura-
cies/c-178601094. February 8, 2019.

27. ibid.

28. Krell, David. *Ty Cobb, the Detroit Tigers, and the Brawl of 1912.* http://davidkrell.
com/uncategorized/ty-cobb-detroit-tigers-brawl-1912/. Accessed February 8,
2019.

29. ibid.

30. ibid.

CHAPTER 13

Johnson Loses His Grip

While Johnson developed many friends and supporters who recognized the value of his contributions, he also built up an army of enemies, people jealous of his power and offended by his rulings. Johnson's eventual demise as the Czar of Baseball was in part the result of his arrogant manner and dictatorial inclinations. Four controversial case rulings by Johnson between 1915 and 1919 paved the way for his loss of power, the fall of baseball's ruling body, the National Commission, and firmly fractured American League owners into pro-Johnson and anti-Johnson camps.

In the first case, occurring during the summer of 1911, George Sisler, a 17-year-old high school star in Akron, Ohio, signed a contract with his home town club. Eventually, Akron assigned the contract to Columbus of the American Association, and Columbus later transferred it to Pittsburgh in the National League. Sisler was a minor leaguer when he signed the contract, and he neither performed for Akron or Columbus, nor did he receive any pay. Instead, Sisler changed his mind about playing professional baseball and entered the University of Michigan in the fall of 1911. The baseball coach at Michigan was Branch Rickey (who would become one of the greatest general managers in Major League history). While playing baseball at the University of Michigan, Sisler earned a degree in Mechanical Engineering, but was a star player, too. Rickey saw Sisler's talent, and urged the National Commission to nullify Sisler's original contract, which they did not do.[1]

After he graduated from Michigan, Sisler sought legal advice from Rickey about the status of his contract with Pittsburgh. The three-time Vanity Fair All-American had become highly sought-after by major league scouts. Rickey talked to Pittsburgh owner Barney Dreyfuss about releasing Sisler from the contract he had signed as a minor, but Dreyfuss maintained his claim on him. Rickey wrote to the National Commission, who ruled that the contract was illegal. Rickey, now managing the St. Louis Browns, signed Sisler to a contract worth $7,400.[2] This enraged Pittsburgh owner, Barney Dreyfuss, who claimed that Sisler belonged to the Pirates because the original Akron contract had been transferred to his club.

Dreyfuss cried foul and vowed to destroy the National Commission. Fellow National League owner, the Cubs' Charles Murphy, agreed with Dreyfuss. Murphy, too, was angry after a National Commission decision. He was quoted by I.E. Sanborn in the *Sporting News* as saying he wanted the entire commission disbanded. His suggestion would later be partially fulfilled. Sanborn claimed that Murphy wanted, ". . . a non-partisan, baseball body of three or five men, among them an ex judge or two, appointed for life to adjudicate all the disputes now coming before the commission."[3] It was the first nail in the coffin for Johnson.

The second case centered on Scott Perry, a journeyman pitcher, who was purchased by the Boston Braves from the Atlanta Crackers of the South Atlantic League, in 1917. Perry was with Boston a few days when he left the club. The following winter, Connie Mack purchased Perry from Atlanta, and he won 21 games for the eighth-place Athletics in 1918.[4] Boston complained, and the National Commission awarded Perry to the Braves. But Mack, with Ban Johnson's approval, secured an injunction blocking the transfer. Both Boston and the National League were furious at this defiance of a National Commission ruling, especially in view of their recent acquiescence in the Sisler case. John Tener, the National League president, insisted that his National League should sever relations with the American League, but when the owners refused to go that far, he resigned.[5]

The issue was finally resolved when the Athletics paid an indemnity to the Braves, but National League bitterness at Johnson was intensified.[6] Once again, the American League had won a contract dispute, leaving some to wonder if the National League could ever win a case brought before the commission.

While the Sisler and Perry cases offended the National League, the other two cases were strictly internal, American League, matters, over which Ban Johnson had complete authority. Johnson's decisions in these cases would eventually upset the American League owners, which would lead to revolt and a shake up the balance of power in the American League.

The third case concerned baseball and the First World War. During the second year of the United States' participation in the war, General Enoch Crowder, who was the draft administrator, had issued a "work-or-fight" order. This order made a distinction between essential and non-essential jobs, which would determine one's eligibility for the draft. Baseball was labeled a non-exempt job, meaning that players would be eligible for the draft. Many other baseball leagues closed down their operations due to the war. The Pacific Coast League was one of these leagues that closed down.

Jack Quinn, a pitcher with the Vernon organization of the Pacific Coast League, went to play with the Chicago White Sox after the Pacific Coast League shut its doors in July of 1918. Hurt by a badly depleted roster due to the drafting of players, and players leaving baseball to work on essential jobs that would make them exempt to the draft for the war, the White Sox needed all the help they could get. Quinn was a welcome addition. Quinn won five games and lost one before the end of the season, and immediately became very much in demand throughout Major League Baseball.[7]

The following winter, the New York Yankees purchased Quinn from Vernon of the Pacific Coast League, which still owned his contract despite his service with Chicago during the 1918 season. Comiskey protested that Quinn belonged to the White Sox, and the case went to Johnson. Johnson, however, awarded Quinn to New York, and Comiskey became irate. Comiskey viewed it as a deliberate stab in the back. Johnson's action effectively ended the close friendship with Comiskey. As the years went by, resentment about the ruling in the Quinn case never ceased for Comiskey. After two decades of a close friendship, as well as both men sharing the same office, Johnson and Comiskey became bitter enemies.[8]

The fourth case occurred on July 13, 1919 in a game between Chicago and Boston. Carl Mays, a submarine-style pitcher for the Red Sox, quit the club during the game. Harry Frazee, the Boston owner, had several offers for Mays while he was away from the team and on July 29 he traded him to the Yankees for $40,000 and two forgotten players (Allen Russell and Bob McGraw). Ban Johnson took no action against Mays when he left Boston, expecting Frazee to either suspend or take disciplinary action against him. When the news of the trade reached Johnson, he nullified it, suspended Mays, and ordered the umpires not to allow the pitcher to play for the Yankees.[9]

The Yankee owners were outraged and they went to court to stop Ban Johnson with an injunction. Ban Johnson stood his ground against the Yankee magnates and the court and attempted to exert his power like a true Czar of Baseball. But several owners sided with the Yankees, and Johnson's grip on power was starting to be wrestled loose from him. Revolution was in the air.

That revolution occurred a few months later when a story broke centering on suspicion that Comiskey's Chicago White Sox had thrown the 1919 World Series. Johnson took some pleasure over his former friend's embarrassment. But when he tried to ride in and save the situation, the owners balked. Ban Johnson had rubbed too many of them the wrong way. The magnates were tired of Johnson's one-sided rulings and influence over the National Commission, along with what some of them saw as abuses of power that undermined the structure of the game.

As a result of Johnson's actions, and to restore integrity and harmony to running major league baseball, baseball's magnates decided to restructure the National Commission by appointing an independent person from outside of baseball to chair the commission. Their choice was a federal district court judge named Kenesaw Mountain Landis. However, Landis didn't just want to sit on a commission. He wanted absolute power to run major league baseball. At a joint meeting without Johnson, held in Chicago on November 12, 1920, Judge Landis was unanimously elected the first commissioner of baseball. Landis had limited baseball experience, but he was every bit as stubborn as Johnson. Of course, Johnson opposed Landis's appointment, as he could see his power over baseball slipping away.

The "imperial years" for Ban Johnson were over; his decline continued as a sad, slow exile into irrelevance. Unfortunately, at the same time, Johnson's health began to decline. As he struggled to carry on as before, he found that his former drive and the strength to persevere had left him. He began to make mistakes and alienate even his most sympathetic supporters.

As for the new commissioner, Landis had established himself as a tough, blunt autocrat. He seemed the sort of person necessary to save baseball from itself. When the 16 club owners tendered him the post of commissioner, they granted Landis's request for absolute power over major league baseball. He never hesitated to use this authority, and clashes with the failing but stubborn Ban Johnson appeared inevitable.

Endnotes

1. Santry, Joe, Thomson, Cindy. Society for American Baseball Research. *Ban Johnson*. http://sabr.org/bioproj/person/dabf79f8. Accessed August 3, 2017.
2. Warburton, Paul. *Signature Seasons: Fifteen Baseball Legends at Their Most Memorable, 1908–1949*. McFarland Publishing Inc, Jefferson, NC. 2010. pp. 68-79.
3. Santry and Thomson, op. cit.
4. Murdock, Eugune C. *The Tragedy of Ban Johnson*. http://library.la84.org/SportsLibrary/JSH/JSH1974/JSH0101/jsh0101c.pdf. Accessed August 3, 2017.
5. ibid.
6. ibid.
7. ibid.
8. ibid.
9. ibid.

This classic shot of Commissioner Kenesaw Mountain Landis has come to symbolize his strength and determination as unilateral leader of major league baseball.

CHAPTER 14

The Making of Kenesaw Mountain Landis

Like his rival Ban Johnson, Kenesaw Mountain Landis had a successful career before he came to major league baseball. Unlike Johnson, Landis was a legal scholar. Landis would bring to baseball a whole different approach to ruling the game than Johnson's. Landis would bring a judicial philosophy to baseball—the same that had been the cornerstone of his decisions as judge. Although no less a dictator than Johnson, Landis brought a sense of evenhanded justice and professionalism that baseball lacked in 1920.

To understand Landis's mode of thinking, and eventually how he came to his decision in the Dutch Leonard Affair, the reader must get a general understanding of Landis's career before baseball, along with the historical time period that contributed to his line of thinking as a judge. There are only a few biographies written about Landis, but an understanding of his thinking and motivations can be gained through an analysis of the decisions he made as a judge. Landis was a complex man, and his opinions showed a range of motivations and beliefs, which when examined closely provide a good roadmap for how he would rule on matters as Commissioner of Baseball.

Kenesaw Mountain Landis was born in Millville, Ohio, the sixth child and fourth son of Abraham Hoch Landis, a physician, and Mary Kumler Landis, on November 20, 1866. The Landis family descended from Swiss Mennonites who had emigrated to Alsace, eastern France, on the west bank of the upper Rhine next to Germany and Switzerland, before coming to the United States. Abraham Landis had been wounded fighting on the Union side at the Battle of Kennesaw Mountain in Georgia. When Landis was born, his parents could not decide on a name for the new baby. Mary

Landis proposed that they call him Kenesaw Mountain. At the time, both spellings of "Kenesaw" were used, but in the course of time, "Kennesaw Mountain" became the accepted spelling of the battle site.[1] In those days, it common to name newborn children after Civil War heroes, or after the war's major battles.

Dr. Abraham Landis worked in Millville as a physician. When Kenesaw was eight, his father moved the family to Delphi, Indiana, and subsequently to Logansport, Indiana, where the doctor purchased and ran several local farms, for his war injury had caused him to scale back his medical practice.

Two of Kenesaw's four brothers, Charles Beary Landis and Frederick Landis, became members of Congress.

As "Kenny," as he was sometimes known, grew, he did an increasing share of the farm work, later stating, "I did my share—and it was a substantial share—in taking care of the 13 acres ... I do not remember that I particularly liked to get up at 3:30 in the morning." Kenesaw began his off-farm career at age ten as a newspaper delivery boy. He left school at 15 after an unsuccessful attempt to master algebra, and from there worked at the local general store. He left that job for a position as errand boy with the *Vandalia Railroad*. Later on, Landis applied for a job as a brakeman, but was dismissed as being too small. He then worked for the *Logansport Journal* and taught himself shorthand reporting, and in 1883 he became an official court reporter for the Cass County Circuit Court. Landis later wrote, "I may not have been much of a judge, nor baseball official, but I do pride myself on having been a real shorthand reporter."[2] He served in that capacity until 1886.

In his spare time, he became a prize-winning bicycle racer and played on and managed a baseball team. Offered a professional contract as a ballplayer, he turned it down, stating that he preferred to play for the love of the game.

Landis spent the next several years getting a law degree and dabbling in politics, while supporting a friend, Charles F. Griffin, in Griffin's effort to become Indiana's Secretary of State, which he did. In March 1893, President Grover Cleveland appointed federal judge Walter Q. Gresham as his Secretary of State, and Gresham hired Landis as his personal secretary. Gresham had a long career as a political appointee in the latter part of the

19th century; though he lost his only two bids for elective office, he served in three Cabinet positions and was twice a dark horse candidate for the Republican presidential nomination.

In Washington, Landis worked hard to protect Gresham's interests in the State Department, making friends with many members of the press. He was less popular among many of the Department's senior career officials, who saw him as brash.

When word leaked concerning President Cleveland's secret Hawaiian policy (When the new Hawaiian government refused to be annexed by the United States, Cleveland sent a new U.S. minister, former Congressman James Henderson Blount, to Hawaii to restore Queen Liliuokalani to the throne. It was an unsuccessful venture), the President was convinced Landis was the source of the information leak and demanded his dismissal. Gresham defended Landis, stating that Cleveland would have to fire both of them, and the President relented, later finding out that he had been mistaken in accusing Landis.[3]

President Cleveland grew to like Landis, and when Gresham died in 1895, he offered Landis the post of United States Ambassador to Venezuela. Landis declined the diplomatic post, preferring to return to Chicago to begin a law practice and to marry Winifred Reed, daughter of the Ottawa, Illinois postmaster. The two married July 25, 1895; they had two children who survived, a boy, Reed, and a girl, Susanne. A third, Winifred, died almost immediately after being born.

Landis built a corporate law practice in Chicago. With the practice doing well, he deeply involved himself in Republican Party politics. He built a close association with his college friend Frank O. Lowden, and served as his campaign manager for governor of Illinois in 1904. Lowden was defeated, but would later serve two terms in the office and be a major contender for the 1920 Republican presidential nomination.

When a seat on the United States District Court for the Northern District of Illinois became vacant in 1905, President Theodore Roosevelt offered it to Lowden, who declined it, but Lowden recommended Landis for the position. Other recommendations from Illinois politicians followed, but Roosevelt took Lowden's advice, and nominated Landis for the seat. According to J.G. Taylor Spink, President Roosevelt wanted "a tough judge and a man sympathetic with his viewpoint in that important court."[4] Lowden and Landis were, like Roosevelt, on the progressive left of the Republican Party. On March 18, 1905, Roosevelt transmitted the nomination to the Senate, which confirmed Landis the same afternoon, without any committee hearing.

The Jurisprudence of Kenesaw Mountain Landis

An analysis of the Landis decisions, both as a judge and as commissioner in baseball, demonstrates that Landis's opinions did not follow a clear-cut pattern, nor were they always consistent with the precedents he had set in the past. While Landis had cracked down on gambling in baseball for his first six years as commissioner, and made it clear doing so was his number one priority, his love for the game and desire for its success made it impossible to predict how he would rule on Cobb and Speaker in the Dutch Leonard Affair.

Kenesaw Mountain Landis's ascension to the bench overlapped with the historical rise of what legal scholars call "the legal realists." As the legal realists gained momentum around the turn of the 20th century, the old ways that judges decided cases, which legal scholars call "legal formalism," was becoming moot. Generally speaking, "legal formalism" is probably what most people think of when they imagine how a judge thinks, which is the idea that all questions of policy have been, and should be, dictated by the legislature alone. Legal formalism, above all, seeks to enforce what the law actually says, rather than what it could or should say. It is a theory that the law is a set of rules and principles independent of other political and social institutions.[5]

In contrast, "legal realism" is the concept that the law is capable of adaptive change according to a pliable body of guidelines, and should be enforced creatively and liberally in order that the law supports good public policy and social interests. Legal realists see the legal world as a means to promote justice and the protection of human rights. Legal realists often believe that judges should develop and update law incrementally, because they, as the closest branch in touch with economic, social, and technological realities, should and can adapt the law accordingly to meet those needs.

They often believe judges should have broad discretion and decide matters on an individual basis, because legislatures are infamous for being slow to move in the direction of change.[6] Landis's opinions as a judge adhered to this standard implicitly; each set of facts, even if nearly the same, warrants a fresh interpretation according to the circumstances.

Tracing its roots back to the writings of Oliver Wendell Holmes, Jr., legal realists gained prominence within the legal world in the 1920s and 1930s.[7] Just as Landis's entrance into the legal profession was affected by the changing nature of legal education, his career as a judge occurred at a time when scholars had begun to critically examine the proper role of judges in the development of the laws, and judges themselves explored new rationales for their own decisions.

In both contexts of law and baseball, Landis's use of the doctrine of legal realism was applied in the following ways: (a) relied on a common set of principles in reaching his decisions; (b) used opinion writing or public pronouncement to rationalize and legitimize results by making them seem inevitable and morally right; and (c) carefully employed the press, guarding some material as private while sharing other information.[8] This methodology both garnered popular support for his judicial acts and allowed the public to see Landis as a leader whose first priority was the integrity of professional baseball.

Landis was a pragmatic judge both on the bench and in baseball. Pragmatism means pursuing practical solutions to problems, even at the expense of intellectual or artistic concerns. Landis often weighed the circumstances surrounding cases he considered against the letter of the law and decided them in a sensible and reasonable manner rather than in some sort of idealistic legal vacuum.

Landis comfortably borrowed from the legal principles and procedures of the federal court when it suited his purposes in governing in the non-legal setting of organized baseball, while ignoring the legal formalism constraints dictated by either the law itself or the presence of higher authority.[9] Landis consistently looked at popular sentiment and opinion when formulating his rulings. He tried to look past the rule of law that acted to constrain his authority. As decision-maker in both the legal and non-legal settings, Landis was not without limitation.

In addition, it is difficult to determine what the proper overlap is of legal rulings into non-legal entities like professional baseball. Power on the bench and the use of legal precedent may or may not be structured to serve that organization's goals. In Landis's case, professional baseball was that organization that enabled him to successfully rule, as Ban Johnson did before him, as a benevolent dictator or "Czar," namely ruling by doctrines to reach an end result by: (1) reliance on contractual relationships; (2) existing quasi-legal structures and processes; and (3) the need for a solution to complex, equal weight on repeat-player games.[10] This laid the foundation for Landis when the reality of various non-legal systems of private ordering suggested that such an extra-legal system is likely to benefit from a dictator.

Landis's employment of the philosophy of legal realism can be seen in his rulings as a judge on the very important railway rate cases and in anti-trust cases involving billionaire John D. Rockefeller's enterprise, Standard Oil.

The Railway Rate Cases

In the early 1900s, the federal government began its efforts to curb some of the economically ruinous practices of corporate trusts and monopolies. An important historical figure in early "trust-busting" was President Theodore Roosevelt, who launched a progressive assault on these trusts from the White House. In 1902, he ordered the Justice Department to bring suit against the Northern Securities Company railroad monopoly under the Sherman Act, during that law's infancy, and supported the creation of the Bureau of Corporations, an investigative arm of the new Department of Commerce and Labor.[11]

The history of the development of the railroad system is littered with corruption. One of the abuses that Congress sought to curtail was the secret dealing and discounting rebates that railway companies would provide to large corporations. The cheaper rates enabled these companies to drive out competitors. While the Interstate Commerce Commission (ICC) was created in 1887, it wasn't until 1903 that Congress passed the Elkins Act, which forbade railroads from receiving rebates. Several years later, the Hepburn Act replaced the Elkins Act, significantly increasing the penalties for illegal rebates.

Many rate cases came before Judge Landis in the district court. In each case, the government was victorious, inevitably from Landis finding a way to punish these corporate heads of business who were doing business in a very shady way. The common theme in the Landis rate decisions was the new legal realism approach that (1) placed the focus on the economics of the underlying arrangement; and (2) accepted progressive notions of equality and uniformity.[12]

The outcome in favor of the ICC was a product of the way Landis felt about the facts in question as informed by the influence of the progressive era at the time. Landis saw it as the greedy car company in cahoots with the even greedier railway company whose tactics must be curbed by the government. In turn, the government must have the authority and ability to prevent the ruinous practices. Landis got to this result by applying a moral purpose to the Congressional regulation—that of uniformity and equality— and through the use of economic analysis. Ever the pragmatist, Landis broke down the transaction to its most basic form to demonstrate the inevitability of his ruling. The methodology sold the result.

United States v. Standard Oil Co. 148 F. at 719 and Standard Oil Co. of Indiana, 155 F. at 305

The Standard Oil railway case was the most high profile of all the cases Landis would preside over during his seventeen years on the federal bench.

Standard Oil was owned by that Gilded Age "Robber Baron" or "Captain of Industry," (depending how one looked at the super-rich at the time) John D. Rockefeller. Standard Oil was the poster child for a monopoly company. Yet Standard Oil had long evaded any penalties for the ruthless methods it used to drive out competition. This included a bevy of practices such as:

(1)   Undercutting the prices of competitors until they either went out of business or sold out to Standard Oil.

(2)   Buying up the components needed to make oil barrels in order to prevent competitors from getting their oil to customers.

(3)   Using its large and growing volume of oil shipments to negotiate an alliance with the railroads that gave it secret rebates and thereby

reduced its effective shipping costs to a level far below the rates charged to its competitors.

(4) Secretly buying up competitors and then having officials from those companies spy on and give advance warning of deals being planned by other competitors.

(5) Secretly buying up or creating new oil-related companies, such as pipeline and engineering firms, that appeared be independent operators but which gave Standard Oil hidden rebates.

(6) Dispatching thugs who used threats and physical violence to break up the operations of competitors who could not otherwise be persuaded.[13]

In 1906, federal prosecutors charged the Standard Oil Company of Indiana with violating the Elkins Act during a period from 1903 through 1905 by paying the Chicago and Alton Railway Company less than its published rates for the transportation of Standard Oil's property. The indictment contained 1,903 counts, each based on the movement of one car of oil.[14]

Standard Oil challenged the indictments on the grounds that the Hepburn Act, which had been enacted in 1906, was the appropriate law to be used in deciding the case. This act contained penalties for parties who offered illegal rebates and superseded the Elkins Act, which made the federal prosecutor's case moot under federal law.

To Landis, Standard Oil's argument was morally incomprehensible. The alleged corruption occurred between 1903 and 1905 when the Elkins Act was the prevailing law, and so Landis believed it was the statue applicable to the case. Landis explained:

> "[I]t is inconceivable that the Congress of the United States, while addressing themselves to the task of drafting a law, the great object of which was to secure to all men fair treatment in respect of the transportation of property on the basis of absolute equality, could possibly have gotten into such a frame of mind that they would divide all prior offenders into two classes, and say that those who had been indicted should be punished, and those who, up to that time, had avoided the

grand jury, should be pardoned. For Congress to do such a thing would be both absurd and unjust."[15]

After knocking down Standard Oil's motion to dismiss the case with the above- mentioned analysis, the jury found the corporation guilty on 1,462 of the 1,903 counts, and Landis ruled on the penalty to be imposed. Turning attention to the matter at hand, Judge Landis laid out the moral obligation that common carriers bear. He noted that the railway company was a "public functionary" that must use the property acquired "for the benefit of the public; not part of the public, but all of the public."[16]

Landis announced his sentence: Standard Oil was fined $29,240,000. This represented the statutory maximum fine ($20,000) multiplied by the number of counts on which the company was found guilty (1,462).[17]

The fine, which was the largest that had ever been issued in the country, created significant debate and controversy. By and large, the press and the public approved of Judge Landis's decision. It is difficult to determine how much of the acceptance was due to Landis's process—combining the moral justification of the law with the economic realities of the Standard Oil's practices—as opposed to the fact that the judgement was consistent with the progressive sentiments as those who applauded him. The rhetoric and content of Landis's opinion did not convince everyone. When he learned of the fine that Landis issued, Rockefeller declared that, "Judge Landis will be dead a long time before this fine is paid."[18]

Rockefeller was correct. Standard Oil appealed Landis's decision, and the Seventh Circuit Court of Appeals reversed the sentence. The court used the opposite judicial philosophy that Landis employed to decide the case. Unlike Landis's use of legal realism, that stretched the law to fit the facts of the Standard Oil case, the appeals court used a formalistic approach (a literal and by-the-books meaning) to define the term "transaction," which undermined the concept of treating each shipment as a separate offense. In the end, the Appeals Court went along with the argument put forward by the attorneys of Standard Oil, who said the Hepburn Act repealed the Elkins act, rendering the argument by federal prosecutors moot.[19] The overturning opinion was penned by Judge Grosscup, a man that Landis thought to be an ally, "but who had established a reputation for not enforcing antitrust laws against the railroad corporations."[20]

Fed. League of Professional Baseball Clubs v. National League of Professional Baseball Clubs, Equity Case No. 373 (U.S.D.C. Chi. 1915).

Even though his decision had been reversed, Judge Landis's ruling earned him a national reputation as a "trust-buster." His philosophy was definitely in line with President Theodore Roosevelt's policy to bust up monopolies and trusts.

When an upstart baseball organization, the Federal League, began losing in court on contractual claims brought by major league baseball teams, it delivered a powerful counter claim: an antitrust suit against the National League.

In a move that could now be considered a strategic legal blunder, the Federal League filed its suit in the Northern District of Illinois, because both the American League and the Federal League were headquartered in Chicago, and secondly, in an effort to forum shop, the league expected to find a sympathetic ear in Judge Kenesaw Mountain Landis.[21] Unfortunately for the Federal League, their assessment of Landis as a "trust buster" proved to be dead wrong.

The Federal League suit forced Landis to weigh his love for baseball with his anti-trust jurisprudence. Organized baseball defended itself on several grounds, including that the labor of baseball players was not interstate commerce, and thus did not fall under the federal antitrust laws.[22] That same argument would prevail many years later in another Federal League case against Major League Baseball, when Justice Oliver Wendell Holmes on the Supreme Court determined that baseball was not interstate commerce.[23]

Though Holmes's ruling was the foundation for the baseball antitrust exemption at the time, it was based on the more restrictive pre-New Deal understanding of Congress's view of commercial powers, which was that baseball did not qualify as commerce under under the Interstate Commerce Clause.

The difference in judicial philosophy between Landis and Holmes was not merely that Landis cared for baseball. The jurisprudence of Landis demonstrates a form of judicial activism that does not exist in the decisions of Oliver Wendell Holmes, Jr. After expanding federal power in the rebate cases, it would have been difficult for Landis to write a federalist opinion declaring baseball off limits from regulation, not because baseball was sacred, but rather because the federal government lacked jurisdictional power over the institution. In addition, Landis struggled to think of baseball as an economic enterprise. The Federal League case created tension between the outcome Landis desired—organized baseball must win—progressive principles of moral justice.[24]

Accordingly, Landis disposed of the case in a manner consistent with his contradictory views of the issue. He left the case on the back burner and intentionally did not rule. He waited with complete and utter silence to see what, if anything, would happen. Ultimately, the parties reached a settlement, sparing Landis the task of matching the principles he normally utilized with a result he could not justify with his prior decisions.

Landis on Gambling

In addition to his judicial philosophy of legal realism, it is also important to analyze Commissioner Landis's views on gambling before the Dutch Leonard Affair. Landis's staunch animosity toward gambling helped provide baseball with the strength it needed to overcome the trauma of the Black Sox scandal. It was a hostility he possessed long before 1919.

In 1909, when Landis had traveled to Milwaukee to address Marquette University law students, he carefully laid out his thoughts on the subject of gambling:

> "I have been going to baseball games for thirty years, I never saw a game or heard of one where somebody did not call the umpire a robber or a thief, and yet no intelligent man doubts the integrity of baseball. . . . It is a great game this baseball—a great game. I have just been thinking about it. It is remarkable for the hold it has on the people, and equally remarkable for its cleanness. You know what happened to horse racing. Gambling killed it. Boxing, wrestling and almost all games of professional sports have unpleasant features connected with

them. It is different with baseball, the managers realize it, and they keep it clean. There is no gambling connected with baseball, and I am glad of it, for it is certainly a wholesome sport. It is a compliment to the nation to love such a clean and thoroughly wholesome sport."[25]

Of course, baseball wasn't all that clean in 1909 when Landis made that speech; however, his view that gambling was a cancer that had to be excised contributed to his tough stance on betting in baseball when he was commissioner. Leo Durocher, player and manager for many years in major league baseball, and notorious gambler (who hung around bookies and organized criminals, including famous actor, George Raft who was connected to the mob) summed it up best about Landis:

"He was an absolute fanatic when it came to gambling... As far as Judge Landis was concerned, it was a gambler who had undoubtedly set Sodom and Gomorrah on the road to ruin."[26]

Landis's own granddaughter, Susanne admitted:

"You know, I don't know if it was because of him or what...but I never even went to a race track until after he died."[27]

His most visible pre-baseball assault on Chicago's gamblers came in 1916 when he had investigated Mont Tennes' bookmaking ring. Tennes was a noted mobster in Chicago.

Landis's war on baseball gambling began as soon as he assumed power as commissioner. In a visit to St. Louis in December of 1920, the judge spoke to reporters about the importance of restoring confidence in baseball:

> "If more stringent laws are needed to prevent gambling in baseball, they can be had through either state or federal statutes. I don't believe there would be any difficulty in having such legislation introduced in Washington for decent people are too fond of the game to pass up an opportunity to do what they can for its good. To help the game we must not only get rid of evil, but every appearance of evil.
>
> I think one highly important matter for baseball men to ponder is the betting which goes on in the stands between friends. For instance, two friends make a bet on the game.

Somebody sees the money pass when the bet is paid. He recalls then that in a certain inning some player made a boner or struck out at a critical time. 'Uh-huh!' says this fan to himself, so it's that way, eh? Then, having in mind what happened at the world's series of 1919, his suspicion grows. To eliminate this sort of thing, and I think it is highly important that it be eliminated, I have great faith in the loyalty of the fan for one thing and such influences as can be devised."[28]

The depth of his hostility was shown in February 1921, when he wrote to a Massachusetts state legislator, Holyoke Representative Hugh J. Lacey. Lacey had introduced a bill mandating a year's prison sentence, a $500 fine, or both, for players who had thrown games. Landis not only supported increasing the penalty to a felony, with penalties of two to five years imprisonment, but making it applicable to betting on games at ballparks, no matter how small the bet. If there was no betting, Landis reasoned, there would be no bribery.[29]

There is no doubt that Landis put the fear of God, and the fear of himself, into the ball players. If the great mass of ball players seemed to be inherently honest, they were more likely to avoid straying from the very fact that they knew that Landis sat in the commissioner's seat and kept them on the path of righteousness. The Black Sox Scandal and the consequences of barring those eight players showed them that.

If the Black Sox Scandal showed the public how harsh penalties could be, the Risberg-Gandil and Cobb-Speaker cases in 1926-1927 had their purposes too. Although six years apart in time, the bridge that linked 1920 and 1926 brought about a general strengthening of the baseball rules. Landis's anti-gambling principles would now be codified in writing.[30]

As a result of these early cases which were heard in Landis's baseball court, he came to hate professional gamblers, or bookmakers, with a determination to stop them that bordered on obsession. Landis summed up his views with this statement:

"Those wormy, crawly creatures [the professional gamblers] once befouled and almost ruined this great game we all love," he said with a depth of feeling. "They thrive and live at race tracks. And I will have no truck with those who consort with them."[31]

Further attempts by Landis to halt the gambling bloodline to baseball occurred in 1923. When the 1923 season began, Landis asked the nation's press to forego printing weekly runs scored totals, as that was a significant component of baseball wagering. He indicated:

"This form of gambling," Landis noted, "by which large sums are taken in by the swindlers, comes from small bettors. You seldom hear of the big man interested in a baseball pool. It is mostly the little fellow. This kind of gambling is most dangerous to baseball and should be eliminated."[32]

When Landis was in Albany, New York, where he traveled to open the Eastern League season alongside Governor Alfred E. Smith, he told the local Elks:

"It's not a gamble, it's a swindle. If the people only knew that less than 30 per cent of the money received is ever paid out from a baseball pool, gambling would soon stop."[33]

Albany was a wide open city and was the center of a huge baseball pool, taking in as much as $50,000 per week. Landis continued with his Elks Club sermon:

"...I suppose that's what some folks think about their chances in a baseball pool. They look easy. But they aren't. The poor sucker hasn't a thing to do with what's happening."[34]

Overall, Landis's dedication to cleansing baseball of gambling issues succeeded during his reign. J. G. Taylor Spink, publisher of the *Sporting News* wrote:

"[Landis] may have been arbitrary, self-willed and even unfair, but he 'called 'em as he saw 'em' and he turned over to his successor and the future a game that was cleansed. And for that, I, as a lifelong lover of baseball, am eternally grateful."[35]

Landis's intolerance of gambling had been already etched in the public's consciousness long before he had to deal with the Dutch Leonard Affair. What people of the time were not sure of was, which Judge Landis would rule in the case of two Baseball Gods, the anti-gambling zealot, or the pragmatist who loved the game?

Endnotes

1. Pietrusza, David. *Judge and Jury: The Life and Times of Judge Kenesaw Mountain Landis*. 2011. Kindle Edition. Locations 301-344.

2. ibid, Location 672.

3. ibid, Location 898.

4. Spink, J. G. Taylor. *Judge Landis and 25 Years of Baseball: The Story of America's First Commissioner of Baseball*. NightHawk Books, Taos, NM. Kindle Edition. Location 298.

5. Schwerd, Fryman & Torrenga, LLP website. *Legal Formalism vs. Legal Realism: the Law and the Human Condition*. http://sftlawyers.com/legal-formalism-vs-legal-realism-the-law-and-the-human-condition/. Accessed April 15, 2019.

6. Sigman, Shayna M. *The Jurisprudence of Judge Kenesaw Mountain Landis*. Marquette Sports Law Review. 15(2);Spring 2005:285.

7. ibid.

8. ibid, p. 280.

9. ibid, p. 279.

10. ibid, p. 280.

11. ibid, p. 289.

12. ibid.

13. LINFO.org. *The Dismantling of Standard Oil Trust*. http://www.linfo.org/standardoil.html. Accessed August 6, 2017.

14. Sigman, op cit., p. 292.

15. Ibid, p. 293.

16. ibid.

17. ibid, pp. 294-295.

18. ibid, p. 295.

19. ibid.

20. ibid.

21. ibid.

22. ibid, p. 295-296.

23. ibid, p. 296.

24. Ibid, p. 297.

25. Pietrusza. op. cit., Locations 7941-7946.

26. Pietrusza, op. cit., Locations 7946-7950.

27. ibid.

28. Pietrusza, op. cit., Locations 7953-7966.

29. Pietrusza. op. cit., Locations 7966-7976.

30. Spink, op. cit., Location 3016.

31. Spink, op. cit., Locations 3016-3021.

32. Pietrusza, op. cit., Location at 8003.

33. Pietrusza, op cit., Locations 8003 to 8011.

34. Richards, Lawrence. The National Pastime Museum website. *Judge Kenesaw Mountain Landis.* a https://www.thenationalpastimemuseum.com/article/judge-kenesaw-mountain-landis. Accessed September 22, 2017.

35. ibid.

CHAPTER 15

The Demise of Ban Johnson and Rise of Kenesaw Landis

Probably the best way to describe Ban Johnson by 1916 was as more of a constitutional monarch than an absolute ruler. His informal title of Czar was becoming less and less apt, and the American League that he created and grown over the years was now a troubled institution.

Ban's own destructive attitude and stubbornness made his fall from baseball's Czar inevitable. His style was to demand absolute subservience. He lacked the ability to compromise, which was so essential to the proper functioning of his title of president. Disagreement over policy matters frequently escalated into personal jealousies, and the string of enemies he built up over the years wanted to see Ban's authority curtailed, as he tried to wield it with reckless disregard for the interests of other owners or players.[1]

There was one National League owner who desperately wanted to see the end of Johnson's reign. He was Pittsburgh Pirates owner, Barney Dreyfuss. Ironically, Dreyfuss was the only National League owner who sympathized with Johnson during the Great Baseball War from 1901 to 1903. But now, Dreyfuss had become disenchanted with the rulings of the National Commission, and since Ban was the dominant figure in the commission, he was the target of Dreyfuss's disdain. After Pittsburgh lost George Sisler to the St. Louis Browns from a decision by the National Commission, Dreyfuss set off on a course to gather support to restructure powers of the league office.

By this time, Ban Johnson was also starting to make huge mistakes. As shown in the Perry case, Johnson backed Connie Mack's decision to go to the court system, which in turn trumped the commission's authority and undermined his status as baseball's most powerful figure. Within a year, dissatisfied American League owners, who at one time accepted all of Johnson's wishes, were now going to court and challenging Johnson.

More disdain for the National Commission and Johnson would come at the Red Sox-Cubs World Series of 1918. By the time of the World Series, the competing Federal League had folded and Major League Baseball had its monopoly again, resulting in lower salaries for the players. The payout from the 1918 Series was cut to the lowest level in World Series history. The players petitioned the National Commission to raise their share. Chairman Garry Hermann told them no changes would be made so late in the process. The players revolted and refused to play Game 5 of the series. When Ban Johnson arrived at Fenway Park to see the game, he was rerouted to the umpires' room where the National Commission, player representatives, and Red Sox manager Ed Barrow were assembled. Two versions on how Ban handled the situation were recorded.

John Heydler told sports writer Fred Lieb that Johnson threw his arm around Harry Hooper, the Boston representative, and appealed to the teams to take the field "for the sake of the public and the wounded soldiers in the stand."[2]

Manager Ed Barrow gave a completely different account. Rather than appealing to the players' better nature, Johnson asserted his authority and commanded the players to return to their clubhouses and start the game at once. Reportedly Johnson said, "With a war going on and fellows fighting in France, what do you think the public will think of you ballplayers striking for more money?"[3]

An hour later, the game commenced. Whether Johnson appealed or demanded did not matter. His behavior at the meeting had left a bad impression on those present. John Heydler, who soon would become President of the National League, later said of the situation:

"I decided after that spectacle in the umpires' room that the old National Commission form of baseball government was outmoded and we needed a strong, one man administrator to run our game."[4]

Eventually, Heydler, as National League President, refused to accept Garry Herrmann as chairman, seeing him as a puppet of Johnson. Inevitably, Heydler did not support Herrmann's re-appointment as Chairman just before the 1919 World Series. Herrmann would eventually resign on January 8, 1920. To make matters worse for the National Commission, no chairman was elected to take his place. In turn, Johnson and Heydler carried on without a third party on the National Commission in 1920. That turned out to be a huge mistake as well, as it made many people skeptical about the validity of the National Commission. If Johnson had learned to accept alternative viewpoints and to compromise when necessary, the National Commission might have continued as baseball's ruling body rather than being replaced by a single commissioner. The National Commission would have needed to be restructured with a different membership and altered channels of power, but Johnson might have remained on the commission with reduced power.

As sportswriter Fried Lieb pointed out, "Barney Dreyfuss had won another important ally in his campaign to dispose of Chairman Garry Hermann."[5] That ally was John Heydler, President of the National League. Dreyfuss's assault on Ban Johnson would have further help from the anti-Johnson faction of the owners in the American League. The Carl Mays incident in 1919 would tear the American League owners apart, which would lead to Ban Johnson's subsequent loss of power and the eventual election of Judge Landis to the baseball Commissionership.

The Carl Mays situation would be the final nail in the coffin for Ban Johnson. Mays, winner of forty-three games in 1917 and 1918 and of two 2-to-1 victories over the Cubs in the 1918 World's Series, had a rocky going in 1919, and at the time of the fateful incident had won only five games while losing eleven. Mays blamed his poor showing on sloppy fielding behind him. There had been errors in the game of July 13, and at the end of an inning Mays said to his manager, Ed Barrow, later the president of the Yankees:

"I'm through with this ball club; I'll never pitch another game for the Red Sox."[6]

Barrow sent another player to the clubhouse to tell Mays to forget the incident and return to the ball game. He found Mays already dressed and about to leave the ball park. Mays took a train for Boston and he responded to appeals by Harry Frazee, president of the Red Sox, and Barrow, to return to his team, by going off on a fishing trip.

In the meantime, the Yankees, as well as all four western American League clubs—Chicago, Cleveland, Detroit, and St. Louis—all sent feelers to Frazee and Barrow on possible deals for Mays.

From the start, Ban Johnson was annoyed that Frazee had not suspended Mays after the latter deserted his club, and communicated with all the club owners clamoring for Mays that there could be no deal involving the pitcher until Carl had returned to the Boston club. In later court testimony, Johnson said that in a conversation in New York, Col. Tillinghast L. Huston, half-owner of the Yankees, had told him the New York club would cease negotiations if the rest of the club owners would do likewise.

Ban believed his wishes in the matter would be respected. Johnson was spending a weekend at the home of J. G. Taylor Spink in the St. Louis suburbs when the bomb fell. As he was having breakfast with Spink and turned to the sports pages, his eyes popped and his hands shook when he read a headline that said: "Carl Mays Traded to New York."

Frazee had swapped the pitcher to the rich owners of the Yankees, Ruppert and Huston, for $40,000 in cash and two other pitchers, Allan Russell and Bob McGraw.[7]

Johnson was furious. "I never saw him more riled," Spink said. It was the most serious threat to Johnson's authority since he expanded the old minor Western League of the nineties into the American League.

Johnson reacted quickly. He suspended Mays indefinitely, notified Presidents Ruppert and Frazee of the New York and Boston clubs to that effect, and issued instructions to his umpires that under no circumstances were they to permit Mays to appear in a game in a New York uniform. In a statement to the press, Johnson said in part:

"Baseball cannot tolerate such a breach of discipline. It was up to the owners of the Boston club to suspend Carl Mays for breaking his contract and when they failed to do so, it is my duty as head of the American League to act. Mays will not play with any club until the suspension is raised. He should have reported to the Boston club before they made any trade or sale."[8]

The Yankees immediately retaliated by getting a temporary injunction restraining Johnson, his umpires and agents, from interfering with the contract between the New York club and Carl W. Mays or with the established schedule between the New York club and the other members of the American League.

The result was a feud that showed a bitterness and intensity rarely seen the world of baseball. After days of wrangling in the courts, a temporary injunction was served on Johnson's umpires before a Yankees-Browns double-header on August 7, and Mays pitched and won the second game for New York, 8 to 2.[9]

As the season wore on, the feud grew in intensity, and the badgering of Johnson continued. On September 5th the New York Supreme Court Justice Robert F. Wagner, who later became Senator from New York, granted the Yankee attorneys a temporary order restraining Johnson from interfering with the Carl Mays case. This injunction, as well as the earlier one, was made permanent by Justice Wagner on October 26, 1919. There would also be an award of damages, as the facts showed that "the New York club had expended $75,000 in money and players in securing the services of Mays."[10]

American League owners were divided over the issue, and sides split into pro-Johnson and anti-Johnson factions. Johnson's supporters were called the "Loyal 5" (St. Louis, Philadelphia, Cleveland, Detroit, and Washington), while the anti-Johnsonites (New York, Boston, and Chicago) were the "Insurrectionists." Though outnumbered 5-3, the Insurrectionists had control of the five-man Board of Directors.[11]

Johnson fought back the best he knew—hard and directly. With eight Yankee victories won by Mays, New York finished third; without those Mays games, Detroit would have had enough wins to secure third place. The Tigers were third in Johnson's book, and as a member of the old three-man National Commission, Johnson had Chairman Herrmann hold back the third-place World Series purse to New York's players.

In turn, the Yankees then filed a $500,000 suit against Johnson and the "Loyal Five" on the grounds that "he [Johnson] conceived the idea of driving the New York club out of baseball and to this end did various acts injurious to the New York club, including the suspension of Mays, making public the plans which the New York club had for a new baseball site, and preventing the acquisition on favorable terms."[12]

As the Mays case festered, the American League grew increasingly tired of Ban Johnson's shenanigans. The Insurrectionists were starting to lean towards the anti-Chairman Herrmann faction in the National League. The threat by the Insurrectionists to defect from the American League to the rival league and form a twelve-club National League was starting to seem more plausible and the pressure to do something about Johnson was becoming too great.

Largely through the intervention of Frank Navin, president of the Tigers and vice president of the American League, the hatchet was temporarily buried in a meeting in Chicago, February 10, 1920, and the solution was almost a complete defeat for Johnson. Mays was reinstated without penalty as

Kenesaw Landis, in 1920, posing with most of the owners of major league teams, shortly after his appointment as commissioner.

a member of the Yankees; New York's third place position was recognized; and third place money was ordered to be paid to Yankees players. And, shattering Johnson's autocratic hold on power, a two-man committee of Jake Ruppert and Clark Griffith was appointed to review all penalties and suspensions in excess of ten days.[13]

Even with Johnson's powers curtailed, Barney Dreyfuss and most of the National League magnates, continued to lobby for a single commissioner, but agreed to go along with the three-man National Commission so long as Ban would play ball with them and help National League President Heydler find that new strong chairman.

On January 15, 1920, a full year before Landis began his reign as commissioner of baseball and eight months before the Black Sox scandal broke, the *Sporting News* ran a picture of Landis, with his characteristic dour expression and battered felt hat on the front page under the heading: "Called Man of the Hour." Underneath the picture was some foreshadowing copy:

> "A big campaign is being waged by admirers of Judge Landis
> to make him chairman of the National Commission. He
> is declared to be just the man to bring peace and order to
> Organized Baseball—a man who will have the respect of the
> magnates, players and public in all leagues. Doubtless he is all
> of that, but in the East there is a strong pull for some 'native
> son'—meaning New Yorker—for the job."[14]

When the Black Sox scandal hit in September of 1920, the whole baseball community was in disarray. Johnson was delighted to see that his arch rival, Charles Comiskey, owner of the Chicago White Sox, was feeling the heat from the scandal. Unfortunately for Johnson, his gloating over Comiskey's woes blinded him temporarily to the big picture. The cataclysmic incident finally pushed league owners over the edge to seek a savior to help save the national past time.

Even before the autumn of 1920, with the Black Sox Scandal dominating the headlines and the fans' consciousness, things were heading in the direction of abandoning the National Commission. There was a great cry for the cleaning up of the game—for its very survival. To many, the game was in need of a savior. Columns were written about it in the nation's press;

the subject was discussed in the halls of Congress, from school platforms, and from the pulpits.[15] From time to time such men as former President Taft, General Pershing, General Leonard Wood, ex-Secretary of the Treasury McAdoo, Senator Hiram Johnson had been suggested as possible chairmanship.

Albert D. Lasker, Chicago advertising executive and a minority stockholder in the Cubs, developed a system of baseball government that became known as the Lasker Plan.[16] On October 2, three days before the start of the 1920 World Series, Lasker submitted his plan to Bill Veeck and Charles Comiskey, presidents of the two Chicago clubs, John Heydler, president of the National League, Barney Dreyfuss, president of the Pirates and pioneer in the campaign for "a change," and John J. McGraw, vice president and manager of the Giants.

Heydler and McGraw were in Chicago as witnesses in the grand jury investigation of the Black Sox. It is worth noting that Lasker did not submit his original plan to Ban Johnson, whose offices were in Chicago.

The Lasker plan, in short, recommended doing away entirely with the old three-man National Commission and substituting for it a three-man board made up of "men of unquestionable reputation and standing in fields other than baseball and in "no way connected with baseball."[17] The names of ex-President Howard Taft, Generals Pershing and Wood, Senator Johnson, former Secretary McAdoo and Judge Landis were mentioned as possibilities. The plan went on to say, "The mere presence of such men on the Board... would assure the public that public interests would first be served, and that therefore, as a natural sequence, all existing evils would disappear."[18]

Lasker proposed that this commission of three would have sole and unreviewable power over players, managers, umpires and club owners, even to the extent of forcing an offending magnate out of baseball. It further would be empowered to establish proper relationship between the major and minor leagues, and would have the sole, unimpeachable right to prescribe the rules of the game and to regulate the conduct of players on the field and in public. It would have provided for the most powerful and absolute tribunal ever thought up to protect and govern a sport in the history of mankind, without the baseball people having the slightest check on the men selected to be the overlords of their sport and business.

The Lasker plan met with immediate favor with the National League, and at a meeting held in Heydler's New York offices shortly after the World Series, the senior league voted unanimously for its adoption and recommended that a joint meeting of the two majors be held in Chicago, October 18, to discuss the new plans and work out the details. However, not surprisingly, Ban Johnson failed to join in the enthusiasm for the Lasker plan.

Johnson, of course, was a proud man, and proud of all he had done for baseball—expanding the Western League of the 1890's into the strong American League, and then ruling over the league for two decades. But Johnson realized the Lasker plan would strip him of much of his authority and would leave him little more than the schedule maker and director of umpires in his own circuit. Few men who have tasted great power willingly stand by idly while they are stripped of it.

Johnson had some arguments on his side. He pointed out what he felt were the weaknesses of the Lasker plan. He believed that no body of civilians, no matter how high-minded, possibly could have a practical, even theoretical, knowledge of the professional game and all of the peculiar conditions that grew up as it evolved into the national sport. He further insisted the time was not ripe, inasmuch as the Chicago grand jury investigating the White Sox scandal had not completed its labor, while the Baltimore Federal League damage suit, which had been appealed, still was pending.

Johnson fought as hard as he could to save something of the old order. However, Frank Navin was in no mood for another war, and persuaded the "Loyal Five" to agree to appoint a new National Commission of non-baseball men. Federal District Court Judge Kenesaw Mountain Landis was appointed as chairman.

Kenesaw Mountain Landis Joins Major League Baseball

Just what did Judge Landis think about all this baseball strife? His name, of course, had been mentioned in connection with the chairmanship of the old National Commission all through 1920, and even before that. While the judge later played a little coy, and seemingly had to be sold on the job, J.G. Taylor Spink thought he was quite receptive—and had appreciated for some time what direction the game was moving in. As early as 1917, before the United States entry into World War I, Landis contemplated resigning from the bench, as he was finding it difficult to live on his $7,500 judge's salary.[19] The financial perks of the new baseball position presented Landis with a great opportunity to serve the game he loved, and also to enjoy more of the good things of life in his later years.

"In view of my 40 years of watching baseball from the bleachers and the grandstand, and my intense love for the sport, I could not say no, if the proposition were made to me."[20]

Two meetings were held in Chicago on November 12th with all of the owners of the National League and the American League present to settle the ongoing baseball feud. It was quickly apparent that four of the Loyal Five to Johnson had no wish for a baseball war and were ready to climb on the Landis bandwagon. The only dissenter was Phil Ball, the rugged ex-Federal Leaguer from St. Louis, but at the later regular meeting, presided over by Bill Veeck of the Cubs, Ball did not prevent Bob Quinn, his vice president and general manager, from making the vote for Landis unanimous. The business of the meeting, which made Landis supreme ruler of baseball, was given out as follows:

"The first order of business at the formal meeting was the election of Judge Landis as the high commissioner of Organized Baseball, the vote upon this being unanimous."[21]

The following resolution then was unanimously adopted:

> "Resolved that the chairman of the Board of Control shall be elected by a majority of the votes of the clubs composing the American and National Leagues...That his successor shall be elected in the same manner and this shall be incorporated in

the new national agreement. It is agreed that upon all questions of an inter-league nature, or in any manner coming up at the joint meeting of the two major leagues that the roll be called, and after voting by clubs of each league, if there be a division, then the American League shall cast one vote and the National League another vote. Should these two votes be at variance, then the Commissioner shall cast the deciding vote and there shall be no appeal therefrom. Further, that the Commissioner shall preside at any and all joint meetings."[22]

It also was decided that the presidents of the two leagues, though not permitted to attend this all-important meeting, should each appoint three men to revise the old National Agreement, or draw up a new one, and to seek the advice and assistance of a similar committee from the minor leagues.

When this business had been finished, a joint committee made up of Ruppert, Comiskey, Veeck, Griffith, Ebbets, Herrmann, Dreyfuss, Mack, Breadon, Dunn and Quinn packed into taxicabs for the Federal Building to wait on Landis.

Later, they were joined by the other club presidents—all but the uncooperative Phil Ball. They first went into the back of the courtroom reserved for spectators, as Landis went on with the hearings in a case. The club owners did considerable buzzing among themselves, and Landis, knowing the purpose of their visit, said: "Will you gentlemen wait for me in my chambers?"[23]

Landis kept them waiting for some time before he adjourned court, and when he came into his chambers, he said almost gruffly: "Gentlemen, what is the purpose of your visit?" Yet it was no secret to him.

Lasker and Col. Ruppert already had met him secretly, sounded him out, and his mood was receptive, provided the call was unanimous. Bill Veeck and Charley Comiskey, the two Chicago club presidents, were spokesmen for the larger delegation. They advised Landis of the action taken by the club owners earlier in the day, and said: "It will make us very happy if you will accept and serve us."[24]

At first Landis refused the offer, saying: "I love my work here as judge, and I am doing important work in the community and the nation."[25]

Someone suggested that perhaps he could take on the chairmanship and still continue his work on the bench. That struck a responsive chord with Landis. Most of the owners felt much of Landis's prestige came from the fact that he was judge of an important Federal Court. The thought was that if he descended from the bench he would be just another "former judge."

After some further conversation, Landis agreed to accept if he was given absolute control over baseball. He further said that inasmuch as he would continue on the bench he would subtract his judge's salary, $7,500, from baseball's $50,000 offer, and take only $42,500 for his baseball job.[26]

Shortly after the club owners had their pictures taken with their new boss. Landis issued a statement to the American public:

> "I have accepted the chairmanship of baseball on the invitation of the 16 major league clubs. At their request and in accordance with my own earnest wishes I am to remain on the bench and continue my work here. The opportunities for real service are limitless. It is a matter to which I have been devoted for nearly 40 years. On the question of policy, all I have to say is this: The only thing in anybody's mind now is to make and keep baseball what the millions of fans throughout the United States want it to be."[27]

Czar Ban Johnson had been overthrown. The new Czar, Kenesaw Mountain Landis, ascended to the throne.

Endnotes

1. Murdock, Eugene C. *Ban Johnson: Czar of Baseball.* (Contributions to the Study of Popular Culture, number 3.) Greenwood Press. p. 159.
2. ibid p. 165.
3. ibid.
4. ibid.
5. ibid at pg. 166.

6. Spink, J. G. Taylor. *Judge Landis and 25 Years of Baseball: The Story of America's First Commissioner of Baseball.* NightHawk Books, Taos, NM. Kindle Edition. Location 806.

7. ibid, Location 815.

8. ibid., Locations 815 to 825

9. ibid., Location 829.

10. *New York Times*, October 26, 1919.

11. Spink, op. cit., Locations at 829-834.

12. ibid., Locations 839-843.

13. ibid., Locations 848-852.

14. ibid., Location 879.

15. ibid., Location 1053.

16. ibid.

17. ibid., Locations 1058-1062.

18. ibid., Location 1062.

19. ibid., Locations 1123-1127.

20. ibid., Location1132.

21. ibid., Locations 1150-1154.

22. ibid., Locations 1154-1159.

23. ibid., Locations 1164-1169.

24. ibid., Locations 1169-1173.

25. ibid., Location 1173.

26. ibid., Locations 1173-1178.

27. ibid.

The media were capable of making light of the battle for baseball supremacy between Johnson and Landis, but to the two combatants, it was no laughing matter.

CHAPTER 16

Johnson's and Landis's Battles, 1920 to 1926

"The hiring of Landis was the thing that turned Johnson into a screaming harridan and had Ban been just a little less arrogant he might have saved himself the crushing burden of dealing with the equally arrogant Landis."
- Bill Klem, Umpire

"That middle name (Mountain) tells you all there is to know about how tough he was and American League President Ban Johnson called Landis 'a wild-eyed nut.'"
– Commissioner Fay Vincent

The New Commissioner Gets Used to the Job

Landis did not start his job as baseball commissioner immediately after accepting the position on November 12, 1920. Before he could, there was the important business of writing a new agreement between the two major leagues, and a new major-minor league agreement. Johnson appointed Herrmann, Dreyfuss, and Ebbets for the National League and Frank Navin, Tom Shibe, and Jim Dunn of the American League to draft the new agreement. It is worth noting that Johnson did not appoint the heads of any of his former three "insurrectionist" clubs.

In the end it, was National League President, John Heydler, who wrote the new agreement. "If I never have done anything else for baseball, I am proud that this was my contribution to the game," said the genial Heydler.[1]

It was Heydler who suggested that the length of the agreement be 25 years. Heydler's penciled notes were put into a more formal format by

George Wharton Pepper, the National League attorney. Heydler designated the new governing body of baseball as the "Superior Tribunal," and wrote into the agreement, "the title of Judge Landis, because of his increased powers, is raised to 'Director-General of Baseball.'" However, when Landis saw the draft of the agreement, he struck out both terms. Of the Director-Generalship title, Landis said, "That sounds too highfalutin." Landis took the more simple title of "Commissioner."[2]

During the course of friendly winter discussions and negotiations, the part of the Lasker plan that provided a commission of three civilians was ignored, and instead the new commissioner was surrounded by an advisory council of the two presidents of the major leagues. That was something of a concession to Johnson, though by nature Landis was not a man to ask for or take advice. He didn't need to. As Landis was in a position to write his own ticket, he did. As a shrewd lawyer and a judge, he knew all the loopholes, and he plugged them to his benefit.

Landis was elected for a term of seven years, and was eligible to succeed himself. His salary was fixed at $50,000 per year, and he was officially named "the first Commissioner." Landis was granted autocratic power over everyone in baseball, from the humblest bat boy to a major league president, the club owners, and both the American and National Leagues. In addition, to avoid the debacle that went on with Ban Johnson and the law suits that tore major league baseball apart, the magnates waived all recourse to the courts of the land no matter what would be the severity of the new commissioner's discipline.

The public was pleased and the nation's press predicted a new and better era for the game. Will Rogers, quaint Oklahoma cowboy-philosopher and American icon, put it this way:

> "Baseball needed a touch of class and distinction. So somebody said: 'Get that old boy who sits behind first base all the time. He's out there every day anyhow.' So they offered him a season's pass and he jumped at it. But don't kid yourself that that old judicial bird isn't going to make those baseball birds walk the chalk-line."[3]

Contrasting the assessment of Landis by Will Rogers, the January 20, 1921 issue of The *Sporting News*, put it this way:

> "Judge Landis in accepting office outlined his plans for the government of the game, dwelling particularly on the big reason for him entering into it, which is to clean out the crookedness and the gambling responsible for it and keep the sport above reproach. The Judge made it plain he would have no mercy on any man in baseball, be he magnate or player, whose conduct was not strictly honest. They must avoid even the appearance of evil or feel the iron hand of his power to throw them out of any part of the game. The Judge will be absolute ruler of the game."[4]

The first big matter confronting the new commissioner was the unfinished business of the Black Sox Scandal. In addition, smaller situations were springing up daily, creating an urgency among the Lasker planners as they tried to introduce Judge Landis into baseball. It took two months from the time Landis accepted the position for the owners to finalize a plan and Landis could finally sign his contract to start the job.

Even before Landis was offered the job, on October 22, 1920, the Chicago grand jury voted its indictments against 13 persons, including the eight accused Black Sox, for throwing the 1919 World Series in conspiracy with gamblers. On October 26, Arnold Rothstein, the New York mobster, thought by many to have been the mastermind behind the "Big Fix," was exonerated by the grand jury. Rothstein's tale in court was that the famous boxer, Abe Attell, and former baseball pitcher, Bill Burns, had approached him with the proposition to finance the White Sox throwing the series, saying it could be done for $100,000. Rothstein testified that he turned it down flat, and was so convinced that a World Series couldn't be fixed that he bet $6,000 on the White Sox.

Joe Gedeon, second baseman of the St. Louis Browns, testified before the grand jury that he had bet $700 on the Reds on the tip of a White Sox player, who said the club wasn't as good as generally supposed, and Gedeon claimed he didn't know the Series was crooked until the third game. Then he admitted he foolishly attended a meeting at the Hotel Sherman in Chicago, instigated by two St. Louis gambler friends, where a further effort was made to raise another $25,000 for the White Sox "throwers."[5]

The story always was that the White Sox culprits were double-crossed and never got anywhere near the money they expected. Gedeon willingly came from Sacramento to Chicago to tell what he knew, but baseball later tossed him out for having guilty knowledge of the nasty business. The jury ended its work on October 29 and made its final report to Chief Justice McDonald on November 6, 1920.

On November 16, four days after Landis unofficially took over as the commissioner of baseball, Maclay Hoyne, the State's attorney, resigned to return to private practice. The general consensus was that Hoyne had been only partially interested in the matter, inasmuch as he permitted one of his assistants, Hartley L. Replogle, to conduct the gambling investigation.

Then, shortly after the shift in the chief prosecutor's office, came the most startling development. It became known that the transcripts in the district attorney's office relating to the gambling cases—including the confessions of Cicotte, Williams and Jackson—had been stolen.

At first a secret was made of the mysterious disappearance of the papers. Ban Johnson seems to have been one of the first who heard of it, and he immediately notified Landis, and the new Commissioner quickly said that if it was found that any of the evidence had been tampered with or was missing, he would insist that federal action be taken against the guilty persons. Landis certainly was sincere in his remarks, but the thieves who stole the papers never were apprehended. Copies of the indictments did get around and reached New York.

About this time, the *Chicago Tribune* wrote to the new District Attorney Crowe as follows:

"The *New York Herald*, through its syndicate, has offered us copies of the grand jury records as they concern the indictments of the crooked ball players in the World's Series of 1919. They offer this to us in eight installments, for the total sum of $25,000. What would happen if we bought the Chicago rights to this material and published it?"[6]

Not so long thereafter, Johnson publicly charged that the papers were stolen and that Arnold Rothstein paid $10,000 for them. The New York gambler issued a wildly-worded denial and said he would sue Johnson for $100,000 libel. "I hope he sues," said Ban. "Then I can get him into court and learn a few things I want to learn."[7]

Rothstein never filed the suit. After District Attorney Crowe couldn't locate the papers, he advised Johnson:

"There is nothing for me to do but dismiss the indictments, inasmuch with the records gone, we have no case against the men. When that is done, it will be necessary to build up an entirely new case against those men."[8]

The Johnson-Landis Skirmishes From 1920 to 1926

If there had been any chance for Landis and Ban Johnson to get along, it blew up in a vitriolic smoke as the Black Sox Scandal was being litigated. Johnson was mortified when Landis was selected during a meeting from which he had been excluded; he saw his crown as Czar of Baseball taken off his head and placed on the white, shaggy-haired dome of the Chicago judge, and he resigned himself to try to play ball with Landis for the sake of baseball and his survival in the game.

Several years later, when the gulf between the two men became unbridgeable, J.G. Taylor Spinks asked Johnson point blank the reason for his continuous feud with the Landis, to which Johnson replied:

"When the Black Sox Scandal broke, the American League voted to prosecute the crooked players...those men had let down the game, and our league, and I wanted them punished to the full extent of the law. Landis had just come into office, and he was given the job. After several months had passed, I asked him what he was doing about the case, and he said, 'Nothing.' I took the case away from him, prosecuted it with the funds of the American League, and never again asked him to help. I decided he didn't want to co-operate, and I never felt the same towards him after that."[9]

Judge Landis, no doubt, had his reasons for not doing anything about the case against the eight players. Like Johnson, he saw the greed and amorality of the guilty players. While the eight players were awaiting trial, the commissioner decided that regardless of the outcome of the court proceedings, the accused octet never again would play in professional baseball. Landis had become the game's court, and did not have to adhere to the actual court itself. He would rule with his unlimited powers on what he felt was needed for baseball and not what a court would lay down as law. Maybe it was his judicial philosophy combined with his love of the game that made Landis feel he could run the game of baseball differently than he would have in a court of law.

Landis also resented any interference from Johnson. If Ban didn't like the judge, the feeling was mutual. And perhaps the judge wanted to show Johnson immediately that he was the new boss of baseball—with no divided authority. Attorney Crowe had pointed out to Johnson that an indictment must be returned within 18 months of the time the crime was committed.

The "crime," the thrown World's Series, had taken place in October, 1919, and the window to indict ended in April, 1921—a matter of a few weeks. It was this disinclination of Landis to act, while the weeks were slipping by, that further irked Johnson.

Johnson got busy, jumped on a train for Texas, induced Bill Burns to come back from Mexico, traveled 10,000 miles, and spent thousands of dollars, much of it his own money, and by March 26, supported by the new District Attorney Robert Crowe and his assistant John Tyrell, he submitted enough evidence to the grand jury to re-indict not only the original thirteen men, but five other gamblers from the midwest.[10]

The eight Black Sox and their gambling associates went on trial in July of 1921 on a charge of criminal conspiracy. Bill Burns, former American League pitcher, was the prosecution's chief witness. He told the sordid story of the fixing to the court. However, failure to bring Abe Attell within Illinois jurisdiction, or to get his sworn statement, weakened the prosecution's case, as did the inability to introduce the stolen signed confessions of the Chicago players.

On August 2, the jury returned a verdict of "not guilty," in so far as criminal conduct on the part of the players and alleged gamblers was concerned. If there was any doubt as to whom the erring players held to be their primary foe, it was revealed in a wild scene in the courtroom after the acquittal.

The players had many friends in court, and some of them treated the acquitted players like returning heroes. There was hand-shaking, back-slapping, and other jubilation. And above the jubilation could be heard the voice of Arnold "Chick" Gandil, the first baseman and generally considered the leader of the Black Sox. "Boys, I want to give you a sailor's farewell," he shouted. "Goodbye, good luck, and to hell with Ban Johnson."[11]

In a statement to the press, Gandil said: "I guess that will learn Ban Johnson that he can't frame an honest bunch of players." A rather disheartening next act to the trial was that after the verdict, the jury and the acquitted players adjourned to an Italian restaurant on Chicago's West Side and made whoopee far into the night. Justice Charles McDonald, who directed the first grand jury investigation, expressed disappointment at the verdict, but felt that it had helped clear the air over baseball and saw a cleansing of the game. Justice McDonald proclaimed:

> "The Grand Jury investigation and prosecution that followed put the fear of God and the law in the hearts of crooked gamblers and shady players and has purged baseball for a generation to come...While the club owners have sustained some monetary loss while the trial was in progress, I believe our national sport would have gone the way of horse racing and boxing due to the same baneful influence had not the strong arm of the law been extended to save it. I am pleased to note that those in control of baseball and club owners interested have decided for all time to keep shady players from the game. I am sure the young men and boys of the country will welcome the purging and will again have confidence in the great American sport."[12]

Unlike Justice McDonald, Commissioner Landis wasn't going to wait around hoping the system had fixed itself. He immediately advised the American League public that no player even remotely connected with the fix would ever play major league baseball again. In essence, with his ruling, he ignored the court's decision completely, and made a statement that Major League Baseball had a new judge, jury and executioner. He issued the following statement:

> "Regardless of the verdict of juries, no player that throws a ball game, no player that entertains proposals or promises to throw a game, no player that sits in a conference with a bunch of crooked players and gamblers where the ways and means of throwing games are discussed, and does not promptly tell his club about it, will ever play professional baseball. Just keep in mind that regardless of the verdict of juries, baseball is entirely competent to protect itself against the crooks both inside and outside the game."[13]

Even if Landis was not as vigilant as Johnson was in prosecuting the Black Sox, he never showed any leniency on the judge's part toward the culprits in the many years that followed. Every now and then moves were movements started up to gain pardons for some of the players. They said Joe Jackson, a poor, illiterate South Carolinian when he first came into baseball, didn't know what he was doing, and had been badly led and advised by more worldly, cunning and avaricious fellow players. But Commissioner Landis was adamant. The biggest case for a pardon was built up for Buck Weaver, and a request for the great infielder's reinstatement was signed by 12,000 Chicagoans. Weaver, who hit .324 in the Series, always claimed that while he was in attendance at the meeting at which it was agreed to throw the series, he had no part of it, took no money, and always played to win. Landis met a committee of the petitioners, and said that Weaver's very presence at the meeting was sufficient to convict him.

After his banishment of the Black Sox Scandal players, Commissioner Landis's power was absolute, even over the game's top players.

With the Black Sox Scandal disposed of by both the court and Landis's ruling, from 1921 to 1924 there was somewhat of a detente between Landis and Johnson. That changed quickly in 1924 with a power struggle that saw Johnson trying to wrestle back some of his power he had lost in 1921.

A tight pennant race, and the mention of a bribe in the National League, ignited a flame again between Landis and Johnson at the close of the 1924 season. The Giants needed two victories to win the National League pennant. On September 27, before a Phillies-Giants game, New York outfielder Jimmy O'Connell approached Phillies' shortstop Heinie Sand and offered him $500 to not bear down during the game. Sand reported the bribe attempt, and the case was before Landis two days later.

At the hearing, O'Connell said he had merely followed the instructions of Giant coach "Cozy" Dolan in approaching Sand. Landis promptly banished both O'Connell and Dolan from organized baseball. Johnson angered Landis by urging that either the World Series be called off entirely or that the second place Brooklyn club be substituted for the Giants as the National League entry. Landis rejected the idea and the series went ahead as planned. So strongly did Johnson feel about the affair, that for the first time in his career in the major leagues he refused to attend the World Series.[14]

The story did not break until Wednesday, October 1, three days before the opening of the World Series. There were rumors in New York that something big was on, but no one knew exactly what. Landis's finding was given out just as he left New York for Washington.

Landis never was much of one to grant interviews, and when he reached Washington he wasn't prepared for his reception by the press. Almost one hundred sports writers, many of them already in Washington for the Series, crowded outside of his door at the Willard, and wouldn't go away until he gave them some kind of an interview. They especially wanted to know whether the thing went deeper, who was behind Dolan, and what further investigations he would undertake. He said his New York finding told the story in full, but that he would reopen the case if additional evidence warranted it.

Coming on the eve of the World Series, the story was a considerable sensation, nearly rivaling the Black Sox Scandal. Ban Johnson and Barney

Dreyfuss, who had fought each other for years over the Garry Herrmann issue, both immediately made statements to the press.

Johnson, again, was peeved that he had been ignored as a member of the Advisory Council, and what made him even more angry was the fact that he knew nothing of the incident until he had read of it in the newspapers. He also had hated John McGraw ever since his disputes with the Giants manager after McGraw jumped leagues during the 1902 season, taking several Orioles players with him.

Ban now offered the suggestion that in view of the attempted bribe, Brooklyn should represent the National League in the World Series instead of the Giants. Johnson was direct to the point: "And if Brooklyn isn't permitted to play, there should be no World Series at all."[15]

Despite the fact that Judge Landis had been given supreme power by the major league club owners on November 12, 1920 to handle all such matters, Johnson called for a federal investigation of the case and announced that he had dispatched the American League attorney to Washington to see what steps could be taken to get such an investigation under way. Naturally, that irritated Landis, and heightened the tension between the two. This time, however, Johnson got some support when Representative Sol Bloom of New York, former chairman of the House's Foreign Affairs Committee, came out with a declaration that baseball should be regulated by federal act. Early in the Senators-Giants Series of 1924, Congressman Bloom made this statement:

> "The nationwide interest in the World Series, now in progress, combined with national chagrin that one of the participating teams is involved in a scandal, convinces me that the time has come when the Federal Government should take a supervisory interest in baseball...Baseball is a matter of inter-state commerce. The two major leagues, and most of the minor leagues, are inter-state affairs. Congress has power to regulate the inter-state operation of railroads and the inter-state movement of foodstuffs, medicines, etc. If Congress can do this, it can regulate inter-state baseball. The sport is a national

pastime and it has taken such a hold on our public that the government should provide some sort of regulation for the good of the sport itself, as well as the protection of the public. Baseball club-owners recognized the demand for some sort of super-regulation when Judge Landis was chosen as Czar, but the game is too big for one man to control. When Congress reconvenes I shall introduce a regulatory bill, and I believe it will be enacted into a law."[16]

This is just what Landis and most of his supporters among the club owners did not want. A federal regulatory board or commission would have taken away much of Landis's great power, just as the judge's elevation to commissioner had reduced Ban Johnson to a mere league president, and a rather feckless one at that. Ban Johnson would have welcomed the law to bring down Landis a few pegs, but it never came to pass, as it got buried in committee with the House of Representatives.

Barney Dreyfuss, the anti-Johnson owner from Pittsburgh, actually joined Johnson in asking that the 1924 World Series be called off, after Landis had paid no attention to Johnson's suggestion to substitute Brooklyn for the Giants. Dreyfuss's club had finished only three games out of the lead, and he said if there were shenanigans in the last fortnight of the race, his club might well have been unfairly deprived of its chance at the pennant.

Following a wire from Dreyfuss urging that he call off the Series, Landis publicly admonished Dreyfuss by telling him "to keep his shirt on." Dreyfuss refused to attend the Series, but while the games were in Washington, he took a train to the capital, not to see any of the games, but to call on Landis. He said he could give the commissioner some additional evidence on the Dolan-O'Connell case. When Dreyfuss called at Landis's hotel, the judge personally sent out word: "The commissioner is not in."

Landis and Dreyfuss later met in the Willard Hotel elevator. Dreyfuss was accompanied by his manager, Bill McKechnie. "When can I talk to you, judge?" asked Dreyfuss. "I came all the way from Pittsburgh to see you." "I will not be in," snapped Landis abruptly.[17]

Landis not only was livid at Ban Johnson for his conduct surrounding the 1924 World's Series, but also for Ban's action in hiring detectives to investigate gambling and alleged approaches made by gamblers to players of the Pacific Coast League.

Johnson learned that a big ring of gamblers, betting thousands of dollars daily, operated out of Los Angeles, and he gave the inference that neither Harry Williams, the new Pacific Coast president, nor Landis, was sufficiently active in seeking to correct the situation. In defense of his conduct, Johnson said:

"I am not so much interested in Coast League gambling in itself, but these gamblers are so strongly entrenched and have so much money, they can reach their slimy fingers right into the American League."[18]

Five years before, two former American League players, Bill Rumler and Harl Maggert, along with Gene Dale, a former Cardinals and Cincinnati pitcher, then with the Salt Lake City club of the Coast League, were all expelled for allegedly conspiring to throw games.

Landis did not deny that there was heavy gambling on the west coast, centering in Los Angeles (which had no horse racing at the time), but Johnson again was infringing on the commissioner's domain. Landis was the game's policeman, and if there was any sleuthing to do in the coast league, he would do it through his own operatives.

William Wrigley, Jr., the chewing gum millionaire, who then was building a new ball park in Los Angeles, took a blast at Johnson. Wrigley, who also owned the Chicago Cubs, always was believed to be the man behind Lasker in the Lasker Plan, and in Lasker's early campaign for Landis as commissioner.

At the annual meeting of the minor leagues at Hartford, Connecticut, on December 22-24, which preceded the major league meetings in Chicago and New York, Coast League President Williams and Bill Lane, owner of the Salt Lake City club, lashed out at Johnson, and an effort was made to put the entire National Association on record in opposition to Johnson.

Landis did not attend the Hartford meeting, owing to the death of a sister-in-law and the fact that Mrs. Landis had to go to the Mayo Clinic for a jaw condition, but he was bristling with anger and ready for a showdown struggle with Johnson when he arrived in New York for the joint major league meetings a week later.

A committee of American Leaguers, headed by the Yankees' Jacob Ruppert, and including Ernest Barnard of Cleveland and Tom Shibe of the Athletics, had been selected by American League club owners at a previous meeting in Chicago to see whether they could patch up the feud between their president and the judge. Ruppert was optimistic enough to give out a statement:

"The quarrel between Judge Landis and Ban Johnson should be patched up. Both are big men and have accomplished much good in baseball. They should work in harmony, instead of pulling in opposite directions, and I feel sure that when spring arrives there will be no further trouble."[19]

Ruppert's statement was well meant but he added fuel to the flames. It insinuated there was a lack of harmony on both sides, and that if Johnson pulled one way, Landis didn't help matters any by throwing his weight in the opposite direction.

The American League's conciliatory committee found an irate, uncompromising Landis when they called on the commissioner at his suite at the Commodore. Privately, Landis confided to friends, "I have tried to get along with that man, but it is just impossible . . . They've got to choose him or me."[20]

Landis implored Colonel Ruppert about the clash:

"Ruppert, you people have got to make up your minds whether you want me or Ban Johnson, I've stood all that I intend to stand. You've promised me repeatedly that you would control Johnson, but this year he has been more impossible than ever."[21]

When Ruppert, Barnard and Shibe reported back to their fellow club owners, the result was a public censure of Johnson which was one of the most humiliating rebukes in the entire history of baseball. Johnson was removed from the game's Advisory Council, and given to understand that he was only being retained on sufferance, and subject to his good behavior.

This action was a unanimous action of the league, except for Phil Ball, who alone declined to sign it. The reason the magnates came down so hard on Johnson is that they thought that baseball might revert to the chaotic conditions of the National Commission. This alone was sufficient to convince the owners that Johnson must be silenced. The magnates thus warned Johnson that his first act of any misconduct would result in his "immediate removal from the office."[22]

The statement, as given to Landis, and released to the press, was as follows:

> "We recognize that conditions have arisen that are gravely harmful to baseball and that must be intolerable to you and that these conditions have been created by the activities of the president of the American League. While you were dealing promptly and efficiently with a most deplorable exception to baseball's honorable record, our president sought to discredit your action and to cast suspicion upon the 1924 World's Series. One year ago you made known to us, in his presence, various of his activities, and that it was our expectation and hope that the unanimous action then taken certainly would operate as a corrective, but in this expectation and hope we have been disappointed. We do not extenuate these things or question their harmful effect on baseball. However, he has been president of our league since its inception and we ask you again to overlook his conduct and accept from us these guarantees:
>
> 1. That his misconduct will cease or his immediate removal from office will follow.
> 2. That legislation will be adopted that will limit his activity to the internal affairs of the American League.
> 3. That any and all measures which you may deem advisable to the above will be adopted.
>
> As expressing our attitude toward your administration of the Commissioner's office, we tender you herewith a copy of the resolution unanimously adopted at its annual meeting in New York, December 10, 1924. (signed):
> THOMAS S. SHIBE, Philadelphia,
> CLARK C GRIFFITH, Washington,

ROBERT QUINN, Boston,
CHARLES A. COMISKEY, Chicago,
E. S. BARNARD, Cleveland
JACOB RUPPERT, New York
FRANK J. NAVIN, Detroit"[23]

It was indeed a cruel ultimatum for Johnson. Landis left the meeting the victor, with banners flying; Johnson was heartsick, disconsolate, and suffering a mental torture. His only statement and public reply to the rebuke was "I am sorry that the American League club owners could not conceive their faithful and exact duty to the public. I have no criticism."[24]

Humiliating as this was for Johnson, it appeared that this might settle the feud between Landis and Johnson. No major or minor clashes occurred for almost two years. The American League owners showed their appreciation by honoring Johnson in December 1925 with a new ten-year contract at $40,000 per year.

Landis, too, would get an extension and a raise the next year. As the fall of 1926 wore on and turned to winter, a lot of politics were playing under the surface, as the major leagues approached their December annual meetings.

At the annual meeting of the American League held in Chicago, on December 14, 1926, a committee consisting of Colonel Jacob Ruppert of the Yankees, Phil Ball of the Browns, and Ernest S. Barnard of the Cleveland Indians was appointed to wait on Landis and ascertain whether the organization could work in greater harmony with him for the general good of baseball. They also were instructed to tell the commissioner, as gently as possible, that the original agreement with him provided that he should have two advisers from the ranks of baseball on the Advisory Council. They felt that the American League was handicapped by not having its league president, Ban Johnson, on the Advisory Council.

Johnson now had been kept off the Advisory Council for two years. The magnates hoped that the improved relations between Landis and Johnson for the last few years would warrant Johnson's return to the Advisory Council. The committee, along with a National League delegation, also queried Landis on his willingness to accept a new term. When the committee reported back to the league, Clark Griffith, who had resumed his early friendly feelings for Johnson, made the motion that Johnson be restored to the Advisory Council, and seven affirmative votes were cast. Only Charles Comiskey of Chicago, Johnson's arch enemy, declined to vote.

This action had an interesting sequel, as Phil Ball, who had fought with Johnson against Landis, and alone among the club presidents refused to sign the original 1921 agreement with the Commissioner, offered the resolution that Kenesaw Mountain Landis be elected to a new seven-year term after his first term ran out on November 12, 1927. Two days later, on December 16, 1926 at the joint meeting of the two major leagues, the same spirit of good will prevailed. Landis not only was given a new seven-year contract, but his salary was boosted from $50,000 to $65,000. And Santa Claus also came to Leslie O'Connor, the Judge's secretary, as his annual stipend was upped from $10,000 to $12,500.

Peace! It was wonderful! The story at the time was that the $10,000 raise given to Johnson a year before was directly responsible for Landis's increase of $15,000. Some of the club owners, especially National Leaguers, felt that when the American League rewarded Johnson with a nice raise, putting him only $10,000 less than what Landis was making, was an indirect slap at the commissioner. They feared an effort was being made to build up Johnson to his former prominence in the game. So they widened the gap between the Judge and Ban to $25,000.

Harmony might have been restored between the leagues, Johnson, and Landis for the time being, but as the fall of 1926 wore on, Ban Johnson's decision and actions over the fates of Ty Cobb and Tris Speaker—made without Landis's knowledge—would spark the final battle between the two titans and bring baseball to its knees with another scandal that became a media sensation.

Endnotes

1. Spink, J. G. Taylor. *Judge Landis and 25 Years of Baseball: The Story of America's First Commissioner of Baseball*. NightHawk Books, Taos, NM. Kindle Edition. Location 806.
2. ibid., Location 1216.
3. ibid., Locations 1216-1220.
4. ibid., Location 1238.

5. ibid., Locations 1243-1247.

6. ibid., Location 1308-1312.

7. ibid., Locations 1321-1326.

8. ibid., Location 1326.

9. ibid., Location 1331.

10. ibid., Locations 1336-1341.

11. ibid., Locations 1350-1355.

12. ibid., Locations 1360-1364.

13. ibid., Locations 1364-1373.

14. ibid., Locations 1373-1377.

15. Murdock, Edward C. *The Tragedy of Ban Johnson.* http://library.la84.org/SportsLibrary/JSH/JSH1974/JSH0101/jsh0101c.pdf. Accessed August 10, 2017.

16. Spink, op. cit., Locations 2173-2183.

17. Spink, ibid., Locations 2197-2022.

18. ibid., Locations 2202-2207.

19. ibid., Locations 2305-2309.

20. ibid., Locations 2322-2326.

21. Murdock, op. cit.

22. ibid., Locations 2322-2326.

23. ibid., Locations 2326-2330.

24. ibid., Locations 2336-2352.

CHAPTER 17

The Battle Over the Cobb-Speaker and Risberg-Gandil Cases

"Speaker and Cobb will never play in the American League, notwithstanding what action Landis may eventually take in this matter."

–Ban Johnson

When the 1926 season ended, as the Dutch Leonard Affair unfolded and Cobb and Speaker resigned from their positions with Detroit and Cleveland, it seemed like the two Gods of Baseball might be leaving the game for good. At the time, of course, few knew that both Cobb and Speaker had been forced to resign by the American League President Ban Johnson.

When Landis released the story to the press after conducting his own investigation, his visit with Leonard, and his hearing with Cobb, Speaker, and Wood, Landis explained that the story took a long time to publish because none of the men involved was involved with major league baseball any more. There was no urgency; Cobb and Speaker had quit the game and resigned the month before, and Smoky Joe Wood had been the coach of the Yale baseball team for the last three years. This, of course, was the smokescreen Landis gave to the public while he conducted his behind-the-scenes political war against Ban Johnson.

When Landis did break the story to the public, Cobb and Speaker were still in Chicago, as it was only the day after they had testified. In addition to the players proclaiming their innocence and anger and embarrassment from by the whole Dutch Leonard Affair, Cobb remarked that he "understood that the American League had paid Dutch Leonard $20,000 for the two letters."

Landis's smokescreen did not assuage the public's curiosity or ire, as the persistent Cobb threw baseball under the bus with his claim of a conspiracy among American League owners over the payment to Leonard for the two letters. The media frenzy intensified. It was bad enough for the fans that two of baseball's biggest stars had suddenly just quit the game, but the charges of a cover-up and payoff made people wonder if there was more to the story still untold.

Furthermore, the very public display of the war of words between Cobb and his former boss, Frank Navin, the month before (when Cobb had resigned), left the impression that even bigger stories would come out later on.

In a scathing opinion written in the *Brooklyn Standard Union* on December 26, 1926, the growing sentiment against Landis's handling of the whole scandal was strongly expressed. To Landis's chagrin, public opinion was going against the commissioner—someone who clearly considered public opinion when in making his decisions, as his legal philosophy dictated. The article said in part:

"The baseball public, sifting the evidence in the baseball scandal case for the greater part of a week, have come to the conclusion that the players involved aren't the only ones who have been shown in an unfavorable light."[1]

Landis's prestige and shiny reputation was unquestionably sustaining a powerful blow. The appearance among fans was that had the newspapers not forced his hand by releasing the information, Landis would have kept it under cover. Of course, this is not true. The press knew nothing of the whole Dutch Leonard Affair, but nevertheless, it was the assumption of some.

The impression was also there that he had not investigated the case as thoroughly as he could have. He made no official statement concerning the $20,000 the American League is said to have paid Dutch Leonard for the letters that involved Cobb, Speaker, and Wood. If the American League had paid Leonard $20,000 for the letters, league officials would then be equally as guilty as players, for that action compounded the crime, not erased it. So if that part of the story were true, why didn't the commissioner—who had all the facts of the case at his disposal since the previous summer—put the owners into public arena the same way had with the players involved?

And finally, as Landis was the public protector and Czar of the game, there was an expectation that he should articulate baseball's official position in the case. Did the powers that be in the game, by forcing the retirement of Cobb and Speaker, judge them to be guilty of the charges?[2]

At this point, in late December of 1926, all Landis had done was to make public the evidence in the case—Leonard's letters and the transcripts of the hearings the judge conducted in Chicago. All of this material was released without any official comment accompanying it.

And there the matter rested, with the public left to decide whether to believe Leonard or Cobb and Speaker, the latter of whom enjoyed impeccable reputations among fans both as ballplayers and as men. But the alleged cover up and Cobb and Speaker's resignations gave credence to Leonard's charges. Yet the judge, in possession of all the facts and supposedly the public protector and guide, refused to aid them in forming an opinion."

Ban Johnson had been mortified that all this information had been made public. He thought that his decision to banish Cobb and Speaker and their resignation would close the matter and baseball could go on untarnished. Even with all Johnson's materials going to Landis, Johnson thought that the evidence he gave to Landis was sufficient to convict Cobb and Speaker and that would be the end of that. Johnson made no formal statement to the press about the affair immediately after Landis released it, but was quoted as saying:

> "I feel deeply sorry for the families of Cobb and Speaker. It is a terrible blow to them. Cobb and Speaker evidently saw the crash coming and stepped out before the scandal became a byword...While it shocked me beyond expression, it simply goes to show that ball players cannot bet on ball games and escape the results that are bound to come. This thing of betting on games was a common condition previous to the 1919 World Series scandal. The type of player who bets has been virtually cleaned out of our league, and every player should know by this time that we will not countenance wagering if we know about it. The club owners are with me on this."[3]

After releasing the documents to the media on December 21, 1926, Landis indicated he would render his decision over the winter. Sources close to Landis said that this was one of the toughest decisions that he had to make as commissioner of baseball. After gathering the evidence and taking the testimony of all the players involved, he understood all the implications. He also knew what a huge blow it would be to baseball if Cobb and Speaker would not be allowed back into baseball like the Black Sox of 1919. Just putting the two in the same categories as those tainted Sox players would not only undo the legacies of Cobb and Speaker, but could permanently damage baseball forever.

With the media circus going mad about the story, and the players hiring high-priced lawyers to defend them, Landis saw the storm that was coming. He also had to factor in the overwhelming support for Cobb and Speaker, by not only the media, but by the public as well. Even Babe Ruth defended his not-always-friendly rival Cobb (most of the unfriendliness it must be admitted came from the surly Cobb). "This is a lot of bull," he snorted from a San Francisco vaudeville stage, "I've never known squarer men than Cobb and Speaker. Cobb doesn't like me and he's as mean as ----. But he's as clean as they come."[4]

Some not only defended Cobb, they attacked Landis for making the matter public. "Judge Landis's act in publishing this story is indefensible and in line with his history of hypocritical sensationalism," charged Detroit Municipal Judge Guy A. Miller.[5]

Another Detroit jurist, E. L. Jeffries concurred, "Landis has fouled his own nest in his desire for sensationalism. He has unnecessarily gone out of his way to destroy two of the greatest idols of the day."[6]

In the Motor City, a petition circulated to censure Landis, who remained publicly unflappable. "Thanks for the information," he responded to reporters' queries on the subject, "Not a word to say about it."[7]

Local jurists, famous comics, evangelists, and the Sultan of Swat himself were the least of Landis's problems if he wished to ban Cobb and Speaker. Landis would have to deal not only with the legacies of Cobb and Speaker in the public eye and in baseball, but would have to face both men head on who had immense power in the game and out of the game. Besides being perhaps the greatest player in major league baseball history, Ty Cobb had also parlayed a brilliant business sense and his connection into a personal fortune. If he was not a millionaire by 1927, he soon would be. Such wealth gave Cobb entrance to circles not normally frequented by mere ballplayers.

One example of Cobb's power beyond baseball is that when the hearings about the Dutch Leonard Affair were over and Landis had rendered his decision, Cobb visited with former Supreme Court Justice Charles Evans Hughes in Washington, D.C. Hughes's advice to Cobb was to sue baseball for "defamation of character." Even though Cobb could not garner the help of Congress and the American Justice Department to get involved in the matter because baseball had been ruled exempt from anti-trust violations, United States Senator Hoke Smith, Democrat of Georgia, stood by Cobb. "Evidently he is in a position to blow the top off a game already riddled with knavery."[8]

As Landis continued to ponder his verdict, in Augusta, Georgia, a massive pro-Cobb, anti-Landis rally held featuring three bands and a roughly-made model Landis, created to be destroyed as an expression of anger over the whole affair.

Tris Speaker also had strong support with the public and the media. The Cleveland press printed ballots asking: "Are Speaker and Cobb innocent? Are they guilty? Should they be reinstated in baseball? Should they be returned to the big leagues? Cleveland fans threw their weight behind their hero, Speaker. The public voted 1,430 to 41 in favor of Speaker's being innocent.[9]

The popularity of the Baseball Gods and the ramifications on the game if they were banished, weighed against Landis's loathing of gambling and the damage it did to institution of baseball, placed tremendous pressure on Landis. And if that pressure was not enough, the possibility of losing the two of baseball's biggest stars to a new upstart, rival baseball league was lurking in the background.

Prominent sportsmen were said to be behind a new circuit, intent on placing franchises in Cleveland, Pittsburgh, Cincinnati, Detroit, Milwaukee, Kansas City, and Minneapolis or Indianapolis. It was rumored that its backers had approached the University of Pittsburgh about renting or even purchasing its new $2 million, seventy-thousand seat stadium. Both Cobb and Speaker were still viable stars, and would certainly shine in any new circuit. Either one was a bigger name than any player who had jumped to the Federal League a decade earlier. And the new circuit was also said to be interested in Rogers Hornsby, who had been part of a messy trade from the Cardinals. This made for a potential firestorm the commissioner most certainly would have rather avoided.

But Landis also knew that if he cleared Cobb and Speaker, he would have to face off with Ban Johnson for a final time. While pondering this monumental matter, threatening to blow his beloved game of baseball to pieces, the Risberg-Gandil controversy arose, suddenly sidetracking Landis away from Cobb and Speaker.

The Risberg-Gandil Case

The Risberg-Gandil matter was a sucker punch that Landis could never have anticipated. Already up to his neck in the highly sensitive and potentially explosive Dutch Leonard Affair, the last thing the commissioner needed was for people or events from The Black Sox scandal to get into the public eye again.

Charles "Swede" Risberg was the shortstop for the 1919 Black Sox, and was expelled from baseball as one of the Chicago Eight for throwing the 1919 World Series. When Risberg got wind of the Cobb-Speaker affair, he decided he could take advantage of the situation by exposing other of baseball's misdeeds. Risberg was living in Minnesota at the time. He contacted the *Chicago Tribune* and gave an interview. The *Tribune* then notified Commissioner Landis of what Risberg insinuated in the interview.

The *Chicago Tribune* reported to Landis that there were brand new allegations against the Detroit Tigers for betting on games. Risberg claimed that in 1917, when Chicago and Boston were battling for the pennant, the Detroit Tigers had "sloughed off" a September series to the White Sox, and were repaid two years later in 1919 after the Chicago club clinched the pennant and Detroit was in a fight for third with the New York Yankees. Risberg also alleged that the 1917 White Sox contributed $45 a man to make up a pot for the Tigers for their play against the Red Sox late in the season.

When an exasperated Commissioner Landis got word of these allegations on December 30, 1926, he exclaimed "Won't these God damn things that happened before I came into baseball ever stop coming up?"[10]

Risberg was not done. In his comments to the press, Risberg was quoted as saying "They pushed Ty Cobb and Tris Speaker out on a piker bet. I think it's only fair that the 'white lilies' get the same treatment."[11] The "white lilies" Risberg was referring to were Eddie Collins, Ray Schalk, and the "clean sox" as they were called, who were believed not to have participated in fixing the 1919 World Series.

Risberg goaded Major League Baseball with the hook and bait, implying even greater scandals remained untold—for the time being. Risberg declared:

> "I can give baseball's bosses information that will implicate twenty big leaguers who never before have been mentioned in connection with crookedness. Landis will never ask me to tell him what I know. The facts are there, but they don't want to know them."[12]

Landis took Risberg's bait and jumped all over his comments. He wanted to know the details, and wanted to know as quickly as possible. He did not even take New Year's Day off. Two days after Risberg's story was printed, he found himself sitting in Landis's Chicago office. The commissioner grilled Risberg for complete information on what he knew about wrongdoings going on in baseball. After his meeting with Risberg, Commissioner Landis summoned Risberg and 35 of the Chicago and Detroit players of 1917 to an open hearing at his office in Chicago before representatives of the press.

The first of these hearings took place on January 5, 1927. Two days later, Chick Gandil, Risberg's partner in crime in throwing the 1919 World Series, came to the Commissioner's office to testify.

It was a feeding frenzy by the press to get a spot in Landis's office to report on the new Risberg allegations. The office was so crowded that a few tables and chairs were wrecked and the carpet was almost ruined.

When the hearings opened on January 5th, Risberg implicated Clarence "Pants" Rowland, who was the manager of the 1917 Chicago White Sox, early in his testimony. Rowland was still in baseball at the time of the hearing, as an American League umpire. Rowland would go on to be the

President of the Pacific Coast League. Rowland was always regarded as a man of high integrity, but Risberg's testimony brought that into question. Risberg claimed that regarding the game on September 2, 1917, Rowland had told him "everything is fixed." "Then we proceeded to win the four games," Risberg added.[13]

In his continuing testimony, Risberg recounted that "about two weeks later, in the Ansonia Hotel in New York, Chick Gandil and I collected $45 apiece from the boys for the Detroit team. Rowland gave us permission to

"Swede" Risberg was only 25 when banished permanently from baseball after the 1920 season, during which he enjoyed the best year of his short career.

go to Philadelphia, and there we gave the money we had collected to Bill James." (James was a pitcher for the Tigers in 1917.)[14]

Risberg also testified that the Detroit pitchers gave up deliveries with nothing on the ball so that the Sox players could hit. Landis asked "Did it look off?" Risberg replied "It seemed they were getting an awful big lead before Oscar Stanage let go of that ball."[15]

Then Risberg referred to the games that the Sox repaid to the Tigers two years later by stating "We paid Detroit back by sloughing off two games to the Tigers. I know I played out of position, and Jackson, Gandil and Felsch also played out of position."[16]

Two days later, when he testified, Chick Gandil backed up Risberg's story. The rest of the 35 men who testified denied Risberg's claim. Some of the greatest baseball men from that time period were interrogated by Commissioner Landis. These included Rowland, Eddie Collins, Ray Schalk, Kid Gleason, Ed Walsh, Harry Heilmann, Donie Bush, and many others.

Landis then questioned ex-White Sox Manager Rowland. "What do you say of Risberg's testimony?" Rowland, who was clearly angry, raised his voice and said in a heated tone, "It's a damn lie. I made no such remark to Risberg as 'It's all fixed.'"[84] Landis reiterated Risberg's accusation and queried Rowland further "Risberg says he and Gandil went to Philadelphia to give this money to Detroit." Rowland's response was "Gandil came to me and asked if he could go to Philadelphia and I said 'All right.' But no one asked me to contribute anything to any pool."[17]

Landis then went straight to the point. "Did you see anything wrong in these Chicago-Detroit games?" Rowland's response was "There was nothing wrong in those games, was no talk about any 'sloughing' of ball games. We were two games ahead before that series, with twenty games to go, and that is considered safe. If I said anything at all to Risberg, it was 'get in there and win this ballgame.'"[18]

When Rowland finished his testimony, Landis turned to Risberg and asked him "Do you want to ask Rowland any questions?" Risberg replied "No sir." Ray Schalk, who succeeded Eddie Collins as the Sox manager, said "What Risberg said, I don't believe." Landis then turned his attention to Eddie Collins and said "Risberg says those four Detroit-Chicago games were 'sloughed' to the [White] Sox. Is that true?" Collins replied "I don't

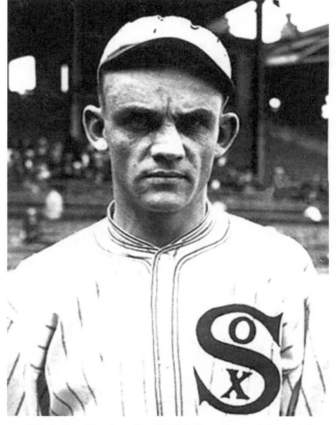

Chick Gandil, who reportedly reaped great financial benefit from the fixed 1919 World Series, retired after the 1919 season after a salary dispute with owner Charles Comiskey, rendering his banishment from baseball by Landis in 1920 moot.

believe it. I played in those games and saw nothing wrong with them." However, Collins did admit that he contributed $45 to the Gandil fund to reward Detroit players, but not until the White Sox-Giants World Series took place in October of 1917, and after Eddie had been assured such a fund had been raised. The practice of rewarding opponents was common during the Deadball Era. It was not unusual for a contending team would reward another for playing harder against a pennant rival in late season games.[19]

Regardless of the outcome of the Risberg-Gandil hearings, it further cast baseball in a negative light, which was the last thing the institution needed as it grappled with the Dutch Leonard Affair. Ty Cobb certainly did not appreciate being asked to testify in a case brought by two of baseball's worst scoundrels right on the heels of his testimony in his own defense. Merely being brought up in the same breath as Risberg and Gandil must have sent shivers up Cobb's spine. When he did testify at the Risberg hearings, Cobb's anger showed in his sarcasm in his responses to Landis, and played up to the media sitting in Landis's office who were covering the hearings. When he declared sarcastically to Landis "You gonna swear me in?"[20] Cobb added fuel to the fire against Landis. Cobb's hostility toward Landis should have come as no surprise to the commissioner, but even if the media reporters laughed at Cobb's comment, Landis didn't.

Landis's ruling on the Risberg-Gandil hearings completely absolved the players on Detroit and Chicago in 1917 of any wrongdoing, In his written decision Landis said:

> "To some it may seem inexplicable that Risberg and Gandil should implicate themselves in these alleged corrupt practices... Obviously the implication may have been conceived upon the theory that they have been incriminated themselves, so it must be true. However, being already on the ineligible list, it would not affect them, and it might blacken the white lily whites. It is the finding of the Commissioner that the fund raised by the Chicago players about September 28, 1917, was not collected or paid to the Detroit Tigers for 'sloughing' the Chicago games of September 2 and 3, 1917, but was paid because of Detroit's beating Boston; and there was no 'sloughing' of the September 2 and 3, 1917 games, nor of the September 26, 27, 28, 1919 games, except possibly by Risberg and Gandil."[21]

Landis also commented on the conversation they said they had with Pants Rowland, Eddie Collins and others regarding the alleged fixed games and the pool, and the commissioner decided that those men were telling the truth and not Risberg and Gandil. In the end, Landis resorted to legalese summarize the whole ordeal: "If the Risberg-Gandil version be correct, it was an act of criminality. If the other version be true, it was an act of impropriety, reprehensible and censurable, but not corrupt."[22]

In the constant battle to win media attention against Landis, Ban Johnson gave a statement to the press regarding his opinion of the whole Risberg-Gandil judgment:

> "It is the same case tried by the commissioner six years ago... The same players appeared before the commissioner when he first was inducted into office and all were exonerated. This is just a retrial on those same charges. At that time, Eddie Collins, Faber, Schalk and the rest of them were absolved from all wrongdoing. With the same evidence submitted there could not have been any other finding."[23]

With the whole Risberg-Gandil hearings properly disposed of, Landis considered the issue of teams being given incentives to try harder against pennant rivals, and pots of money (such as collected by Risberg and Gandil which amounted to $1,100) being used as rewards. He didn't like it. Landis called on baseball to banish the practice and implemented penalties on those who broke this law.

Out of the hearings came four written suggestions by Landis to be made part of baseball's moral code. The four suggestions were[24]:

1. A statute of limitations with respect to alleged baseball offenses, as in our state and national statutes with regards to criminal offenses.
2. Ineligibility for one year for offering or giving any gift or reward by the players or management of one ball club to the players or management of another ball club for services rendered or supposed to be, or have been rendered, in defeating a competing club.
3. Ineligibility for one for betting any sum whatsoever upon any ball game in connection with which the better had no duty to perform.
4. Permanently ineligibility for betting any sum whatsoever upon any ball game in connection with which the better has any duty to perform.

The statute of limitations clause reflected Landis's utter distaste for in dealing with the Risberg-Gandil case and Dutch Leonard Affair. If the limitation had been in place before both affairs were sent to Landis's office, they would not have been taken up by the commissioner. The statute of limitations was set at five years after an incident occurred.

The second clause was put in to stamp out the old custom of one team rewarding another for playing harder against a division rival.

The third and fourth clauses are similar in structure but differ in punishment. Clause 3 makes it clear that betting on a game a player was not involved in would result in a year banishment from baseball, The fourth clause cemented the harshest penalty for those who bet on games they were involved in, that is, a lifetime ban. The message was, a player betting on a game his team team is involved in is nothing short of a criminal act.

Endnotes

1. *Brooklyn Standard Union*, December 26, 1926.
2. ibid.
3. Spink, J. G. Taylor. *Judge Landis and 25 Years of Baseball: The Story of America's First Commissioner of Baseball*. NightHawk Books, Taos, NM. Kindle Edition. Locations 2652-2657.
4. Pietrusza, David. *Judge and Jury: The Life and Times of Judge Kenesaw Mountain Landis*. 2011. Kindle Edition. Location 7479.
5. ibid.
6. ibid.
7. ibid., Locations 7479-7486.
8. ibid., Location 7486-7493.
9. ibid., Location 7493-7502.
10. Spink, op. cit., Location at 2668.
11. Gay, Timothy, *Tris Speaker: The Rough and Tumble Life of a Baseball Legend*. Guilford, Connecticut, The Lyons Press, 2006. p. 236.
12. Spink, op. cit., Location 2680.
13. Spink, ibid., Locations 2694-2699.
14. Spink, ibid., Location at 2699.
15. Spink, ibid., Locations 2699-2704.
16. Spink, ibid., Location at 2704.
17. Spink, ibid., Location 2713.
18. Spink, ibid., Locations 2713-2718.
19. Spink, ibid., Locations 2718-2733.

20. Spink, ibid., Location 2730.

21. Spink, ibid., Locations 2783-2793.

22. Spink, ibid., Locations 2793-2798.

23. *Chicago Daily Tribune*, January 13, 1927.

24. Spink, op. cit., Locations 2803-2808.

CHAPTER 18

The Judge Rules, Johnson Gets Knocked Out, and Major League Baseball Is Changed Forever

After Landis cleared the Risberg-Gandil matter off his desk, he turned his attention to Cobb-Speaker and Ban Johnson. If what the public saw in the handshake between Landis and Johnson (when Johnson was put back on the Advisory Council after two years) a month before at baseball's winter meeting as a sign of enduring peace, they were greatly mistaken.

Despite the temporary cooperation among baseball's powers that be, the whole Cobb-Speaker affair clouded the winter meetings. The fact that Johnson withheld information from Landis for over four months, only handing over the documents over to him after the urging of the American League owners, did not sit well with Landis. He stewed over it, but was not vindictive against Johnson in any way. To some degree he trusted the American League magnates, and they had him convinced that Johnson must return to the Advisory Council. Shockingly, Landis obliged.

One would think Johnson would be grateful that Landis let him come back to the Advisory Council, but he wasn't. Even with his return, Johnson broke this temporary peace by mouthing off again against Landis. This time, however, the commissioner was not going to cut him any slack or give him any sympathy. Johnson was playing Russian Roulette, but had spun the chamber one time too many.

All of Johnson's current public ranting after Landis released the story to the press stemmed from his belief that a strong case was made against Cobb and Speaker in the Dutch Leonard letters. Johnson seemed to believe that he, and he alone, had the power to toss Cobb and Speaker out of baseball. Even though Johnson was aghast that he had been forced to turn the evidence over to Landis by the American League magnates, Johnson blindly believed that the commissioner would side with him and declare the players ineligible.

If there were ever a moment when silence would be golden, this was it. But silence was never an option for Johnson, who ignored common sense and a sense of self-preservation and lashed out against Landis to the press. The only precaution Johnson took was to ask the press to publish his remarks anonymously. Johnson referred to himself to the press as "a leader in organized baseball" and stated:

"Landis had made a mess of the Cobb-Speaker case...Speaker and Cobb never again will play in the American League, notwithstanding what action Landis may eventually take in this matter."[1]

To throw fuel onto the fire, the unsigned letter suggested that Landis was weighing a decision without all the evidence presented, which introduced a sense of doubt to the public about the validity of the investigation and implied that Landis was an inept investigator. It was an explosive accusation to make against the commissioner who had by now held the job for six years and was very highly respected.

The public's imagination was sparked by Johnson's anonymous remarks, and new rumors began to circulate about the affair. One example of the frenzy came on January 15, 1927, in an article by Bert Walker, the sports editor of the *Detroit Times*. In the article, Walker declared that the resignations of Cobb and Speaker were not due to the investigation of the whole scandal, but for being accused of negotiating with a third baseball league that was preparing to rival the American and National Leagues. The article downplayed the whole Dutch Leonard inquiry and the hearings over the two letters that Leonard produced. Walker emphasized that the alleged bet and thrown game occurred before Landis took office in 1920, and that more than six years had passed without anything about it surfacing. This smelled funny to him. Walker believed that Cobb and Speaker were actually being punished for disloyalty to major league baseball.

The article went on to say: "Ty Cobb himself seems to verify the suspicion, for he told the writer that he knew he was slated to leave baseball more than a year ago, and that only the testimonial banquet given to him in Detroit, when he was highly praised, saved him for the time being. Thus, he managed and played in the 1926 season."[2]

Walker insinuated that this new information would explain why both Landis and Johnson had been so secretive regarding the status of Cobb and Speaker. Walker accused both Landis and Johnson of not talking about the Cobb and Speaker situation for so long due to financial reasons, fearing that it might lead encouragement to prospective rivals of the major leagues.

Articles like these popped up all over the newspapers across the United States, as speculation ran rampant after Johnson's anonymous interview to the press. One thing was true, there really was talk of a third league. What was not true was that the resignations stemmed from the accusations of Cobb and Speaker from this planned formation of a third league.

When Landis got word of this anonymous "leader's" statements accusing the commissioner of handling the Cobb-Speaker case in a negligent manner, he didn't have to think twice who the "anonymous leader" was. He knew right away it was Ban Johnson, even if he couldn't prove it.

Landis blew a gasket. Of all the years of wrangling with Johnson, he exercised patience and sympathy towards the old Czar. This horrendous display by Johnson was more than Landis could swallow, however. He immediately called for a special meeting in Chicago on January 24, 1927, for the purposes of ascertaining what basis, if any, there was for the story to have been printed. J.O. Murfin, Cobb's attorney and W.H. Boyd, Speaker's counsel, were both invited to attend this special meeting.

When Landis told the press that he was calling this meeting, he lashed out against Johnson for having himself be quoted anonymously. This only spurred Johnson on more. In his next message to the press, which was not anonymous, Johnson said:

> "The American League is a business...When our directors
> found two employees who they didn't think were serving them
> right, they had to let him go. Now isn't that enough? As long as

I am President of the American League, neither one of them will manage or play on our teams."

Then Johnson took the liberty with the press to tell his side of the story of what happened. Well, at least half of the story:

"I called a meeting of the directors of my league...We met September 9th in a prominent Chicago club and we met secretly. We wanted secrecy, not because it meant anything to us, but because we felt we should protect Cobb and Speaker as much as we could."

Johnson went on further saying:

"They had done a lot for baseball. We had to let them out, but we saw no reason for bringing embarrassment upon their families. We wanted to be decent about it... The Directors voted to turn the results of the Leonard investigation over to Landis. We did that in compliment to him, not to pass the buck. We acted, but we thought [Landis] should know about it...When Landis released that testimony and those letters, I was amazed. I couldn't fathom his motive. The only thing I could see behind that move was a desire for personal publicity...The American League is a business. It is a semi-public business to be sure, and we try to keep faith with our public. Certainly we had the right to let two employees go if we felt they had violated a trust. But Landis had no right to release Leonard's charges...

He had taken no part in the ousting of the two men. It was merely a league, not an inter-league matter, and there was nothing to be gained by telling the world that we felt Cobb and Speaker had made mistakes which made them unwelcome employees...

When I take the stand Monday [at Landis's specially called meeting] I may tell the whole story of my relationship with the judge. If he wants to know when I lost faith with him, I'll tell him this 'When the Black Sox scandal broke, the American League voted to prosecute the crooked players. Landis was given the job. After several months passed, I asked him what he was doing and he said 'nothing'...

I took the case away from him, prosecuted it with the funds of the American League, and never asked him for help. I decided he didn't want to cooperate. My second break with Landis came over a financial matter. I do not care to discuss it now, but I will tell about it Monday if he wants me to."[3]

It was an epic breakdown—and Ban Johnson didn't stop there. He continued to rant and rave even though he had made a mockery of himself with the anonymous statements he made to the press. And it was all untrue. Johnson had no more information. He never did release anything from his so-called detectives. With Johnson slated to appear before Landis, the press hyped it like a heavyweight fight. But even Johnson had to admit he had been bluffing. He saw the writing on the wall.

Johnson never made it to Landis's office at the January 24th meeting. The American League club owners met the night before in order to rein him in. It was more or less a repeat of the punishment they handed to Johnson two years earlier in the Dolan-O'Connell business, but this time it was a real showdown. Johnson had misbehaved, thereby violating the agreement from 1925 that dictated he would be punished severely if he acted out. Landis again made an ultimatum to the American League magnates by stating "You've got to take Ban Johnson or me." This time, the American League owners eliminated Johnson.

As a result of Landis's ultimatum to get rid of Johnson, the American League club owners gathered at the Blackstone Hotel in Chicago on January 23rd, a day before the Judge Landis's meeting. The owners weighed the facts very carefully, as well as taking into consideration the stressful events that were plaguing baseball at the time. The Risberg decision was still lingering, and the entire nation awaited Landis's decision on Cobb and Speaker.

Two meetings were held during that day at the Blackstone Hotel. Interestingly, Charles Comiskey, who was the most staunch hater of Ban Johnson, was excluded from the first meeting. It was no surprise that Johnson also was not invited, though he submitted a written statement.

It was probably agreed upon by the owners that Comiskey would be so prejudicial in his judgment over presiding Johnson's fate that it would be in everyone's best interest to exclude him to attempt to make the discussion about Johnson as impartial and emotion-free as possible.

The outcome of the meeting was that Johnson should continue as president of the league in name only, and keep his salary under his contract he signed the year before, but that he would have no further part in shaping the policy of the league, and that his voice would be silenced.

Frank J. Navin would serve as acting American League president. The club owners then called Comiskey into their second meeting, in order to make the league's decisions unanimous.

The committee then asked Landis if he would join the meeting. Landis came in and Navin read him the resolution that the club owners adopted. Landis took in the words that Navin read and when he was done, the commissioner asked the owners in a stiff manner: "This time do you gentlemen really mean this?..I believe I recall hearing such language before." "Ban will give you no further trouble, Judge," said Yankees owner, Jacob Ruppert, which was echoed by Navin, Shibe, Barnard and others.[4]

Landis then agreed to postpone indefinitely the meeting called for the following day. The league then gave out a formal statement of its new policy to the press:

> "A meeting of the eight club owners of the American League was held Sunday (January 23) at the Blackstone Hotel, Chicago.
>
> The members of the league unanimously repudiated any and all criticism appearing in the public press as emanating from Mr. Johnson, reflecting in any way upon Judge Landis or his handling of his several investigations concerning the integrity of ball players in the American League, and commended Judge Landis for his efforts in clearing baseball of any insinuation of dishonesty...
>
> Mr. Johnson submitted to the meeting a formal written statement in which he announced that all evidence involved in the matter of Cobb and Speaker investigations had been

submitted to the Commissioner and had been by him published...

Dr. Robert B. Drury, Mr. Johnson's personal attending physician, certified to the meeting that Mr. Johnson's health was such that he should immediately take a much-needed rest...

Thereupon the duties of the president were entrusted for the time being to Mr. Frank J. Navin of Detroit, vice president of the league....

At our request, Judge Landis indefinitely postponed the meeting of the American League called for tomorrow (Monday)."[5]

With the press release showing that the AL owners were united with Landis against Johnson, Ban knew he was sunk. His league sided with Landis and made him look foolish. The expectation from the meeting and press release was that after a reasonable amount of time, Ban Johnson would tender his resignation, saying his health would not permit his return to the game.

J.G. Taylor Spink certainly felt that way, and in the February 3, 1927 issue of The *Sporting News*, the magazine published nearly a page of observations from the nation's top sports writers on the passing of baseball's former strong man, under a heading: "Comment from the Nation's Press on 'Retirement' of Ban Johnson." The *Sporting News*' New York correspondent, Joe Vila, seemed to think the jig was up. He quoted Frank Farrell, the first owner of the New York American League club, as saying:

"I fear Ban is losing his grip. The American League men are not standing by him as they used to. His heart will be broken and he can't stand that thing very long. I wish I was in there to fight for him."[6]

Johnson had miraculously survived the rifts between him and Landis for the last seven years. Why would this be different? He always came back like a cat with nine lives. Johnson must have felt that there was still hope for a return to the league with his powers intact when the ill feelings blew over. Johnson went down to Excelsior Springs, Missouri, for the remainder of the winter, and seemed to thrive under the treatments. His health improved steadily and he gained energy and hope that he could get back into baseball again.

The Sunday meeting at the Blackstone, in which Johnson was relieved of his baseball duties, preceded Landis's verdict on the Cobb-Speaker case by four days. After the American League passed its resolution, repudiating Johnson and extolling Landis and his conduct of the investigation, there was a general belief in newspaper circles that Cobb and Speaker would be acquitted. That surmise proved correct, as Landis's decision gave the nation his answer on the Cobb Speaker affair which had become a national issue, on the subsequent Thursday, January 27th.

When Judge Landis cleared Cobb and Speaker, he summed it up in his last two paragraphs of his decision:

> "This is the Cobb-Speaker case. These players have not been, nor are they now, found guilty of fixing a ball game. By no decent system of justice could such finding be made.
>
> Therefore, they were not placed on the ineligible list. As they desire to rescind their withdrawal from baseball, the releases which the Detroit and Cleveland clubs granted at their requests, in the circumstances detailed above, are canceled and the players' names are restored to the reserve lists of those clubs."[7]

At the very start of his finding, Landis explained that he had acted on the case not because Johnson or the American League had turned its evidence over to him, but because the accused players had requested that he define their baseball status.

He also took occasion to explain why he had not acted before, saying:

> "Tyrus R. Cobb and Tris Speaker have asked that their baseball status be defined. This request is in contemplation of possible future service and is in accordance with the Commissioner's statement of December 21, 1926, as follows: 'These men being out of baseball, no decision will be made unless changed conditions in the future require it.' Preceding that announcement, both players had been released, that action

following a resolution of September 9, 1926, by the American League's Board of Directors."[8]

Landis then permitted it to be known that it was with his knowledge and acquiescence that Cobb and Speaker first expressed their desire to retire from the game in the fall of 1926, rather than to permit their illustrious names to be dragged into a scandal. Landis also revealed that he had gone into the case long before his hearing with Cobb and Speaker, back on December 20th.

Through his entire report on the case, Landis showed his displeasure and resentment with Dutch Leonard for failing to come East and face the men he accused. As a result, Landis paid little attention to the Leonard letters, which Ban Johnson had considered so important when he placed them before his league's board of directors.

Landis continued in his finding that:

> "Cobb, Speaker and Wood were available, but Leonard, a retired player, residing in California, declined to attend a hearing. Therefore, his statement was taken in California and in substance was that this game (September 25, 1919) had been fixed.
>
> Cobb, Speaker and Wood branded this charge as false. A wager had been made, but they vigorously denied that the game had been fixed and they insisted upon an opportunity to face their accuser. Leonard, however, persisted in his refusal to come, and despite the fact that his attendance could not be forced, the hearing was finally set for November 29, and all parties, including Leonard and the American League president and directors, duly notified. Leonard replied that he would not be present.
>
> Cobb and Speaker appeared on November 27 and were informed of Leonard's attitude, whereupon they canvassed the whole situation with the Commissioner and reached the conclusion that they would rather quit baseball than have a hearing with their accuser absent. Their reason was: The mere announcement of charges of this character, whatever

the personality or motives of the accuser, or the scarcity or even absence of evidence supporting the charges, would be harmful to the accused persons, experience having shown that a vindication by baseball authority, based upon a manifest insufficiency or even a total failure of supporting proof, has been labeled a 'whitewash.'

While they insisted they had no doubt of their ability to answer the charges, they were concerned about the possible effect upon themselves and others in whom they were deeply interested. They appeared to be particularly disturbed respecting the situation of Joe Wood.

These considerations, as Cobb and Speaker represented the matter to me, brought about their desire to quit baseball, despite their appreciation of the fact that such action might be misconstrued.

Inasmuch, therefore, as Leonard's attendance could neither be induced nor enforced, the Commissioner consented that the hearing be put over indefinitely, and it was understood that would be the end of the matter, unless conditions thereafter should so change as to require a different course. It was pointed out at the time that a number of people knew or had heard of the Leonard charges and of the Cobb and Wood letters and the likelihood of suspicion and rumor resulting from a retirement in these circumstances of two players of such prominence was discussed. And it was definitely understood that the interests of all concerned might thereafter require a public statement setting forth the charges and answers.

The American League directors were informed of the status of affairs and that Cobb and Speaker desired to leave baseball for the reasons stated. Accordingly, the Detroit and Cleveland clubs granted releases and the American League directors rescinded their resolution calling for a hearing, with the same understanding that this ended the matter unless subsequent developments should necessitate a hearing and publication.

Shortly thereafter, the gossip and rumor mills got busy. As usually transpires when these two sympathetic agencies are at work, they leave in their wake a variety of progeny infinitely more harmful to the individuals concerned than the truth could possibly be. Many press associations and scores of newspapers were persistently demanding the facts. Therefore, Cobb, Speaker and Wood were called to Chicago and the situation laid before them. They all realized that untrue, distorted, and garbled accounts were being advanced and agreed that a hearing had become desirable, even with Leonard persisting in staying away.

Accordingly, a final effort was made to induce Leonard to attend, but again he refused. The hearing was held, and the Commissioner at once issued the record for publication, in accordance with his definite understanding with Cobb, Speaker and Wood."[9]

Addressing the media attention and public discontent with the whole ordeal, Landis said in the finding, "Players of such prominence as Cobb and Speaker don't just drop out of baseball without the nation's fans and the country's sports writers demanding to know the reason."[10] Landis's long experience with the press, gained in Washington, his years on the Federal bench, and in his job as Commissioner, taught him that a story of such great magnitude could not just go away without a substantive explanation.

While the Black Sox ruling forced Landis to declare independence from the American judicial system, the Cobb-Speaker affair and its surrounding events reaffirmed Landis's commitment to the general principles of due process.

Conversely, Landis's judicial philosophy of legal realism was employed in the Cobb-Speaker case, but the opposite way. With Cobb and Speaker, he used his judicial philosophy to find a way not to convict the Baseball Gods, but rather to exonerate them. Seven years had gone by and baseball recognized Landis as the ultimate authority of the national pastime. The questionable evidence that Ban Johnson relied on to discipline Cobb and Speaker was insufficient in Landis's eyes. Dutch Leonard's refusal to face his accusers cast further doubt on the accusations.

Landis relied heavily on his philosophy of legal realism by considering the social and political aspects of the whole Dutch Leonard Affair. Landis did not "find" law in the affair itself. There were no written rules that prevented such an incident from happening. And through his decision, Landis created what would become the law. After the dust from the affair had settled later in 1927, Landis and the Steering Committee established rules to address such situations. The Dutch Leonard Affair served as the starting point for these new baseball laws, and as a reminder to guard against the use of hunches or innuendo rather than the underlying truths.

In fact, both Cobb and Speaker owed a debt of gratitude to the writers of 1926 and 1927, who refused to permit the matter to be hushed up. The judge, in his finding, admitted he was willing to take this way out. Landis spoke scornfully and with his well-known irony of those "two kindly sympathetic agencies, gossip and rumor." Without them there would have been no final decisions, no vindication, and fans and writers always would have known only that the careers of Cobb and Speaker ended abruptly with the 1926 season under suspicious circumstances.

Modern historians have advanced a number of theories to explain Landis's verdict. Fred Lieb agreed with Landis "That to expel these superstars...on less than conclusive evidence might have given professional baseball a blow from which it could not recover."[11]

Some contend the entire case was a mere pretext to humiliate Ban Johnson. David Quintin Voigt in his *American Baseball: From the Commissioners to Continental Expansion*, makes the point that whereas in the early years of his tenure Landis had to expel players in virtual wholesale fashion to restore public confidence in the game, by 1927, the Black Sox Scandal was receding somewhat into history. The fans no longer feared crookedness in the game. "Sensing this," noted Voigt, "Landis pragmatically abandoned his punitive role and became the efficient priest. As priest-judge, he evolved [a more flexible] operational code that spelled out his notion of 'conduct detrimental to baseball.'"[12]

Although the media and the public were happy that Cobb and Speaker were reinstated, the judgement was still viewed with some cynicism.

Cobb and Speaker both played two more years in the American League, despite Johnson having insisted that such a thing would not happen. While the players, on Landis's order, were returned to their former clubs, Detroit and Cleveland gave the men permission to entertain offers for their services from other American League teams.

Landis had passed the word around that he didn't want either Baseball God to play in the National League, though John McGraw had been one of the first to express a wish to have Cobb on his team. But Landis did not want it to look as though Johnson had scored even a partial victory, that these stars had been drummed out of the American League. However, the hint was unnecessary, as many of the six other American League clubs promptly put in bids for the two stars.

Cobb eventually went to the Athletics and Clark Griffith landed Speaker for Washington. In 1928, Speaker joined Cobb on the Athletics. Cobb made $70,000 from the Athletics in 1927 in salary, bonus for signing, and another bonus on the size of the Athletics' gate. Though Cobb was 42 in December, 1928, he could have continued playing, but Connie Mack no longer wished to pay Cobb his big salary. That Cobb and Speaker were far from being washed up as players when they "resigned" at the end of the 1926 season is apparent from their batting averages in 1927 and 1928. Cobb, a .300 hitter to the end, hit .357 and .323 and Speaker closed his career with .327 and .267, though it should be remembered that those seasons were in the heart of an era of domination by the offense and inflated batting numbers. After giving his decision on Cobb and Speaker, Landis said wearily, "That cleans up the cases in my docket."[13]

Other significant cases reached Landis's desk over the next 17 years, but there were no others in which a player, either in the majors or minors, was charged with throwing, or attempting to throw, a game. Most of the cases in which Landis figured so prominently were inherited from an earlier era in baseball, especially during the late rule of the old National Commission, with 1919 being an especially unhappy season in that respect. There is no doubt that Landis put the fear of God, and the fear of Commissioner Landis, into the ball players. The great majority of players always have been inherently honest, but if there were any inclined or tempted to stray, the very fact that they knew the white-haired Landis sat in the commissioner's seat kept them on the path of righteousness.

So in the end, the Cobb-Speaker and Risberg-Gandil cases served the purpose of a general strengthening of baseball's rules of conduct, with the additional edict of making it an offense to reward one club for beating a contender's rival.

Meanwhile, Ban Johnson officially tendered his resignation on July 8th, due to take effect at the end of the 1927 season. As Johnson had an ironclad contract, running to 1935 at $40,000 per year, he could have collected a good part of $320,000 even after the league requested his resignation, but he notified his owners he wanted no compensation after the 1927 season was over.

As Ban Johnson faded into obscurity, on November 2, Ernest Barnard, former Cleveland Indians' president, was elected president of the American League. Landis had a cordial relationship with Barnard and looked forward to working with him on the Advisory Council. It must have been a relief for Landis to see Johnson go.

In a gesture of courtesy, American League owners sent Johnson a telegram thanking him for his years of faithful service and praising him as a gallant, constructive figure in American baseball. Vengeful and holding his hate to the end, Johnson's former crony Charles Comiskey alone refused to sign it.

Baseball Laws Change

With a friendly, cooperative American Leaguer on the Advisory Council, Landis concentrated his energies on having the four suggestions he made at the time of the Risberg finding incorporated in baseball's fundamental law. As time went on and he turned the Risberg-Gandil and Cobb-Speaker cases over and over in his mind, the need for even stronger anti-gambling legislation became an absolute must on his calendar. Before the major league meetings in New York in December, 1927, the two presidents appointed what was termed the game's "Steering Committee" to work with Landis in eradicating abuses and throwing new safeguards around the game. The National League representatives were made up of league chief Heydler, and club presidents Bill Veeck of the Cubs, Barney Dreyfuss of the Pirates and William Baker of the Phillies. On the American League side was the new executive, Barnard, Frank Navin, the league's vice president and Tiger owner, Col. Ruppert of the Yankees and fiery Phil Ball of the Browns.

The *Sporting News* ran a picture of the Steering Committee at the time. Landis and Dreyfuss alone were seated at a table; the others stood up around them.

"Gentlemen, you know what I was up against last winter," Landis told the other members of the committee. "I feel some of these players got into these difficulties because there were no specific rules covering such conduct.

But, we learn as we go on, and from now on there can be no more 'gifts' in baseball, or bonuses for 'bearing down' or 'making it easy for us.' That's got to stop, and stop now."[14]

The Commissioner didn't need to sell the Steering Committee on his program. Landis's original suggestion of making a player ineligible for a year "for offering or accepting any present or reward" was increased to three years. It covered players, league and club officials, and now appears under Rule 21 of the Major League Rules, under the heading: "Conduct Detrimental to Baseball." Any person seeking to influence an umpire's decision with a reward or gift also was to be permanently barred from baseball, as was an umpire accepting or soliciting such a gift. But, the judge always had a wholesome respect for the "men in blue." "What a grand bunch of fellows they have been, and what a record for honesty and integrity they have made through the years!" he used to say with admiration. No major league umpire ever had been involved in any scandal in which he was accused of trying to influence a game with his decisions. Not only players, but all officials of a club, were to be barred for life if they were caught making a bet on a game in which they had a duty to perform.[15]

This rule caught up with William D. Cox, President of the Philadelphia Phillies, 16 years later. When Landis heard about Cox gambling on his own team, he immediately launched an investigation. Initially, Cox denied any wrongdoing, claiming the wagering had been done by associates. As the investigation went on, Cox admitted making some "sentimental" bets on his team and claimed he didn't know it was against the rules. Landis was unmoved, and he suspended Cox indefinitely on November 23, 1943. The commissioner thought the rule should be even more stringent, and once thought of asking that the rule give him power to toss anyone out for making any bet on a baseball game, but this was never done.

At the subsequent joint meeting of December 15, 1927, all of Landis's and the Steering Committee's suggestions were passed, while still more legislation was adopted. Players and managers were now prohibited from owning stock in any club other than the one in which they were engaged, while another amendment provided that "no employee, umpire, president, treasurer, secretary or other official of a major league shall, directly or indirectly, have any interest in a club."[16] It prevented an old custom of having umpires scout players, especially those they might see while umpiring in college games. At this point, Landis and his committed had established as many rules and safeguards as he and the legalistic minds of baseball could think of.

The Risberg-Gandil hearings and especially the Dutch Leonard Affair had laid the groundwork for such rules.

Endnotes

1. Spink, J. G. Taylor. *Judge Landis and 25 Years of Baseball: The Story of America's First Commissioner of Baseball.* NightHawk Books, Taos, NM. Kindle Edition. Location 2823.
2. *The Detroit Times*, January 15, 1927.
3. Spink, op. cit., Location at 2833-2851.
4. ibid., Location 2870.
5. ibid., Locations 2880-2885.
6. ibid., Location 2890.
7. ibid., Locations 2940-2944.
8. ibid., Locations 2944-2949.
9. ibid., Locations 2953-2985.
10. ibid., Locations 2985-2990.
11. ibid., Locations 2990-2995.
12. David Pietrusza, *Judge and Jury: The Life and Times of Judge Kenesaw Mountain Landis.* Kindle edition. Locations 7904-7910.
13. Spink, op. cit., Location 3005.
14. ibid., Locations 3089-3093.
15. ibid., Locations 3098-3103.
16. ibid., Locations 3108-3112.

Joe Wood's good friend Tris Speaker helped Wood (pictured above) land a
job at Yale in 1923 as baseball coach, where he remained until 1942.

CHAPTER 19

Smoky Joe Wood—On and Off the Record

What follows is the interview between Smoky Joe Wood and Lawrence Ritter that appeared in *The Glory of Their Times*, published in 1966. This interview was taken on October 1, 1965.

Ritter: The other book I read was a biography by, uh, Ty Cobb, and at the end of the book, he has a whole section, and it was all news to me, on some mess-up, with him, you, and Tris Speaker and Dutch Leonard. Would you tell me what that was all about?

Wood: I will. I'm not going to tell you details, because I wouldn't tell you too much about this thing because it stinks. When Dutch Leonard got through in Detroit, Cobb was manager. And for that reason he had a gripe against Cobb, and then he wanted Speaker to take him on over in Cleveland, and Spoke wouldn't take him on. For that reason he got sore at both of them. Well, in '20, there was a dispute over some betting, and in order to get even, Leonard claimed this and that, and so on, and, there was a bet placed on the ballgame, but it wasn't against our club, it was on our club. I was the guy who bet the . . . I had charge of the money. Well, I handled this through a gate tender, in Detroit, who contacted the bookies, and the money was bet, the money was collected, and this little son-of-a-gun come down, I know him very well, this gate tender, and brought this money down to the train as we were leaving Detroit, and I gave him, after keeping equal splits, for 3 fellas, I gave him, the extra money, which amounted to about $30 or $40 bucks, for placing the bet. This was just the same as betting on a prize fight or anything else. We bet on ourselves. There was nothing crooked about it on our part.

Ritter: How often did teams bet on themselves?

Wood: Never! Never, that's the only bet I ever made in my life. And just because someone else wanted to bet on it and I handled the money. But this thing in '20 [post-Black Sox scandal], it wasn't exactly on the up and up, I have to admit that. Because I knew from what Cicotte had told me in Cleveland that the White Sox didn't dare win. But I didn't know through a couple of other fellas on the Detroit ball club that they weren't going to play their heads off trying to beat us. I'm not saying that they were going to lay down and give us the game (garbled). Well anyhow, I knew that the White Sox didn't dare win that year. And this got back to Landis, and he had a letter that I had written, and, uh, Landis called me over to New York says, 'You write that letter,' I said I sure did, there was my name on it, and Leonard had blackmailed Navin in Detroit for so much for that letter, and he still kept copies of it, and then he went ahead and tried to blackmail, I don't know how the hell he, small amount of money somebody out there, by going after Cobb and spilling this whole story. Which was true. I was at a World Series, with Landis down in New York and he says, I know Landis very well, Judge says, 'We gonna have any trouble over this thing, Joe?' I said 'I don't think so.' 'You let me know and if ya do, I'll come make a trip up to New Haven.'

Ritter: What was the letter you wrote?

Wood: Leonard. Here he kept this letter that I had written him, after I got home here one winter, I wrote him, out in Fresno, a letter, same as I write to my brother, I trusted him, I wrote him this letter, he kept it and cashed in on it. I understand he got $12-15,000, the first from Navin in Detroit, then they closed it for awhile and came out with it again. And he kept the letter through all of that.

Ritter: The letter had that much dynamite in it?

Wood: Yeah. The letter quoted me the amount of money was bet, his share was enclosed in the letter. I loaned that son-of-a-bitch $200 to buy his first motorcycle in Boston when he first joined us. And he made the crack that he didn't mind what he was doing to Cobb and Speaker but he hated to hurt Woodie. But nevertheless he did it. That dirty little son-of-a- bitch of a Leonard. He died a millionaire, but he died young [60]. A great little pitcher too. But he was a first class . . . crook.

Ritter: How did Speaker and Cobb get involved on it?

Wood: Cobb and Speaker put up some of this money to make the bet. And Leonard broadcast this thing, because Cobb let him go, and Speaker wouldn't take him on.

Ritter: Is it for this reason that both Cobb and Speaker left their jobs at Cleveland and Detroit?

Wood: Yeah, yeah. But they didn't get out of baseball. They went to the Athletics. I'd like to see what Cobb had to say about it, because (garbled). They got together with an attorney in Detroit, my greatest friend, Spoke and Cobb, and they got a bunch of stuff written up, type-written and deposited in a vault in a bank in Cleveland, and if they'd a chased Cobb and Speaker outta baseball this would'a all come out.

Ritter: Cobb has a whole chapter on it. He doesn't hide it at all.

Wood: Well, he didn't hide some of it. But he doesn't tell it as it was, I'll bet you a million dollars. I don't think Cobb could afford that to tell the story. Cause I know the story. I never told that to a soul in my life. I haven't even told it to my . . . brother. Well I didn't tell you anything that wasn't straight and on the level, I'll tell you that. That's one reason why this thing did really hurt me. It's the first and only accusation in my life that I ever had against me, that I know of."[1]

Smoky Joe Wood's Unpublished Transcript

Here, published for the first time, is Smoky Joe Wood's previously hidden conversation that sheds new light on the Dutch Leonard Affair, on the reputations of Baseball Gods Ty Cobb and Tris Speaker, and on the state of baseball in the 1910's and 1920's.

Wood: Now this ain't for publication, hear! Our last series with the White Sox in 1919, we saw they weren't out to win. Now, that was the greatest aggregations of great ballplayers that was ever together. I know enough about that to know that they didn't dare win in '20. I think they could have beaten us.

Now I wouldn't want to say this for publication for anything in the world!

I don't believe we ever could have won in '20 if that thing did not happen to the White Sox. Cause they had one of the finest ball clubs, my God, that was ever put together! They knew. In fact Cicotte, who used to be in Boston when I was there, told me in the hotel, we don't dare win. Before the season '20.

They didn't need money! It was Chick Gandil. He instigated it all. Cicotte was on the same order. Only not so openly. Cicotte was a fixer you know. Not only in that, but his pitching too. He was the one that parafinned the ball, you know. They used to call him knuckles. Threw a fingernail ball. Then threw the shiner and was practically invincible. You can't hit that sailer ball. That's the only thing that made Cicotte a great pitcher.

Now, Jackson, to me, was a pitiful case. He couldn't read nor write, you know. They used to tell me in the dining room, he'd listen to his roommate to order a meal and then he'd say bring me the same...couldn't even read the menu! That was a sad case for me.

Happy Felsch was that type of fellow too. But not Eddie Cicotte, not Risberg, not Buck Weaver, not McMullin. When you think about it, I can't understand how Weaver could have been connected to that thing. The only way I figured was the time he did not report it.

There was only two fellows that were really morons on that club, and they were Happy Felsch and Joe Jackson. Gandil never had a friend in baseball. He was a terrible crook.

Yessire, Joe Jackson was one of the very best that lived. He'd stand up there and swing from his tail and practically throw himself down. If you had two strikes on him, he'd choke up a little on his bat!

Now I've said alot here I wouldn't want to see written up anywhere!

Well, in 1911, on that All-Star club, Hal Chase was on that club. We got down to Baltimore and he was begging me to get Walter Johnson in a crap game and I wouldn't do it. But I saw him get into this crap game.

Well, we finished our series with the Athletics, and I think we were going down to Richmond or something. Well, we started playing poker, pretty fair game, about a one dollar limit I think. Anyhow, I was a $40 or $50 loser and Hal was a good friend of mine. Well, he says to me, don't cut my cards this time I deal. So, well, I didn't cut the cards by Christ, and he dealt me a set of fours! So I says to myself, well, may be coincidence, maybe, maybe not.

Well, so I played the cards and the next deal, I did not cut his cards and he dealt me another set of fours. After that, I cut them. So, you see, I knew he can handle those cards.

He used to hang around in New York when he was with the Highlanders. Jack Doyle and all of them. Well, Hal Chase took me up to that billiard room, and Jack Doyle was the fellow that set the odds on horse races and World Series and all that. Now, I knew Jack like that. I knew he was kind of rowdy too and the fellows who worked for him too. Well, Jack was one of the biggest bettors in New York. He'd have men going to all the race tracks and keep in touch with him by telephone. He'd tell them what to bet here, and what to bet there, you know. Well, Chase took me up there, Well, I knew Jack Doyle, but I never pulled one of those deals with him. Visited Jack Doyle's place for years and years after that, but Jack never approached me! Jack never did anything that I can say wasn't on the up and up, but, a ballplayer shouldn't even think about those placed.

Now Chase and Harry Lloyd. Oh they pulled some. But, see, Harry Lloyd, he was up with me at Boston and he never pulled anything like that up there. But, Hal Chase and him got mixed up with some of them on the White Sox club, well they chased them out. Oh, he was a wonderful fielder. He was strictly an individual player. He could be playing first base and he'd go over and field a ball on his right, and he'd go and throw that ball to the base, and whether there was someone on that base or not...Now that's what I mean individual...he shouldn't throw that ball till he can see who he'd throw to, but he'd throw that ball right over the bag, someone to catch it or not. I've seen him do this many times.

Now I'll tell you about that thing with Cobb, Speaker, Dutch Leonard and myself. When Dutch Leonard got through in Detroit, Cobb was manager. This is Dutch Leonard, the left-handed pitcher, with me up in Boston. Married the toe dancer in vaudeville. Well, for that reason, cause he was through when Cobb was managing, he had a gripe against Cobb. And then he wanted Spoke to take him on over at Cleveland but Spoke wouldn't take him on. Well, then he got sore at Spoke.

In the 1920 World Series, there was a dispute over some betting on the game and Leonard claimed this and that and so on, not important and it stinks. In order to get even with Cobb and Speaker, even though it involved me, he made the crack he was only sorry about this because it implicated Woody and he didn't want to do that. Well, there was nothing wrong about it or anything, as far as our side was concerned, but was only a case of sour grapes cause Cobb let him go and Speaker would not take him on.

This got back to Landis and he had a letter that I had written to him and Landis sent his man, President of the Pacific Coast League for years, sent him to New York to read the letter and ask me about it. Well, he says, did you write that letter? I sure did, I says, there's my name right there, isn't it? Well, Leonard had blackmailed Navin in Detroit for so much for that letter, and he kept a copy of it. Don't know how the hell he tried to blackmail, I guess by telling Cobb that he'd spill the whole story or something.

Well, I was at the World Series with Landis in New York. He says, Joe, are we going to have any trouble over this whole thing? And I says, I don't think so. He says, well let me know if you do. Well, I says, I'll let you know, but of course I knew that I was in the clear.

But there was alot of it that didn't jibe as far as I was concerned. The judge was for me and as I say, there was nothing crooked in it on our parts.

There was a bet on a ballgame, but it was not against our club, it was on our club, see. And for it, it would have absolved all of us, see. I don't think the letter was ever made public.

See, Spoke and Cobb were supposed to have put up some of this money to make the bet. Leonard broadcast this thing cause he was sore, cause of what I told you. And for that reason both Cobb and Speaker left their jobs in Detroit and Cleveland. But, they didn't get out of baseball. They went to the Athletics. Then that dirty little sonofabitch, that Leonard that did that thing, he died a millionaire. Had a huge fruit ranch. Used to ship out these prize dried fruits to friends. But he died young. I don't know if the good lord had something to do with it or not, but he died young and a millionaire.

Well, he dropped it after he got all of it out that he could. There he kept this letter that I written him, one winter. Same as I wrote to my brother, I wrote to him. I like people, I like to think I can trust them, you know. Well, I wrote that I had accepted the cash and quoted the amount of his share and everyone else's share. See, I kept charge of the money. About $12,000 involved you know.

Now what are you going to do with all this? Can't be printed, you know! Don't want to bring this all out. Shouldn't have said anything at all!

See, this money that was to go up on this certain game, same as betting on a prize fighter or anything else. We'd bet on ourselves! Well, I handled this through a gate tender in Detroit, who contacted the bookies. The money was bet. The money was split. This son of gun, this gate keeper in Detroit, he come out very well. Well, he brought this money down to the train as we were leaving Detroit and, after keeping equal splits, the three of us, I gave him all this extra money, which amounted to $40 for picking the bet. And when Landis called Cobb and Speaker, and myself in Chicago to talk about it and question us, this sonofabitch denied knowing anything about the money, and denied getting anything.

Now, that's the only bet I ever made on myself in my life, Never did it before or after. Never! I had a friend was in amateur ball for years and years, and he used to bet on himself all the time. But that's a different thing. But this thing is just a little more complicated than what you would think. I got to admit that it wasn't exactly on the up and up. I got to admit that. I knew, from Cicotte told me in Cleveland that the White Sox didn't dare win, see. Well, a few of the fellows from the Detroit club let it be known that they were not going to beat their heads off to beat us, see. If everything was on the up and up they'd rather see us win, anyway, put it like that.

See they got together with an attorney in Detroit, my friend Spoke and they got a bunch of stuff together and typewritten and deposited it in a bank vault in Cleveland, and if they would have chased Cobb and Speaker out of baseball, it would have all come out.

Now, I've never told that to a soul in my life, not even my brother. So for Christ sake don't ever mention that. Don't even say anything about it at all.[2]

Endnotes

1. Burgess III, Bill. The Baseball Guru website. *Leonard, Cobb, Speaker Affair.* http://baseballguru.com/bburgess/analysisbburgess05.html. Accessed April 16, 2019.

2. Hesburgh Libraries - Department of Special Collections, at Notre Dame University. Notre Dame University, South Bend, IN.

Detroit Tigers vs. Cleveland Indians
September 25, 1919

Detroit Tigers 9, Cleveland Indians 5

Game Played on Thursday, September 25, 1919 (D) at Navin Field

```
CLE A    0  0  2    0  1  1    1  0  0   -   5 13  3
DET A    2  2  0    0  2  1    0  2  x   -   9 18  0
```

BATTING

Cleveland Indians	AB	R	H	RBI		BB	SO		PO	A
Graney lf	5	1	3	1		0	0		1	1
Lunte ss	4	1	1	0		0	0		2	5
Speaker cf	5	2	3	1		0	0		6	0
Harris 1b	5	0	1	2		0	0		11	1
Gardner 3b	3	0	0	1		0	0		0	3
Wambsganss 2b	3	0	1	0		1	0		2	4
Smith rf	4	0	1	0		0	0		0	0
O'Neill c	3	1	2	0		1	0		2	4
Myers p	4	0	1	0		0	0		0	3
Totals	36	5	13	5		2	0		24	21

FIELDING - E: Lunte 2 (6), Harris (6).
BATTING - 2B: Graney (22); Harris (14). **3B:** Speaker 2 (11). **SH:** Lunte (4); Gardner (30). **Team LOB:** 8.

Detroit Tigers	AB	R	H	RBI		BB	SO		PO	A
Bush ss	5	2	3	2		0	0		2	1
Young 2b	4	0	2	1		0	0		4	6
Cobb cf	5	2	1	1		0	0		1	1
Veach lf	4	1	3	1		0	0		4	0
Heilmann 1b	4	0	1	0		0	0		9	2
Shorten rf	4	1	3	1		0	0		3	0
Jones 3b	4	0	1	0		0	0		1	2
Ainsmith c	3	2	3	0		0	0		1	1
Boland p	2	1	1	2		0	1		2	2
Totals	35	9	18	8		0	1		27	15

FIELDING - DP: 1. Bush-Young-Heilmann.
BATTING - 2B: Heilmann (31). **3B:** Boland (1). **SH:** Young (45); Ainsmith (11); Boland 2 (4). **Team LOB:** 6.
BASERUNNING - SB: Cobb 2 (27).

PITCHING

Cleveland Indians	IP	H	R	ER	BB	SO	HR	BFP
Myers L(8-7)	8	18	9	6	0	1	0	39

Detroit Tigers	IP	H	R	ER	BB	SO	HR	BFP
Boland W(14-16)	9	13	5	5	2	0	0	40

WP: Boland (4)

Umpires: HP - Dick Nallin, 1B - Brick Owens

Box score courtesy of retrosheet.org.

Major League Rules Changes Adopted After the Dutch Leonard Affair and Risberg-Gandil Hearings

Rule 21

MISCONDUCT

(a) MISCONDUCT IN PLAYING BASEBALL. Any player or person connected with a club who shall promise or agree to lose, or to attempt to lose, or to fail to give his best efforts towards the winning of any baseball game with which he is or may be in any way concerned; or who shall intentionally fail to give his best efforts towards the winning of any such baseball game, or who shall solicit or attempt to induce any player or person connected with a club to lose, or attempt to lose, or to fail to give his best efforts towards the winning of any baseball game with which such other player or person is or may be in any way connected; or who, being solicited by any person, shall fail to inform his Major League President and the Commissioner.

(b) GIFT FOR DEFEATING COMPETING CLUB. Any player or person connected with a club who shall offer or give any gift or reward to a player or person connected with another club for services rendered or supposed to be or to have been rendered in defeating or attempting to defeat a competing club, and any player or person connected with a club who shall solicit or accept from a player connected with another club any gifts or reward for any such services rendered, or supposed to have been rendered, or who having been offered any such gift or reward, shall fail to inform his League President or the Commissioner immediately of such offer, and of all facts and circumstances therewith, shall be declared ineligible for not less than three (3) years.

(c) GIFTS TO UMPIRES. Any player or person connected with a club, who shall give, or offer to give, any gift or reward to an umpire for services rendered, or supposed to be or to have been rendered, in defeating or attempting to defeat a competing club, or for the umpire's decision on anything connected with the playing of a baseball game; and any umpire who shall render, or promise or agree to render, any such decision otherwise than on its merits, or who shall solicit or accept such gifts or reward, or having been solicited to render any such decision otherwise than on its merits, shall fail to inform the League President or the Commissioner immediately of such offer or solicitation, and all facts and circumstances therewith, shall be declared permanently ineligible.

(d) BETTING ON BALL GAMES.

1. Any player, umpire, or club official or employee, who shall bet any sum whatsoever upon any baseball game in connection with which the bettor has no duty to perform shall be declared ineligible for one year.

2. Any player, umpire, or club or league official or employee, who shall bet any sum whatsoever upon any baseball game in connection with which the bettor has a duty to perform shall be declared permanently ineligible.

(e) VIOLENCE OR MISCONDUCT IN INTERLEAGUE GAMES. In case of any physical attack or other violence upon an umpire by a player, or by an umpire upon a player, or of other misconduct by an umpire or a player, during or in connection with any interleague Major League game or any exhibition game of a Major League Club with a club or team not a member of the same league, the Commissioner shall impose upon the offender or offenders such fine, suspension, ineligibility or other penalty, as the facts may warrant in the judgment of the Commissioner.

(f) OTHER MISCONDUCT. Nothing herein contained shall be construed as exclusively defining or otherwise limiting acts, transactions, practices or conduct not to be in the best interests of Baseball; and any and all other acts, transactions, practices or conduct not to be in the best interests of Baseball are prohibited and shall be subject to such penalties, including permanent ineligibility, as the facts in the particular case may warrant.

(g) RULE TO BE KEPT POSTED. A printed copy of this Rule shall be kept posted in each clubhouse.

Index